Batsford Chess

The King's Indian
for the
Attacking Player

GRAHAM BURGESS

An Owl Book
Henry Holt and Company
New York

Henry Holt and Company, Inc.
Publishers since 1866
115 West 18th Street
New York, New York 10011

Henry Holt ® is a registered trademark
of Henry Holt and Company, Inc.

Copyright © 1993 by Graham Burgess
All rights reserved.
First published in the United States in 1993 by
Henry Holt and Company, Inc.
Originally published in Great Britain in 1993 by
B. T. Batsford Ltd.

Library of Congress Catalog Card Number: 93-77847

ISBN 0-8050-2936-2 (An Owl Book: pbk.)

First American Edition—1993

Printed in the United Kingdom
All first editions are printed on acid-free paper. ∞

10   9   8   7   6   5   4   3   2   1

Adviser: R. D. Keene, GM, OBE
Technical Editor: Andrew Kinsman

Contents

Bibliography

Books

The recent appearance of the lines considered in this book means that very little previous literature provides more than a very rudimentary coverage. The following provided some useful material:

Burgess, *The Classical King's Indian Defence* (Chess Enterprises 1990). Covers all lines after 1 d4 ♘f6 2 c4 g6 3 ♘c3 ♗g7 4 e4 d6 5 ♘f3 0–0 6 ♗e2.

Nunn, *The Classical King's Indian* (Batsford 1990). Covers all lines after 6 ... e5 7 0–0 ♘c6 8 d5 ♘e7.

Encyclopaedia of Chess Openings, vol. E (Šahovski Informator 1991).

Keene & Jacobs, *The Complete King's Indian* (Batsford 1992).

Periodicals

Informator

New in Chess Magazine

New in Chess Yearbook

Inside Chess

Shakhmatny Byulleten

Shakhmaty v SSSR

Chess in the USSR

Byulleten TsSK SSSR

British Chess Magazine

Pergamon Chess

Skakbladet

Fynsk Skak

Dragon

Die Schachwoche

Schach Echo

ChessBase Magazine

Introduction

Recent years have witnessed an increasing willingness on the part of players of all levels to play for a win with Black, following the World Champion's lead — Kasparov has demonstrated that ambitious play by Black, if backed up by sufficient expertise, may not involve an unnecessary risk of disaster. As a result the King's Indian has experienced an enormous surge in popularity.

King's Indian players are always looking for new ways to surprise their opponents, so in the quest for startling ways to lead the opponent onto unfamiliar ground analysts have dug so deep that entirely new ways of playing the King's Indian have been uncovered. It should not be a great surprise that these systems have lain waiting to be discovered. Chess theory (mainly based on the practice of masters and grandmasters) tends to take a relatively small number of plans and examine them exhaustively — only when they lose their appeal for one side or the other do analysts return to an earlier point and begin the hard work of looking for something new.

These entirely new systems constitute the subject matter of this book. A fortunate side-effect of investigating these lines is that, since these ideas have touched all branches of the King's Indian tree, the book provides Black with a repertoire against all of White's major options. Players with White may also use the book to provide the heart of a repertoire, especially with the Classical, though will have to look up the older lines elsewhere — to cover the whole of the King's Indian in detail in one volume would be impractical!

The first section of the book considers lines in which Black plays an early ... ♘a6. In the mid-1980s this move was entirely unexplored, except for a few specific cases, or when following a preparatory ... a6-a5. Investigations, however, have shown that the apparently bizarre position of the knight has a great deal of flexibility and constitutes an entirely viable interpretation of the King's Indian against many of

White's principal options. Maybe in future years chessplayers will wonder why it took so long for their predecessors to recognise the merits of playing the knight to a6; Black's queenside is made sturdier from the point of view of both defence and counterattack, his other pieces are not obstructed, while the icing on the cake is that Black's ... e7–e5 is indirectly, but highly effectively, supported.

In the second section we investigate pawn sacrifice ideas with ... c5 against the Sämisch and Averbakh. These have been known for quite a while, but only recent analyses have made them respectable. Black is in no hurry to prove his compensation or to win back the pawn, but calmly develops, waiting for White's attempts to do the same — this will generally reveal where Black should strike. For example, in the Sämisch lines, when Black has a knight on d7, White has to reckon with it moving to e5, c5 or sometimes b6. Though it is natural for Black to make an active move with this knight, it may cause White more inconvenience to leave it on d7 for a while, keeping open options of various plans. A careful study of the games of Gelfand, Khalifman and Shirov is essential for an understanding of the subtlety and effectiveness of Black's methods.

The Classical Main Line is the subject of the third section. This is of course by no means a new line,

but recent practice has witnessed entirely new approaches by both sides. For instance, we see Black in no hurry whatsoever to block the kingside with ... f5–f4 when there is anything to be gained from manoeuvring (particularly with the move ... ♔h8). Black will also, where appropriate, take prophylactic measures on the queenside, or even seek counterplay there. In the 9 ♘e1 line, this approach is partly (at least) in response to White's idea of meeting Black's ... f5–f4 with g2–g4, a refined version of the old Benko/Pinter line, which denies Black the possibility of maintaining pressure against e4. Also considered are a variety of lines in which White's queenside play involves an early a4.

For many years Black's most popular choices against the Fianchetto line were the Panno and the Yugoslav lines, characterised by the development of Black's knight on c6. In recent years, the more traditional treatment with ... ♘bd7, which avoids these heavily theoretical lines, has re-emerged, fortified by new ideas, as a popular way to try to unsettle White. In the fourth section, together with a few rarer options, we consider White's response 7 ♕c2, and in the main line (White plays h3 and ♖e1) an idea for Black involving rapid queenside mobilisation.

The major chapters in the book begin with a selection of diagram positions illustrating the tactical methods which most characterise the new ideas in the variation under consideration. These will hopefully help to orientate the reader in the theoretical and practical material which follows, and also to assimilate future developments in these topical lines. At present, the variations considered in this book are still very new, and while the theory may already have a firm backbone, or indeed skeleton, there is a good deal of 'fleshing-out' to be done in future years.

It is, of course, easier to study older lines. However, practical success tends to be enjoyed by those who come to grips quickest with variations when they are still 'hot', and refine them with their own input. This is true at all levels — in a club match, simply playing ... ♘a6 (for instance) will force many players largely onto their own resources; one then only needs to have absorbed the important ideas to enjoy a significant head-start.

I hope readers find much that is stimulating in this book, and have practical success with the lines considered. I would like to thank those who helped by supplying original source material: Carsten Mikkelsen, Carsten Buch, Rikard Winsnes, and the many people who gave valuable help with analysis. Andrew Kinsman and Batsford should also be thanked for showing interest in this project, which is my fourth book.

Graham Burgess
Svendborg 1992

Symbols

+	Check
++	Double check
#	Checkmate
$\pm$ ($\mp$)	Slight advantage to White (Black)
$\pm$ ($\mp$)	Clear advantage to White (Black)
$\pm\pm$ ($\mp\mp$)	Winning advantage to White (Black)
=	Level position
∞	Unclear position
!	Good move
?	Bad move
!!	Outstanding move
??	Blunder
!?	Interesting move
?!	Dubious move
$\triangle$	Intending
OL	Olympiad
corres	Postal game
Ch	Championship
Wch	World Championship
Z	Zonal
IZ	Interzonal

1 Ideas with ... ♘a6: Introduction and Modern Exchange Variation

The main reason for putting the knight on a6 is flexibility. Black's other pieces are not obstructed, while the knight is well-placed in a variety of scenarios: when Black plays on the kingside, the knight is a serious obstacle to White's queenside play; in lines where White plays on the kingside it can participate in queenside counter-play, while if the centre becomes open the knight has the c5 and c7 squares for manoeuvring.

There are a few variations in which a ... ♘a6 treatment is not especially appropriate. These are ones in which there is no real chance of a subsequent ... ♘c5 causing an inconvenient threat to the e4-pawn, e.g. the Fianchetto System (there is no white pawn on e4!) and the Sämisch (White has spent a tempo ensuring that e4 is always well guarded).

The play in the ... ♘a6 system is generally a little slower than

in the more traditional lines, as Black's queenside is a good deal more resilient, but the counterplay less quick. As a result, the King's Indian has recently found many new adherents among players who have little faith in the race type of situation which charac-terises many of the older lines. There is plenty of scope here for out-manoeuvring the opponent before the game degenerates into a typical King's Indian dog-fight.

There are many specific tactical ideas associated with the move ... ♘a6, which are discussed in the introductions to the chapters in which they are most relevant. In this chapter we discuss the ... ♘a6 approach to a variety of minor variations, together with the Modern Exchange Variation where the knight goes to a6 a little later, but the ideas are typical of the whole ... ♘a6 complex.

Larsen Variation

1 d4 ♘f6 2 c4 g6 3 ♘c3 ♗g7 4 e4 d6

5	♘f3	0-0
6	♗e3	*(1)*

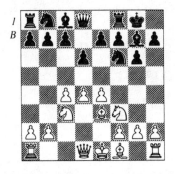

Assuming White is not simply using an unusual move order to reach the Gligorić Variation (viz. 6 ... e5 7 ♗e2), the answer to **6 ... e5** would be **7 de de 8 ♕xd8 ♖xd8 9 ♘d5** and now:

(a) **9 ... ♖d7** 10 ♘xf6+ (10 ♘xe5? ♘xd5 11 ♘xd7 ♘xe3) 10 ... ♗xf6 11 c5 ♘c6 12 ♗b5 ♖d8 (12 ... ♔f8 13 ♔e2 ♔e7 14 a3 ♗g7 15 ♗c4 h6 16 h3 ♘d8 17 b4 ♘e6 18 g3 ♖d8 19 ♖ad1 ♗d7 also gave Black fine prospects in Kosten–King, Hastings 1990/1) 13 ♗xc6 bc 15 ♖d1 ♗a6! 15 ♖xd8+ ♖xd8 16 ♘d2 ♗e7 which gave all of Black's pieces good play in Barbero–Khalifman, Plovdiv 1986.

(b) **9 ... ♘a6** 10 0-0-0 (10 ♖d1 ♖f8 11 ♘xf6+ ♗xf6 12 a3 b6 13 ♗d3 ♗d7 14 ♔e2 ♖fd8 15 h3 ♖ab8 16 b4 c5 was fine for Black in Cifuentes–Nijboer, Wijk aan

Zee 1991) 10 ... ♗e6 (After 10 ... ♗g4, 11 c5?! ♘xd5 12 ed ♘b4 13 ♗c4 b5! gives Black excellent counterplay, as in Rivas–Blees, Amsterdam 1986, whilst 11 ♘xf6+ ♗xf6 12 c5 ♖d1+ 13 ♔xd1 ♖d8+ 14 ♔c1 ♘b4 15 ♗c4 ♘d3+ gives Black no problems, as in a number of Kupreichik's games) 11 ♘xf6+ ♗xf6 12 ♖xd8+ ♖xd8 13 a3 c5 14 ♗e2 ½-½ J. Horvath–Groszpeter, Hungarian Ch 1991.

With **6 ... ♘a6** instead of 6 ... e5 Black avoids this simplifying line. White has a choice of transpositions: **7 ♗e2** e5 (7 ... ♘g4!?) is the Gligorić System with ... ♘a6; **7 h3** e5 8 d5 is the main line of the Makogonov System (see the next chapter), whilst other moves are untried; maybe **7 ♕d2** is worth a thought, while **7 ♗d3** is feasible with Black unable to attack d4 with a knight. Note that **7 ♘d2**, which is White's most consistent answer to 6 ... ♘bd7, here walks into 7 ... ♘g4∓.

'Semi-Averbakh' Variation

1 d4 ♘f6 2 c4 g6 3 ♘c3 ♗g7 4 e4 d6

5	♗e2	0-0
6	♗e3	*(2)*

This is such a rarely-played variation that it does not even have an accepted name. Clearly it is similar to the Averbakh, except that the bishop is less active, but also less exposed, on e3 than on

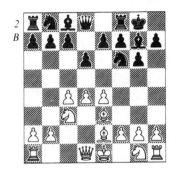

2
B

g5. Also, a possible advance of the g-pawn to g5 is not impeded. A natural response is **6 ... c5** (compare with the variation 6 ♗g5 h6 7 ♗e3 c5, considered in a later chapter).

Black may consider **6 ... ♘a6**, retaining the option of a Benoni approach (... c5) if White tries a kingside advance. Naturally, 7 ♘f3 e5 is the Gligorić System with ... ♘a6, considered below.

After **6 ... e5 7 d5**, Black may deploy the knight to a6 immediately, or delay this a few moves:

(a) **7 ... ♘a6:**

(a1) **8 g4!? ♘c5** 9 f3 (9 ♗f3 a5 10 h3 Doroshkevich–Isupov, Kuybyshev 1990) 9 ... h5 10 h3 ♘h7 11 ♕d2 h4= Hazai.

(a2) **8 h4 ♘c5** (8 ... c6) 9 f3 (9 ♕c2 ♘g4 10 ♗xg4 ♗xg4 11 f3 ♗d7 12 h5 f5= Hazai) 9 ... a5 10 ♕d2 ♘fd7 (10 ... ♘h5!? is more natural) 11 g4 f5 12 g5! ♖f7 13 0-0-0 ♘f8 14 ♘h3 ♗d7 15 ♕c2 ♘a6 16 ♔b1 ♕c8 17 ♘f2 left Black struggling to find any sort of plan in Gomez Esteban–J. Polgar,

Pamplona 1990/1.

(b) **7 ... c6.** Now **8 ♘f3 ♘g4** 9 ♗g5 f6 10 ♗h4 ♘a6 is line (b) in the Gligorić System. Others:

(b1) **8 h4 cd 9 cd ♕a5** 10 ♕d2 ♘a6 11 a3 b5 12 f3 b4 13 ♘a2 ♘h5!? 14 ♘xb4 ♘xb4 15 ♕xb4 ♕d8 16 ♗b5 ♖b8 17 ♗xa7 ♖b7 18 ♗e3 ♗d7 19 a4 ♕b8 20 ♕d2 ♗xb5 21 ab ♖xb5 22 ♖a2 f5 gave Black excellent play in Tolush–Geller, Garga 1953.

(b2) **8 g4 cd 9 cd ♕a5** 10 ♗d2 (10 ♔f1!?) 10 ... ♘a6 11 h4 ♘c5 12 f3 ♕b6 13 ♖b1 a5 14 ♗e3 h5 15 ♘h3 a4 16 ♘f2 ♕a5 17 ♕d2 ♗d7 18 ♗g5 b5 19 ♗xf6 ♗xf6 20 gh b4 (20 ... ♔g7!? 21 hg fg 22 h5 ♖h8) 21 hg?! bc failed to give White anything real for the piece in Sadler–McDonald, British Ch (Eastbourne) 1990.

Gligorić System

1 d4 ♘f6 2 c4 g6 3 ♘c3 ♗g7 4 e4 d6

5	**♘f3**	**0-0**
6	**♗e2**	**e5**
7	**♗e3**	**♘a6** *(3)*

Now, the normal continuation is **8 0-0**, considered under the move order 7 0-0 ♘a6 8 ♗e3. White has also tried:

(a) **8 de** (rather feeble) 8 ... de 9 ♕b3 c6 10 ♘xe5 ♕a5 11 ♘d3 ♘xe4 12 ♖c1 ♗f5 13 0-0 ♘xc3 14 bc ♖fd8 15 ♖fd1 b6 was extremely comfortable for Black in Groszpeter–P. Schlosser, Kecskemet 1990.

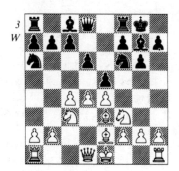

(b) **8 d5** is more critical. The pawn sacrifice **8 ... ♘c5 9 ♘d2 a5 10 a3!? a4!? 11 ♗xc5 dc 12 ♘xa4 ♕e7 13 ♘c3 ♘e8 14 h4 f5 15 h5 ♘d6** gave Black reasonable play in Bandza–Yuneev, Frunze 1989, but more natural is **8 ... ♘g4 9 ♗g5 f6 10 ♗h4** (10 ♗d2) **10 ... c6** (10 ... ♘h6 11 ♘d2 c5 12 f3 ♕e8 13 a3 f5 was roughly equal in Wirthensohn–Gallagher, Bern 1991), which has arisen a number of times from a different variation (7 ... c6 8 d5 ♘g4 9 ♗g5 f6 10 ♗h4 ♘a6). Now:

(b1) **11 0–0** is considered under the move-order 7 0–0 ♘a6 8 ♗e3 c6 9 d5 ♘g4 10 ♗g5 f6 11 ♗h4, and may be White's best.

(b2) After **11 ♘d2 ♘h6** (11 ... h5!? 12 h3 ♘h6 13 g4? hg 14 hg ♘f7 △ ... ♗h6∓) **12 a3 ♘f7 13 f3** (13 ♕c2?! ♗h6 14 ♘f1 ♗g5) **13 ... ♗h6 14 ♗f2 f5 15 ♕c2**, we have:

(b21) **15 ... ♕g5!?** intending a pawn grab, is Gurevich's suggestion, viz. **16 h4 ♕xg2 17 ♖g1 ♕h2 18 ♗f1 ♘c5!** or **16 ♘f1 ♕xg2 17**

♖g1 ♕h3 18 ♖g3 ♕h5 19 f4 ef 20 ♗xh5 fg∞.

(b22) **15 ... ♗d7 16 b4 c5! 17 ♖b1 b6 18 ♘f1!? ♗f4! 19 g3** (19 ♘e3? is well met by 19 ... ♕g5, but Gurevich proposes 19 h4!? and 19 ♗d3 ♘h6 20 ♘g3±) **19 ... ♗h6 20 h4 ♘c7 21 g4 fg 22 fg ♗f4 23 ♘e3 ♘e8 24 ♘cd1!?** (24 h5 g5; 24 ♘g2 ♘f6) **24 ... h6! 25 h5 g5 26 ♖g1 ♘f6 27 ♖g2 ♕c8!** gave Black fine prospects in Karpov–Kasparov, Lyon Wch (19) 1990. A few moves later he opened lines on the queenside with ... cb, ab a5.

Petrosian System

1 d4 ♘f6 2 c4 g6 3 ♘c3 ♗g7 4 e4 d6

5	**♘f3**	**0–0**
6	**♗e2**	**e5**

After **6 ... ♘a6**, White can try to maintain a Petrosian theme with **7 0–0** e5 8 d5 (line (a) in the next note), or **7 ♗g5** (Averbakh with 6 ... ♘a6 7 ♘f3) 7 ... h6 8 ♗h4 e5 9 d5 (9 de de 10 ♕xd8 ♖xd8 11 ♘d5 g5 is harmless) 9 ... g5, which is line (c) in the next note. Note that this avoids the line 6 ... e5 7 d5 ♘a6 8 ♘d2.

7	**d5**	**♘a6**

This is not in fact a very new move, but has increased in popularity recently in line with the trend for ... ♘a6 in many related variations. Now:

(a) **8 0–0** transposes, after 8 ... ♘c5, to the variation 7 0–0 ♘bd7

8 d5 ♘c5 which has long been considered satisfactory for Black. However, in Pekarek–Schandorff, Odense Scandic Cup 1991, Black, a ... ♘a6 specialist, preferred **8 ... ♕e8 9 ♘h4?!** (9 ♘d2!? c6!?) 9 ... ♔h8 10 ♗d2 ♘c5 11 ♕c2 a5 12 ♖ae1 ♕e7∓ 13 g3 ♗h3 14 ♘g2 ♘fd7 15 ♗d1 f5 when White's most consistent continuation was **16 f4!?**. Instead **16 f3?!** f4 17 ♖f2 g5 18 b3 ♘f6 19 a3 ♘h5 20 b4 ab 21 ab ♘d7 clearly favoured Black.

(b) **8 ♘d2** c6 (8 ... ♘e8?! 9 a3 c5 10 h4 f5 11 h5 f4? 12 hg hg 13 ♗g4± Speelman–Ivanchuk, Linares 1991; 11 ... ♘f6±) 9 a3 cd 10 cd ♗d7 11 ♘c4 ♘e8 12 b4 f5 13 0–0 ♘ac7 14 ♘a5 b6 15 ♘c6 ♕h4 16 g3 ♕h3 17 ♗f3 fe 18 ♘xe4 ♗xc6 19 dc ♕f5 20 ♘g5 h6 led to complex play in Aleksandrov–Neverov, USSR Ch (Moscow) 1991.

(c) **8 ♗g5 h6 9 ♗h4 g5 10 ♗g3** *(4)* is the traditional Petrosian System approach. Black has two main ways to try to profit from the knight's position on a6 rather than d7:

(c1) **10 ... ♘h5** 11 h4 ♘xg3! 12 fg gh 13 ♘xh4 ♕g5 14 g4 ♗f6 15 ♕d2 ♔g7 16 g3 ♕xd2+ 17 ♔xd2 ♗g5+ 18 ♔d1 ♗e3 19 ♖b1 ♗d4 20 ♔c2 ♘c5 21 b4! and now a draw was agreed in M. Ivanov–Yurtaev, USSR 1989, in view of the perpetual check after 21 ... ♗xc3 22 bc ♗d4 23 cd cd 24 ♖xb7! ♗xb7 25 ♘f5+ ♔g8 26 ♘xh6+ ♔g7 27 ♘f5+.

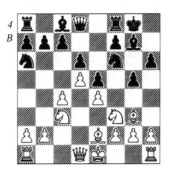

(c2) **10 ... ♘xe4!?** 11 ♘xe4 f5 12 ♘fd2 fe 13 ♘xe4 ♗f5 14 ♗d3 g4!∓ 15 0–0 h5 16 f3 ♗xe4 17 ♗xe4 ♘c5 18 ♗c2 e4! 19 ♗xe4 ♘xe4 20 fe ♗xb2 21 ♖b1 ♖xf1+ was very promising for Black in Rogers–Mortensen, Vejstrup 1989 (a tournament organised by the author's current club, Sydøstfyn).

Modern Exchange Variation

P. Cramling—Wahls
Hamburg 1991

1 d4 ♘f6 2 c4 g6 3 ♘c3 ♗g7 4 e4 d6

5	♘f3	0–0
6	♗e2	e5

Those who are desperate to avoid the exchange variation might experiment with **6 ... ♘a6**. In reply, **7 e5** is untried and appears harmless, while **7 ♗e3** may be met by 7 ... ♘g4 in addition to 7 ... e5 with a ... ♘a6 Gligorić System.

7	de	de
8	♕xd8	♖xd8

9 ♗g5 c6 *(5)*

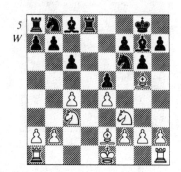

9 ... ♘a6 is also possible, but the text has many more ideas in common with other ... ♘a6 lines, especially the Four Pawns variety, as we shall see.

10 ♘xe5

What else? White's normal ideas, ♘d5 and 0–0–0, are infeasible.

10 ... ♖e8

10 ... ♘a6? is well met by 11 ♘xf7!.

11 0–0–0

White has also tried:

(a) **11 ♗f4 ♘a6!** 12 0–0–0 (12 f3 ♘h5 13 ♘d3 f5∞) 12 ... ♘c5 13 f3 (13 ♗f3 g5! 14 ♗xg5 ♖xe5 15 ♖d8+ ♘e8 16 ♗f4 ♗f6∓) 13 ... ♘h5 14 ♗e3 ♘xe4! and now **15 ♘xe4?!** ♗xe5 (△ ... f5) 16 ♗d4 ♗f5 17 ♗xe5 ♖xe5 18 ♘c3 ♘f4 19 ♗f1 ♖ae8 was very good for Black in Bouaziz–Nunn, Szirak IZ 1987; Nunn gave instead **15 fe** ♗xe5 16 ♗xh5 gh 17 h3 ♗e6∓.

(b) **11 f4** can be met by **11 ... ♘a6** when White has nothing

better than 12 0–0–0, transposing back to the game P. Cramling–Wahls, or Glek's **11 ... ♘h5!** 12 ♗xh5 (12 ♘d3 h6! 13 ♗h4 ♘xf4 14 ♘xf4 g5) 12 ... gh 13 ♗h4 ♘d7! 14 ♗g3 (14 ♘xd7 ♗xc3+ 15 bc ♖xe4+ 16 ♔d2 ♗xd7∓ Glek) 14 ... ♘xe5 15 fe ♗xe5 16 ♗xe5 ♖xe5 17 0–0–0 ♗e6 18 b3 b5! 19 cb cb 20 ♖d4 a5 21 ♖hd1 ♔g7∓ Maliutin–Glek, Moscow Ch 1989.

11 ... ♘a6 *(6)*

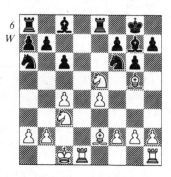

This is the basic position of the whole variation.

12 f4

This is White's most natural move. The critical 12 ♖d6 is considered in the next game. Two lesser options:

(a) **12 f3** ♖xe5 13 ♖d8+ ♖e8 14 ♗xf6 ♖xd8 15 ♗xd8 ♗h3 is level.

(b) **12 ♘f3?!** ♗g4! 13 ♗d3 (13 h3 ♘xe4!; 13 ♗e3 ♘xe4 14 ♘xe4 ♖xe4 15 ♖d2 ♗f6 16 ♖hd1 ♖ae8 17 b3 ♖xe3!? led to a win for Black in Szymczak–Khalifman, Groningen 1989/90) 13 ... ♘c5 14

♖he1 ♞fd7! (△ ... ♞e5) 15 ♗f4 ♞b6 16 ♔c2!? (16 ♗f1?! ♗xc3 17 bc ♞xe4∓; 16 h3 ♗xf3 17 gf ♞xd3+ 18 ♖xd3 ♞xc4 19 ♖d7 ♗e5∓) 16 ... ♗xf3 17 gf ♞xd3 18 ♖xd3 ♞xc4 19 ♗g3 (19 ♖d7 b5∓ Watson) 19 ... ♖ad8 gave Black a very promising ending in Barlov–W. Watson, Bor 1986.

12 ... h6
13 ♗h4 g5

13 ... ♞c5 14 ♗f3 g5 15 ♗f2 gf 16 ♗xc5 ♖xe5 17 ♗d6 ♖e8 18 ♗xf4 ♞d7 19 ♞e2 ♞e5 20 b3 a5 gave Black very reasonable compensation in Finegold–Barbero, Wijk aan Zee 1991.

14 ♗f2

Again White has a choice:

(a) **14 fg hg** 15 ♗g3 ♞c5 16 ♖he1 (16 ♖hf1 ♗e6 and 16 ♞f3 ♞cxe4 17 ♞xe4 ♞xe4 18 ♗d3 ♞xg3 19 hg are both fine for Black) 16 ... a5 (16 ... ♗e6 17 ♗f1 ♞h5 gave Black good play in Keilhack–Kupreichik, West Berlin 1987) 17 ♞f3 ♞fxe4 18 ♞xe4 ♞xe4 19 ♗d3 ♗f5 (△ ... ♞xg3) 20 ♗c7 (Setterqvist–Sandström, Sweden 1989) and now either 20 ... ♗g6∓ or 20 ... ♗h7 21 ♗b6 g4 22 ♞h4 f5 (Winsnes).

(b) **14 ♗g3 ♞c5 15 ♗f3 g4 (7)** gives White these options:

(b1) **16 ♗e2** ♞cxe4 17 ♞xe4 ♞xe4 18 ♗xg4 (18 ♗h4?! h5∓ Germanivičus–Shchekachev, USSR 1987) 18 ... ♞xg3 19 hg ♗xe5 20 ♗xc8 ♗xb2+ 21 ♔xb2 ♖axc8=.

(b2) **16 ♗f2 ♗f8!?** (16 ... gf=)

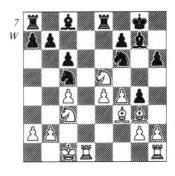

17 ♗e2 ♞cxe4 18 ♞xe4 ♞xe4 19 ♗d4 h5 20 ♖he1 ♗h6 21 g3 c5 22 ♗d3 (22 ♗f1? cd 23 ♖xe4 f6 0–1 Helgason–M. Schlosser, Tecklenburg 1987/8) 22 ... ♞xg3 23 hg cd 24 ♔c2 f6 and if 25 ♗g6 then 25 ... fe 26 ♗xe8 ♗f5+.

14 ... gf
15 ♞f3 ♗g4

15 ... ♞g4 16 ♗d4 ♗e6 17 g3 fg 18 ♖hg1 ♗xd4 19 ♖xd4 ♖ad8 20 ♖xg3 ♔h8 gave Black decent play in Bellón–Pomes, Terrassa 1990.

16 h3 ♗h5

16 ... ♞xe4 17 ♞xe4 ♖xe4 (Hoeksema–Nunn, Groningen 1988) 18 ♗d3 ♗xf3 19 gf=. Wahls was not curious to discover Cramling's improvement.

17 e5 ♗xf3
18 gf ♞h5
19 ♖hg1! ♔f8
20 ♞e4 ♗xe5
21 ♗d3 b6?!

21 ... ♞g3 22 ♞xg3 fg 23 ♗xg3 ♞c5 24 ♗h7 ♗xg3 25 ♖xg3 is fully equal. The text gives White more chances.

22	c5	b5
23	♘d6	♖ed8?!
24	♘xf7	

Pia analysed **24 ♖de1!** as giving Black more serious problems. **24 ... ♗xd6?** 25 cd ♖xd6 allows 26 ♗h7! with a strong attack, so Black must select from **24 ... ♗g7** 25 ♗e4!? and **24 ... ♘b4** 25 ♗h7 ♗g7 26 ♗h4 ♖d7 27 ♖g4!?.

24	...	♔xf7
25	♗g6+	♔f8
26	♗xh5	♘b4
27	♗h4	♘xa2+
28	♔b1	♖xd1+
29	♖xd1	♘b4
30	♖d7	

Now Black should try **30 ... a5** intending to secure counterplay by advancing this pawn further.

Instead there followed **30 ... ♘d5?** 31 ♖f7+ ♔g8 32 ♖f5 ♗c7 33 ♗f7+ ♔g7 34 ♗xd5 cd 35 ♖xd5 with a clear advantage for White. However, after 35 ... ♖c8 36 ♔c2 a5 37 ♔d3 a4 38 ♗e1 ♔f7 39 ♗c3 ♗d8 40 c6 ♗e7 41 ♖xb5 ♖xc6 42 ♖a5 ♖e6 43 ♗d4 ♗f6? 44 ♖f5 ♔g6, Black was let off the hook with **45 ♖xf4??** ♗xd4 46 ♖xd4 ♖a6 47 ♔e4 a3 48 ba ♖xa3 49 ♖d6+ ♔g7 50 h4 ½–½. Instead **45 ♖xf6+** ♖xf6 46 ♗xf6 ♔xf6 47 h4! gives a won king and pawn ending.

Korchnoi–Kasparov
Tilburg 1991

1 d4 ♘f6 2 c4 g6 3 ♘c3 ♗g7 4 e4 d6 5 ♘f3 0–0 6 ♗e2 e5 7 de de 8

♕xd8 ♖xd8 9 ♗g5 c6 10 ♘xe5 ♖e8 11 0–0–0 ♘a6

12	♖d6	♗e6

Of the alternatives, one is bad, one boring, and one highly ambitious:

(a) **12 ... ♖xe5?** 13 ♗xf6 ♗xf6 14 ♖xf6 ♘c5 15 ♖d6! (15 f3±) 15 ... ♘xe4 16 ♖d8+ ♔g7 17 ♘xe4 ♖xe4 18 ♗f3! ♖xc4+ 19 ♔d2 c5 20 ♖c1 ♖xc1 21 ♔xc1 h5 22 h4 ♖b8 23 ♖e8! left Black completely tied up and defenceless against White's bishop eventually reaching the h3–c8 diagonal in Tal–Smirin, Podolsk 1990.

(b) **12 ... ♘xe4** 13 ♘xe4 ♗xe5 14 ♘f6+ ♗xf6 15 ♗xf6 ♘c5= emphasises the harmless nature of White's play, but is rather tedious.

(c) **12 ... ♘h5!?** 13 ♘g4 (13 ♘f3 ♘c5 14 ♗e3 ♗xc3 15 ♗xc5 ♗f6!?; 13 ♘d3 ♗f8=) 13 ... ♘c5 14 ♘h6+ (14 ♗e3 ♗xc3 15 ♗xc5 ♗xg4 16 ♗xg4 ♗e5!) 14 ... ♔f8 15 ♗xh5 (15 ♗e3 ♘xe4 16 ♘xe4 ♖xe4) 15 ... ♗xc3 16 ♗f3! ♗e5 17 ♖d2 (17 ♖dd1!?) 17 ... ♗e6 18 b3 (18 ♗e3 b6 19 ♘g4 ♗xg4=) 18 ... a6 19 ♗e3 b6 with ideas of ... a4 gives Black good play against the white king: **20 h3?** a4!∓ Onischuk–Golubev, Leningrad 1989; **20 ♔c2** a4 (M. Marković–Golubev, Belgrade 1991) 21 b4 ♘a6∞; **20 ♘g4** ♗xg4 21 ♗xg4 a4!; **20 ♖hd1** a4 21 b4 ♘b3+ 22 ab ab 23 ♗d4 ♗f4; **20 ♔b1** a4 21 b4 ♘b3!? 22 ♖dd1 ♗xc4 23 ♘g4 ♗c3 24 e5 h5!? 25 ♗h6+ (25 ♘f6 ♖ed8) 25 ... ♔e7

26 ♗g5+ ♔f8 27 ♘f6 (27 ♗h6+ repeats) 27 ... ♘d4!∞ (Golubev).

13 f4!

This is an improvement on **13 ♘f3 ♘g4 14 ♘d2** (△ ♖xe6) and now:

(a) **14 ... ♘e5** 15 f4 h6 16 ♗h4 g5 17 ♗g3 gf 18 ♗xf4 ♘g6 19 ♗g3 ♗f8 20 ♖d3 ♘c5 21 ♖f3 h5 22 h3 ♖ad8 with roughly balanced play in Lalev–Kupreichik, Lvov 1988.

(b) **14 ... ♘c5** 15 ♗h4 ♗c8 16 ♗xg4 ♗xg4 17 f3 ♗e5 18 ♗g3 ♗xd6 19 ♗xd6 ♘d3+ 20 ♔c2 ♖ad8 21 c5 ♘b4+ 22 ♔b3 ♘d3 23 ♔c2 ♘b4+ 24 ♔b3 ♘d3 ½–½ Haag–Pirisi, Balatonbereny 1988.

13 ...   h6! *(8)*

13 ... ♘c5? is inferior due to 14 ♗f3 ♘h5 (14 ... h6 15 ♗h4 g5 16 ♗f2! attacks the knight) 15 ♗xh5 gh 16 ♘d3! when Kasparov gives **16 ... ♗xc3** 17 ♘xc5 ♗b4 18 ♘xb7± and **16 ... ♘xd3+** 17 ♖xd3 h6 18 ♗h4 ♗xc4 19 ♖g3±.

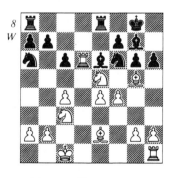

14   ♗xf6

More natural is **14 ♗h4**, but

Kasparov's analysis demonstrates excellent counterplay for Black: 14 ... g5! 15 fg (15 ♗g3 ♘c5) 15 ... hg 16 ♗xg5 ♘c5 17 ♗xf6 (17 ♗f3 ♘fxe4 18 ♘xe4 ♘xe4 19 ♗xe4 ♗xe5 20 ♖d2 ♗xc4 21 b3 ♗e6=) 17 ... ♗xf6 18 ♘d3 (18 ♘g4 ♗xc3 19 bc ♘xe4 20 ♖d4 ♘xc3 21 ♘f6+ ♔f8∓) when Black can choose between **18 ... ♗xc3** 19 ♘xc5 ♗b4 20 ♘xb7 ♖eb8! 21 a3 ♗xd6 22 ♘xd6 ♖b3∞ and **18 ... ♗e7** 19 ♖d4 ♗f6 20 e5 (20 ♖d6 ♗e7 repeats) 20 ... ♘xd3+ 21 ♖xd3 ♗xe5 with plenty of compensation.

14   ...   ♗xf6
15   ♖hd1

15 ♘f3 ♗xc3 16 bc ♘c5 17 ♘d2 (17 ♖d4? ♗g4! 18 h3 ♘xe4∓) 17 ... ♗f5! 18 ef (18 e5 ♖ad8) 18 ... ♖xe2 gives Black good play after **19 g4** gf 20 gf ♖ae8! 21 ♖xh6 ♖g2 and **19 fg** ♖xg2 20 gf+ ♔xf7 21 ♖e1 ♖xh2.

15   ...   ♗xe5
16   fe   ♖ac8

White's only possibility to make something of this position is with a ♘d5 sacrifice, liberating a mass of pawns. Kasparov is naturally alert to this possibility.

17   ♔d2   ♖e7
18   ♔e3   ♖ce8
19   ♖d8   ♔f8!
20   h4   ♘c5!

White's idea is revealed if Black tries to regain the pawn immediately: 20 ... ♗c8? 21 ♖xe8+ ♔xe8 22 h5! forcing weaknesses in Black's kingside.

21	**♖xe8+**	**♖xe8**
22	**b4**	**♘d7**
23	**♔f4**	**♔e7!**

The apparently active 23 ... a5? only weakens Black's queenside: 24 b5 ♔e7 25 bc bc 26 ♖b1± (Kasparov).

24 ♘d5+

Black's position hangs together beautifully after **24 g4** g5+ 25 hg hg+ 26 ♔xg5 ♘xe5 27 ♔f4 ♘xc4 28 ♘d5+ cd 29 ed ♘b2! 30 ♖d2 ♖d8=.

24	**...**	**cd**
25	**cd**	

25 ed?! allows Black to keep the piece: 25 ... ♗f5 26 g4 ♗c2 27 ♖d2 g5+ 28 hg hg+ 29 ♔xg5 ♗h7 30 ♔f4 ♖d8 when White's drawing chances are due only to the small number of black pawns.

25	**...**	**♖c8!**

25 ... g5+?! only gives White chances here: 26 hg hg+ 27 ♔xg5 ♖g8+ 28 ♔f4 ♖xg2 29 de fe 30 ♗c4!±. The text keeps the idea in reserve, e.g. 26 ♗b5?! is met by 26 ... g5+! 27 hg hg+ 28 ♔xg5 (28 ♔e3 ♘xe5∓) 28 ... ♖g8+ 29 ♔f4 ♗g4 when Black saves the bishop, with some winning chances. Therefore White decides to kill the position.

26	**de**	**fe**
27	**♖d2**	**♖f8+**
	½–½	

2 Systems with h3

There are a number of motivations for an early h3 by White. Firstly, by preventing ... ♘g4, White prepares ♗e3. Secondly, g2–g4 is supported, with the point that a later ... f5 by Black may only succeed in opening the g-file against his own king. Leaving the bishop on f1 for a while robs Black's ... ♘h5–f4 of some of its potency, while keeping open the possibility of ♗d3. These are similar ideas to the Sämisch; the obvious difference is that White's pieces retain use of f3, but e4 is less well covered.

Playing the knight to a6 makes a great deal of sense in these variations, as White generally meets ... e5 with an immediate d5, after which Black aims for quick piece play on the kingside, with such moves as ... ♘h5 and ... ♕e8 (to which ♘b5 will never be an irritating reply, with the knight on a6). Often Black has tactical reasons for recapturing on f5 (after ... f5, ef) with the bishop, perhaps linked with ... ♘b4.

Note that the theory of these ... ♘a6 ideas is not so radically new

as in other systems. This is because the manoeuvre is very natural with the c5-square already available (following ... e5, d5); moreover some of the positions are known by transposition from lines with ... ♘bd7.

In the first game we consider lines in which White avoids an early ♘f3. The rest of the chapter is devoted to the Makogonov Variation, 5 ♘f3 0–0 6 h3.

Knaak–J. Piket
Hamburg 1991

1 d4 ♘f6 2 c4 g6 3 ♘c3 ♗g7 4 e4 d6 5 h3 0–0

6 ♗e3

6 ♗g5 ♘a6 may transpose, after **7 ♘f3**, to lines considered below under the Makogonov move order 5 ♘f3 0–0 6 h3 ♘a6 7 ♗g5. An alternative is **7 ♗d3** which may be met by **7 ... e5 8 d5 ♘c5** (8 ... ♕e8) **9 ♗c2 a5**, or the flexible **7 ... c6**. Another idea is **7 ... h6 8 ♗e3 e5**, but ♕d2 is likely to gain a useful tempo: **9 d5 ♘c5** (9 ... c6 10 ♕d2 ♔h7 11 ♘ge2 cd 12 cd ♘c5 13 ♗c2 a5 14 g4 ♗d7

15 ♘g3 b5 16 g5 ♘g8 17 h4± Volke–Schäfer, German Ch 1991) 10 ♗c2 a5 11 ♕d2 ♘h7 12 g4 (12 ♘ge2?! ♘cxe4!? 13 ♘xe4 ♘xe4 14 ♗xe4 f5∓ Andruet–Murey, Royan 1988) 12 ... c6 13 ♘f3 ♘g8 14 ♖g1 ♘e7 15 h4± Averbakh–Bondarevsky, USSR Ch 1951.

A reliable method against **6 ♗g5**, though not on our theme, is **6 ... c5 7 d5 e6 8 ♗d3 ed 9 ed ♘bd7** and now:

(a) **10 ♘f3 ♖e8+ 11 ♔f1 h6 12 ♗f4** (12 ♗e3 a6 13 a4 ♘e5 14 ♘xe5 ♖xe5 15 ♕d2 ♕f8! — Nunn) 12 ... ♘e5 13 ♘xe5 de 14 ♗e3 b6 15 ♕d2 h5 16 a4 (Suba–Nunn, Dubai OL 1986) when Nunn recommends 16 ... ♗d7 or 16 ... ♘h7 △ ... f5 as unclear.

(b) **10 f4!?** a6! (prevents a later ♘b5) 11 a4 ♕e8+! 12 ♘ge2 ♘h5 13 ♘e4 f6 14 ♗h4 ♘xf4 15 ♘xf4 f5 16 ♘e6 fe 17 ♘xf8 ed!+ 18 ♘e6 ♘b6 19 ♕g4 (19 0–0 ♗xe6 20 ♖e1 ♗e5 21 de ♕xe6) 19 ... ♗d4 20 ♖f1 ♘xc4 21 ♕e4 (Tacu–Marin, Romania 1989) 21 ... ♘e3! 22 ♖f8+?! ♕xf8 23 ♘xf8 ♗f5∓ (Marin).

6 ...   ♘a6 *(9)*

6 ... e5 7 d5 ♘a6 generally transposes.

7 ♗d3

Also sometimes seen are:

(a) **7 g4** e5 8 d5 c6 (8 ... ♘c5!? 9 ♕c2 c6 10 ♘ge2 cd 11 cd ♗d7∞ — A. Kuzmin) 9 ♘f3 cd 10 cd ♗d7 11 ♘d2 ♖c8 (11 ... ♘e8 12 h4 f5 13 gf gf 14 ef ♗xf5 15 ♘de4 ♘f6 16 ♘g3 ♗d7 17

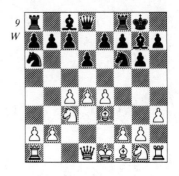

♗e2 ♕c8 18 ♖g1 ♔h8 19 ♘ge4!± Knaak–Istratescu, European Club Cup 1991) 12 ♖c1 ♘c5 13 b4 ♘a4 14 ♘xa4 ♖xc1 15 ♕xc1 ♗xa4 16 ♕a3 b5 17 ♗d3 h5 18 f3 ♕d7 19 ♔f2 ♘h7 20 ♖c1 ♗f6 21 ♕c3 ♗g5 22 ♕c7 ♕xc7 23 ♖xc7 h4 24 ♖c6 ♖d8 25 ♘b1 ♗xe3+ 26 ♔xe3 ♘g5 gave Black counterplay against the h3-pawn in Grinshpun–Yurtaev, Tashkent 1988.

(b) **7 ♗e2** e5 (7 ... ♕e8 8 ♘f3 e5 9 0–0! transposes to the Classical line 5 ♘f3 0–0 6 ♗e2 e5 7 0–0 ♘a6 8 ♗e3 ♕e8 9 h3, which is difficult for Black) 8 d5 ♘c5 (8 ... c6!?) 9 ♕c2 a5 (This is unnecessary; 9 ... c6 10 b4? ♘cxe4 11 ♘xe4 ♘xe4 12 ♕xe4? ♗f5∓ ∓) 10 g4 ♘fd7 (10 ... c6) 11 ♘f3 f5 (rather obliging) 12 gf gf 13 ef ♘b6 14 ♖g1 ♗xf5 15 ♕d2 ♔h8 16 0–0–0 ♕d7 17 ♘h4 a4 18 ♘xf5 ♕xf5 19 ♖g4! a3 20 b3 ♘bd7 21 ♖hg1± Gutman–Degenhardt, Frankfurt 1990.

7 ... e5
8 d5 ♘h5

8 ... ♘d7 works well after **9 ♘ge2 ♘dc5 10 ♗c2 f5 11 ef** (11 f3 ♗h6) **11 ... gf 12 0–0** (12 f4 ♕h4+ 13 g3 ♕h6) **12 ... f4 13 ♗xc5 ♘xc5 13 f3∞** (Kuzmin), or **9 g4?! ♘dc5 10 ♗b1?** (10 ♗c2 f5 11 ef gf 12 a3) **10 ... f5 11 ef gf 12 ♘ge2 ♕h4 13 a3 e4! 14 gf ♗xf5 15 ♘d4 ♗g6 16 ♗c2 ♘d3+ 17 ♗xd3 ♗xd4!∓** Avshalumov–Kupreichik, Blagoveshchensk 1988. However, in Barlov–Kir. Georgiev, Yugoslavia 1991, the simple **9 a3** denied the black knights squares on the queenside; there followed 9 ... ♘ac5 10 ♗c2 f5 11 b4 ♘xe4 12 ♗xe4! fe 13 ♘xe4 ♕h4 14 g4! with a positional edge.

8 ... ♘c5 9 ♗c2 a5 *(10)* (9 ... ♘h5 10 g3 ♗d7 11 ♕e2 a5 12 ♘f3 a4?! 13 ♘d2 a3 14 b4 ♘f4 15 ♕f1± was Neverov–Ivanchuk, USSR 1985; Black should try 12 ... ♕e8) and now:

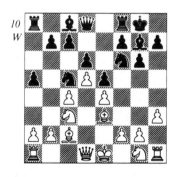

10
W

(a) **10 ♘ge2** occurred, by transposition, in P. Cramling–Kindermann, Dortmund 1986; 10 ... c6 11 a3 cd 12 cd ♗d7 13 b4? (13 ♗xc5?! dc 14 ♗a4 b5!; 13 0–0 followed by ♕d2, ♖c1 and b4 is equal — Kindermann) 13 ... ab 14 ab ♘a6 15 ♖b1 ♘h5!∓ then gave Black a strong and straightforward attack, since the loose knight on c3 means that f4 is a secure post for Black's knight.

(b) **10 g4** is the critical move, though in Gerusel–Heim, Bundesliga 1987/8, White neglected his development and suffered: 10 ... c6 11 a3 (11 ♘ge2) 11 ... cd 12 cd ♗d7 13 b4 ab 14 ab ♘a6 15 ♖b1 ♖c8 16 ♘ge2 h5 17 f3 ♘h7 18 ♕d2 ♕h4+ 19 ♗f2 ♕f6∓.

9   g3!   ♘c5

9 ... ♕e8 10 ♗e2! ♘f6 11 ♘f3 ♗d7?! (Now Black's pieces get in each other's way; better 11 ... ♘c5 12 ♘d2 a5) 12 ♘d2 c6 13 g4 ♗c8 14 ♘f1 ♕d8 15 ♘g3 cd 16 cd ♗d7 17 h4 ♕a5 18 h5± Neverov–Podgaets, USSR 1985.

10   ♗e2!   ♘f6
11   ♕c2   a5
12   0–0–0   a4! *(11)*

12 ... ♘e8?! invites White to push forward: 13 h4 f5 14 h5 f4 15 gf ef 16 ♗xc5 dc 17 hg hg 18 ♘f3± (Piket).

13   g4   ♘e8?!

Piket preferred **13 ... ♗d7**, and only after 14 ♘f3 to move the knight, since it is then more difficult for White to advance; after 14 ... ♘e8 15 ♖dg1?! c6! Black's counterplay is fast enough.

14   h4!   f5!
15   gf   gf
16   ♘f3   a3!

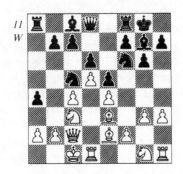

after the text White's king becomes completely exposed. The rest is slaughter: 27 ... d5! 28 ♘c5 ♘xc5 29 ♗xc5 ♖f3 30 ♕c2 d4 31 ♖g3 ♗f5! 32 ♕e2 ♖xg3 33 fg d3 34 ♕d2 (34 ♕b2 e4 35 ♕b3 ♕c7! 36 ♗f2 ♕e5 with the devastating threat ... ♗h6+) 34 ... ♕e6 35 g4 ♕xc4+ 36 ♕c3 d2+! 0–1.

Makogonov System

The traditional ... ♘a6 approach is 6 ... e5 7 d5 ♘a6, which is considered in the second game. The first game deals with the more modern treatment of keeping maximum flexibility with 6 ... ♘a6. After 7 ♗e3, Black is happy to transpose to normal lines (7 ... e5 8 d5), while 7 ♗g5 allows Black a couple of interesting alternatives to the line 7 ... e5 8 d5 ♕e8 9 g4 which denies Black counterplay with ... ♘h5.

Bronstein–Nijboer
Wijk aan Zee 1992

1 d4 ♘f6 2 c4 g6 3 ♘c3 ♗g7 4 e4 d6

5	♘f3	0–0
6	h3 *(12)*	
6	...	♘a6

6 ... e5 7 d5 ♘a6 is very often equivalent, but by playing 6 ... ♘a6, Black avoids the rather tedious 7 de de 8 ♕xd8, and keeps open possibilities of delaying ... e5 still further. White's development is rather slow, so it will be a

---

17 b4   fe!

17 ... ♘xe4?! 18 ♘xe4 fe 19 ♘g5± gives White a preponderance of attacking pieces.

18 ♘e1!

Now 18 ♘g5 can be met by 18 ... ♘d3+ 19 ♖xd3!? (19 ♗xd3 ed 20 ♕xd3 ♗f5) 19 ... ed 20 ♗xd3 e4!?.

18	...	♘a6
19	♕b3	♗f5
20	♘c2	♔h8
21	♘xa3	♘f6
22	♖hg1	♕d7!
23	♘ab1?!	

The position after **23 ♘c2! ♘g4 24 a4** (Piket) is rather messy, but should be pleasant for White. Now Black has the chances.

23	...	♘g4
24	♗xg4	♗xg4
25	♖de1	c5!

Now White has to decide which lines must be kept closed. In time trouble Knaak guessed wrong. **26 a3∓** is necessary.

26	dc?	bc
27	♘xe4?!	

27 ♘d2 is met by 27 ... d5!, but

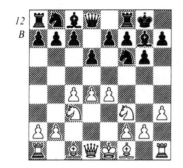

while before e5 is a threat.

It is worth mentioning, however, that **6 ... e5 7 de** de 8 ♕xd8 ♖xd8 9 ♗g5 (Or 9 ♘d5 ♘a6 10 ♗g5) 9 ... ♘a6 10 ♘d5 ♖d6 gives Black no objective difficulties: 11 ♗xf6 (11 ♘xf6+ ♗xf6 12 ♗d2 ♗e6 13 b4 c5 Karklins–Byrne, New York 1986) 11 ... ♗xf6 12 b4 c6 13 ♘xf6+ ♖xf6 14 a3 c5 15 b5 ♘c7 16 ♗e2 (16 ♖d1 ♖e6 17 ♖d8+ ♔g7 18 ♔d2 ♖e7 19 ♔c3 ♘e6∓ Bely–Baturin, Ukraine 1986) 16 ... ♖e6 17 0-0-0 ♖e8= 18 a4 f6 19 a5 ♗e6 20 ♖d2 ♔f8 21 ♖hd1 ♔e7 22 ♘e1 ♖ed8 led to a draw in Larsen–Hellers, Esbjerg 1988.

7   ♗g5
7 ♗e3 e5 is normally met by **8 d5**, transposing to the next game, Hansen–Kasparov. Instead, **8 de** de gives White very little with the bishop already committed to e3, e.g. 9 a3 c6 10 ♕xd8 ♖xd8 11 c5 ♘c7 12 ♖d1 ♖xd1+ 13 ♔xd1 ♗e6 14 ♘d2 ♘d7∓ Pieterse–J. Piket, Dutch Ch (Eindhoven) 1991.

7 ♗d3 may be met by 7 ... ♕e8!? or 7 ... e5.

7   ...   ♕e8!?
With this move, Black prepares 8 ... e5 and is ready to meet 9 d5 with 9 ... ♘h5, having already stepped out of the pin.

7 ... c5 is an interesting alternative. It is worth making a comparison with the variation 6 h3 c5 7 d5 e6. Then White generally plays 8 ♗d3 ed 9 ed, meeting 9 ... ♖e8+ with 10 ♗e3. However, with the bishop already on g5, the possible rook check is much more of an inconvenience. After **8 d5 e6** *(13)*, Yurtaev has been successful in two games:

(a) **9 ♗e2** (not a very effective square) 9 ... ed 10 ed h6 11 ♗e3 ♖e8 12 0-0 ♗f5 13 ♗d3 ♘e4 14 ♘xe4 ♗xe4 15 ♗xe4 ♖xe4 16 ♘d2 ♖e8 17 ♖b1 ♖b8 18 a3 b5 19 cb ♘c7 left Black at least a little better in Cherniak–Yurtaev, Leningrad 1989.

(b) **9 de** ♗xe6 10 ♗e2 ♕b6 11 ♕d2 ♕b4 12 a3 ♕b3 13 ♖c1 ♖fe8 14 0-0 ♘c7 15 ♖d1 ♖ad8 16 ♖b1

♗c8 17 ♗f1 ♖d7 18 ♖e1 ♘e6 19 ♗h4 ♘d4 20 ♘xd4 cd 21 ♘d5 ♘xd5 22 ed ♖f8 was certainly not bad for Black in Chekhov–Yurtaev, Tashkent 1987.

7 ... e5 gives White the choice between a form of exchange variation (8 de de 9 ♕xd8 ♖xd8 10 ♘d5) considered in the note to 6 ... ♘a6 above, and the more critical 8 d5 which is considered in the note (8 ♗g5) to White's eighth move in the next game, Hansen–Kasparov.

8   ♗d3

With the centre not yet closed, 8 g4 (hoping to transpose after 8 ... e5 9 d5 to the line 7 ... e5 8 d5 ♕e8 9 g4) can hardly be a good idea, e.g. 8 ... c5 9 d5 e6 10 de ♗xe6 11 ♕xd6? ♗xg4 12 hg ♘xe4 13 ♘xe4 ♕xe4+ 14 ♗e2 ♖fe8. After the text, however, all of Black's pieces obtain active play, so it seems that the untried 8 e5 must be the critical response.

| 8 | ... | e5 |
| 9 | d5 | ♘h5 (14) |

10	g3	f5
11	♗d2	♘c5
12	♗c2	fe
13	♘xe4	♘xe4

| 14 | ♗xe4 | ♘f6 |

Black wins the vital square e4 and so White's underdeveloped position falls apart remarkably quickly.

15	♗c2	e4
16	♘g5	h6
17	♘e6	♗xe6
18	de	♕xe6

Black has a safe extra pawn and will attack the white king wherever it seeks shelter. The game concluded 19 ♕e2 ♖ae8 20 ♗e3 ♔h7 21 0–0–0 b5! (And why not?) 22 ♗b3 bc 23 ♕xc4 d5 24 ♕c5 c6 25 ♔b1 ♘d7 26 ♕a5 ♘e5 27 ♖d2 ♘d3 28 ♖c2 ♕f6 29 ♖d1 c5 30 ♗xd5 ♘xb2 0–1.

C. Hansen–Kasparov
Tåsinge (Valdemars Slot) 1990

1 d4 ♘f6 2 c4 g6 3 ♘c3 ♗g7 4 e4 d6 5 ♘f3 0–0 6 h3

6	...	e5
7	d5	♘a6
8	♗e3	

Since one point of 7 ... ♘a6 is to wait for White's bishop to reach e3, to provide a target for the f-pawn's advance, 8 ♗d3 has its logic. In Hort–Kunze, German Ch 1991, there followed 8 ... ♘h5 9 g3 f5 10 ♕e2 ♕e8 11 ♗c2 ♗d7 12 ♗d2 ♘f6 13 ♗e3 ♘h5 14 ♗d2 ♘f6 15 ef gf 16 ♘h4±. More traditional play may be in order, viz. 8 ... ♘c5 9 ♗c2 a5 10 g4 ♗d7 11 ♗e3 ♘e8 12 ♖g1 (Kluger–Szabo, Budapest 1937 — the oldest game reference you'll find in this book!) whereupon *ECO* suggests 12 ... ♔h8!? to prepare ... f5.

A very important alternative approach is **8 ♗g5** *(15)*:

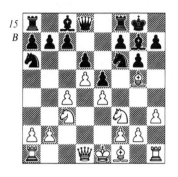

(a) **8 ... h6 9 ♗e3 ♘c5** (9 ... ♘h5 10 ♘d2 ♕e8 11 ♘b3 f5 12 c5 f4 13 ♗d2 ♘xc5 14 ♘xc5 dc 15 b4!? ♕e7?! 16 ♕b3 was promising for White in P. Cramling–K. Arakhamia, Biel 1991, but compare the related line in the note to White's ninth move. Note that the pawn on h6 allows White the additional possibility 10 ♘h2 ♕e8 11 ♕d2 ♔h7 12 0-0-0± Høi–Mortensen, Copenhagen 1984) **10 ♘d2 a5**. Now:

(a1) **11 g4 ♗d7** 12 ♕c2 (12 ♗e2!?) 12 ... h5!? 13 g5 (13 f3 ♘h7=) 13 ... ♘h7 14 ♖g1 f6 15 gf ♖xf6 16 0-0-0 ♕f8! gave Black good play in D. Werner–Kožul, Frankfurt 1990.

(a2) **11 ♗e2 c6** (11 ... ♗d7 can be met by 12 ♕c2 ♘e8 13 g4 f5= *ECO* or 12 g4!? c6 13 ♕c2 ♖c8 14 dc ♗xc6 15 ♗xc5 dc 16 0-0-0 a4!? Høi–Nørgaard, Copenhagen

1991) 12 a3 ♘fd7 13 b4 f5 14 ef gf 15 dc bc 16 bc f4 17 ♘de4 fe 18 0-0 ef+ 19 ♖xf2 ♖xf2 20 ♔xf2 ♘xc5 ½-½ Speelman–Spraggett, Hastings 1989/90.

(b) **8 ... ♕e8 9 g4** appears to keep an edge:

(b1) **9 ... ♗d7** 10 ♗d3!?± (Gulko).

(b2) **9 ... ♘d7** 10 ♖g1!? ♔h8 11 ♕d2 ♘dc5 12 ♘h4! ♗d7 13 ♖b1 ♘a4 14 ♘xa4 ♗xa4 15 f3 ♗d7 16 ♖c1± Østenstad–Maki, Haifa 1989.

(b3) **9 ... ♘c5** 10 ♘d2 a5 11 ♕f3 ♘fd7 12 ♖g1± King–Brunner, Geneva 1990.

(b4) **9 ... ♔h8** 10 ♘d2 (10 ♘h4 c6 11 ♕f3 ♘g8 12 0-0-0 cd 13 ♘xd5 ♗e6 14 ♔b1 f6 15 ♗c1 ♘e7 16 ♕a3 ♖d8 17 b4 ♘xd5 18 cd ♗d7∞ Lerner–Kruppa, USSR Ch (Moscow) 1991) 10 ... ♘g8 11 h4 f5 12 gf gf 13 ♗h3 ♘c5 14 ♕e2 ♘f6 15 ef! (15 ♗xf5 ♗xf5 16 ef e4 17 0-0-0 ♕e5∞ Bagirov–Lukin, Leningrad 1989) 15 ... ♘h5 16 ♘de4 ♘xe4 17 ♘xe4 ♗xf5 18 ♗xf5 ♖xf5 19 0-0-0± (Lukin).

8 ... ♘h5
9 ♘h2

The other knight retreats have been seen:

(a) **9 ♘g1** looks peculiar, but is it a worse square than h2? After **9 ... ♕e8 10 ♗e2 ♘f4 11 ♗f3 f5**, White has tried:

(a1) **12 g3 fe** (12 ... ♘b4!? seems healthier) 13 ♘xe4 ♗f5 14 ♘e2. Now Black ought, in Andonov–Hazai, Camaguey 1987, to have settled for equality with 14 ... ♘b4 15 ♕d2 ♘xe2.

(a2) **12 ♘ge2 ♕e7 13 ef** (13 0-0 ♘xh3+ gives Black a dangerous attack) **13 ... ♗xf5** (13 ... gf) **14 0-0 ♘d3 15 ♘e4 ♘ac5 16 ♗xc5** ½-½ Vilela–Pecorelli Garcia, Havana 1991.

(b) **9 ♘d2 ♕e8 10 ♘b3 f5 11 c5:**

(b1) **11 ... ♘f4!?** 12 cd (12 g3 ♘h5 intends ... f4) **12 ... cd 13 ef gf 14 ♗xf4** (14 g3 threatens nothing) **14 ... ef+ 15 ♗e2** (15 ♕e2 ♘b4! 16 0-0-0 ♘xa2+! 17 ♘xa2 ♕a4) **15 ... f3!** (Else White castles short with a good position) **16 gf ♗d7 17 ♖g1 ♔h8 18 ♕d2 ♖c8 19 0-0-0 ♘b4 20 ♔b1 f4 21 ♘d4** (21 ♖xg7 ♗f5+!) **21 ... ♕e5!∓** Koopman–Burgess, Biel 1987.

(b2) **11 ... f4 12 ♗d2 ♘xc5 13 ♘xc5 dc 14 b4** (14 ♗e2 should be met not by 14 ... ♘f6?! 15 b4!, but 14 ... ♖f6 15 ♘b5 ♕e7 16 ♗a5 f3! 17 ♗xf3 ♘f4 18 ♗xc7 c4∓ Markov–Sirota, corres 1987) **14 ... cb 15 ♘b5 f3 16 g4 ♘g3 17 ♘xc7 ♕f7 18 ♘xa8 ♘xh1∞** (Koopman).

9	...	♕e8
10	♗e2	f5!

10 ... ♘f4 11 ♗f3 f5 *(16)* is the older approach:

(a) **12 h4?!** ♕e7 13 g3 ♘b4! 14 ♕b3? (14 0-0 g5! is messy but Black seems to have the initiative) **14 ... ♘fd3+ 15 ♔e2 f4 16 ♗d2** is the famous game Kavalek–Kasparov, Bugojno 1982; now 16 ... ♘xf2! would have given Black

a decisive attack.

(b) **12 0-0** is evidently the correct move. There may follow:

(b1) **12 ... g5 13 ♖e1 ♕g6 14 ♘f1 ♕h6 15 ef ♗xf5 16 ♗g4 ♗g6 17 ♘g3 ♘b4 18 ♘ge4 ♘bd3 19 ♗xf4 ♘xf4 20 g3** forced Black to sacrifice unsoundly with **20 ... ♘xh3+ 21 ♔g2 ♘xf2 22 ♘xf2 ♖xf2+** in Kalantarian–Peshina, Blagoveshchensk 1988, since retreating would have been positionally horrible.

(b2) **12 ... ♕e7** can be met by **13 a3, 13 ♔h1 ♘c5, or 13 ♖e1 ♕f6 14 ♔h1** intending h4 and g3 (Romanishin).

(b3) **12 ... b6 13 ♖e1** (13 a3!?; 13 h4 [Korchnoi–Romanishin, Tilburg 1985] 13 ... ♕e7 14 g3 ♘h3+ 15 ♔g2 f4 16 ♗c1 h5∞ — Romanishin) **13 ... ♘c5!?** (13 ... ♕f7 14 a3! ♘c5 15 ♗xc5 bc 16 b4 cb 17 ab± Anastasian–A. Kuzmin, Blagoveshchensk 1988) **14 ♗xf4** (14 ef ♘cd3 and 14 ♗xc5 bc 15 a3 a5 are both pleasant for Black) **14 ... fe 15 ♗xe5 ♕xe5 16 ♗xe4 ♕d4** gives Black compensation according to Kuzmin; one point is 17 ♕xd4 ♗xd4 18 ♘f3? ♗xc3 19 bc ♗xh3!∓.

(b4) **12 ... ♘c5** is Kuzmin's latest try. He gives **13 ef** ♗xf5 16 ♗xc5 dc and **13 ♗xc5** dc 14 ♕d2 ♗d7 both as unclear, whilst **13 ♕c2** a5 14 ♖ad1 b6 15 ♖fe1 ♕f7 occurred in Guseinov–A. Kuzmin, USSR 1991; 16 ef ♗xf5 17 ♘e4 is then equal.

11 ef

White has two other main possibilities:

(a) **11 ♗xh5?!** gh 12 ♘f3 (12 f3) 12 ... fe 13 ♘d2 ♕g6 14 ♕e2 ♗f5 15 0–0–0?! (15 a3) 15 ... ♘b4∓ 16 ♖dg1 c6 17 ♔b1 cd 18 ♘xd5 ♘xd5 19 cd ♗d7 20 g4 hg 21 hg a6 21 g5 ♗b5 22 ♕d1 ♖xf2! was devastating in Anastasian–Neverov, Minsk 1990.

(b) **11 0–0** ♘f6 (11 ... f4 12 ♗d2 ♘f6 13 ♘g4 h5 14 ♘xf6+ ♗xf6 15 a3 ♖f7 16 b4 ♖h7 17 c5 gave White a useful queenside initiative in Vilela–Hernandez, Havana 1991) 12 ef gf 13 f4 ef! (13 ... e4?! 14 g4!±) 14 ♗xf4 (Gheorghiu–Cooper, Novi Sad OL 1990) 14 ... ♘c5!∞ 15 ♘b5 ♕f7 16 ♘d4 ♘ce4 (Gheorghiu).

11 ... ♘f4
12 0–0

In Chernin–J. Polgar, New Delhi 1990, White decided to test Black's pawn sacrifice but found that Black's compensation was excellent: **12 ♗xf4** ef 13 fg ♕xg6 14 ♔f1 (Hansen considers 14 ♗g4 ♗xg4 15 gh ♖ae8+ 16 ♔f1

♘c5 good for Black) 14 ... ♘c5 (14 ... ♗f5) 15 ♖c1?! (15 ♘f3!? ♗d7) 15 ... ♗f5 16 ♘f3 ♗f6!. The game finished **17 ♔g1?!** ♔h8 18 ♔h2 ♖g8 19 ♖g1 ♕h6! 20 ♗f1 (20 b4 ♖xg2+!) 20 ... ♖g7 21 b4 ♘d7 22 ♗d3 (Judit analysed 22 ♘d4 ♗xd4 23 ♕xd4 ♘e5 24 ♗e2 f3∓∓) 22 ... ♖xg2+!! 23 ♖xg2 ♗xh3 24 ♘e4 ♘e5! 25 ♘xe5 ♗xe5 26 ♘g5 ♗xg2+ 27 ♔xg2 ♕xg5+ 28 ♔f3 ♖g8 29 ♔e2 f3+ 0–1. Polgar gave as a better try for White **17 ♘d4** ♗xd4 18 ♕xd4 f3! 19 gf (19 ♗xf3 ♖ae8 20 ♔g1 ♘d3 21 ♖d1 ♘e1!∓∓) 19 ... ♖f7 though Black's threats are ominous.

12 ... ♗xf5

Kasparov prefers never to allow his opponents to settle, so rejects the more obvious **12 ... ♘xe2+** 13 ♘xe2 gf 14 f4.

13 ♖e1! ♕f7!

Black's queen steps out of opposition with the white rook, and prepares threats against f2.

14 ♘f1 *(17)*

White aims with this move to control the e4-square with ♘g3. Ibragimov–Kruppa, Kherson 1991 saw an alternative method: **14 a3** ♘c5 15 ♗xc5 dc 16 ♗f3, which allowed a standard line opening: 16 ... e4 17 ♘xe4 ♗xb2 18 ♖b1 ♕g7 19 ♕d2 ♗e5 20 ♖xb7 ♗xe4 21 ♖xe4 ♘xh3+ 22 ♔h1 ♗f4 and Black was fine.

14 ... ♗xh3?

As Kasparov's analysis shows,

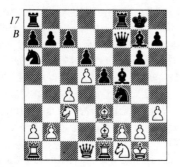

this sacrifice is unsound. The correct way to prevent White winning the battle for e4 was **14 ... ♘b4!** 15 ♘g3 ♘c2 16 ♗xf4 ♘xe1 17 ♘xf5 gf 18 ♗d2 ♘xg2 19 ♔xg2 ♔h8, which Kasparov considered unclear.

15	**gh!**	**♘xh3+**
16	**♔g2**	**♘xf2**
17	**♕b1!**	

White must not allow 17 ... ♕f5.

17	**...**	**e4**
18	**♘g3!**	

Threatens to round up the knight with 19 ♖f1.

18	**...**	**♕d7**
19	**♗xf2**	**♖xf2+**
20	**♔xf2**	**♕h3**
21	**♕xe4!**	

White has found a series of 'only' moves, and would now have been able to reap the reward,

except for the damage they had caused to Hansen's clock time.

21	**...**	**♘c5**

An interesting alternative is **21 ... ♖f8+ 22 ♗f3!** (22 ♔g1 ♗d4+! draws) **22 ... ♕h2+ 23 ♔f1**, but Black has nothing better than **23 ... ♕xg3 24 ♔e2 ♕h2+ 25 ♗g2 ♘c5 26 ♕g4±**, since **23 ... ♗d4 24 ♘d1 ♕g1+ 25 ♔e2 ♕h2+ 26 ♗g2 ♘c5 27 ♕xd4 ♕xg2+ 28 ♘f2 ♕xg3** (△ ... ♖xf2+) **29 ♖f1** (Kasparov) gives Black no more tricks.

22	**♕e7**	**♗e5**
23	**♖g1**	**♖f8+**
24	**♔e1**	**♗xg3+**

Now **25 ♖xg3 ♕xg3+ 26 ♔d2** (Kasparov) would have snuffed out Black's counterchances.

However, there followed an horrendous time scramble: **25 ♔d2?** ♖f7? (25 ... ♗f4+) 26 ♕e8+ ♖f8 27 ♕e7? (27 ♖xg3) 27 ... ♗f4+ 28 ♔c2 ♕f5+ 29 ♔d1 ♖f7 30 ♕e8+ ♖f8 31 ♕e7 ♖f7 32 ♕e8+ ♔g7? (32 ... ♖f8=) 33 ♖f1 ♕f6 34 ♖xf4! ♕xf4 35 ♔c2 ♕g5 36 ♖d1? (36 ♕c8±) 36 ... ♖e7?? (36 ... ♖f8∓) 37 ♕c8 ♕f6 38 ♗d3 ♕f2+ 39 ♖d2 ½–½. White is now winning, but Hansen, with only seconds left, had no idea how many moves had been made.

3 Four Pawns Attack with 6 ... ♞a6

1 d4 ♞f6 2 c4 g6 3 ♞c3 ♝g7 4 e4 d6

| | 5 | f4 | 0-0 |
| | 6 | ♞f3 | ♞a6 *(18)* |

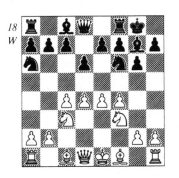

18 W

For more than half a century it was believed that Black had no real choice but to attack the centre with 6 ... c5 (generally leading to Benoni positions) since 6 ... e5 doesn't work: 7 de (7 fe de 8 d5±) 7 ... de 8 ♛xd8 ♜xd8 9 ♞xe5 ♜e8 (9 ... ♞xe4 10 ♞xe4 f6 11 c5!±) 10 ♝d3! ♞xe4? (10 ... ♞a6 11 0-0!± Mikkov-Vooremaa, Tartu 1962) 11 ♝xe4! f6 12 ♝d5+! ♚h8 (12 ... ♚f8 13 0-0!) 13 ♝f7! ♜f8 14 ♞xg6+ hg 15 ♝xg6±± (Geller). Nor is there any obvious way to prepare ... e5, since 6 ... ♞bd7 is strongly met by 7 e5.

However, some lateral thinking by Belov and Glek provided the solution: the point of ... e7–e5 is to fix the e4-pawn as a target, so it is logical to prepare to attack this square *before* actually committing oneself to ... e5. Thus 6 ... ♞a6!. None of White's replies are ideal: 7 ♝e2 puts the bishop on a bad square from the point of view of defending e4; 7 ♝d3 weakens d4 and may leave this bishop rather exposed, whilst after 7 e5 the knight happily retreat to d7, preparing ... c5.

This position, from Gorelov–Belov, Moscow 1987, demonstrates some typical ideas *(19)*: 12 ... ♝e6! gave White immediate problems defending c4, since 13 b3 weakens the long diagonal (13 ... ♞fd7). Thus there followed 13 ♝e3 ♞fd7! 14 ♞d5 ♞xe5 15 fe (15 ♝xc5 ♞xc4) 15 ... ♞d7 16 ♝g5 (16 ♞xc7 ♝xc4+) 16 ... ♝xd5! 17 cd ♜e8 when Black

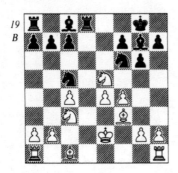

secured a clear positional edge. It seems in this line that White had clearly put his king on the wrong square, but in fact Black's pieces are just so active that the king only has a choice between squares which are less than ideal; examine the third game below!

In practice, White has achieved nothing by accepting the gambit pawn, so attention has been directed towards 7 ♗d3 (considered in our first game), the sharp 7 e5 (second game), and 7 ♗e2 e5 8 fe de 9 d5, which is examined in the notes to the third.

J. Petronić–Belov
Pravets 1989

1 d4 ♘f6 2 c4 g6 3 ♘c3 ♗g7 4 e4 d6 5 f4 0–0 6 ♘f3 ♘a6

7   ♗d3   ♗g4

7 ... e5!? is a more thematic continuation, activating the a6-knight. There may follow **8 fe de 9 d5 c6 10 ♗g5** (10 0–0 cd 11 cd ♘e8=) 10 ... ♕b6! 11 ♕d2 ♘c5 12 ♖b1 cd 13 cd ♘g4 (Sokolin) with good play for Black, or **8**

de de 9 ♘xe5 (9 fe ♘c5!) when, compared with the line 7 ♗e2 e5 8 de de (see Cherniakov–Belov, below), White has e4 securely defended, but the bishop on d3 is a pleasant target for Black's knights:

(a) **9 ... ♘g4!?** 10 ♘xg4 (10 ♘f3 ♘c5) 10 ... ♗xg4 11 ♗e2 ♗xc3+ 12 bc ♕xd1+ 13 ♗xd1 ♗xd1 14 ♔xd1 ♖ad8+ 15 ♔c2 ♖fe8 (Sokolin).

(b) **9 ... ♘c5** 10 ♗e3 (10 0–0? ♕d4+ 11 ♔h1 ♘g4!∓; 10 ♗c2 ♕xd1+ 11 ♔xd1 ♘g4!∓) 10 ... ♘xd3+ 11 ♕xd3 (11 ♘xd3 ♖e8) 11 ... ♕xd3 12 ♘xd3 ♖e8! 13 ♘e5 (13 e5 ♘g4 14 ♗g1 ♗f5) 13 ... ♘g4 and a draw was agreed in S. Ivanov–Sokolin, Leningrad 1991 in view of the line 14 ♘xg4 ♗xc3+! 15 bc ♗xg4 16 e5 f6=.

8   0–0

8 ♗e3 has perhaps been underestimated:

(a) **8 ... ♘d7** 9 ♗e2 (9 0–0 e5 10 fe transposes to the main line) 9 ... c5 10 d5 ♗xf3 11 ♗xf3 ♕a5∞ Kakageldiev–Glek, USSR 1984.

(b) **8 ... c5** 9 d5 e6 and now **10 0–0** ed 11 ed ♖e8 12 ♗d2 ♕d7 13 a3 ♘c7 14 b4 cb 15 ab b5!? 16 ♖a5 a6 17 ♕b3 ♗xf3 18 ♖xf3 ♘g4 19 ♘d1 cb 20 ♗xc4 ♘b5 was more than OK for Black in Vaiser–Gallagher, Suhr 1990; Vaiser proposed **10 de** fe 11 0–0±.

However, **8 h3?!** is illogical: 8 ... ♗xf3 9 ♕xf3 e5! 10 fe ♘d7 11 ♗e3 (11 ed ♗xd4 12 dc ♘xc7∓)

11 ... c5 12 d5 ♘xe5 13 ♕e2 ♘c7∓ Barsov–Maier, Grodno 1984.

8	...	e5
9	fe	♘d7
10	♗e3	c5! *(20)*

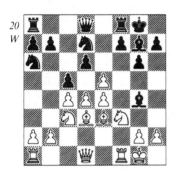

11 d5

11 dc is rather harmless: 11 ... dc 12 ♗e2 ♘xe5= (Belov), or 11 ... de 12 ♗e2 ♗xf3 13 ♗xf3 ♘dxc5 14 ♖f2 ♘e6= Ca. Hansen–Reeh, Gausdal 1990.

11	...	♘xe5
12	♗e2	

Black must now be careful not to allow White's kingside intiative to become too powerful; meanwhile 13 ♘xe5 ♗xe2 14 ♘xf7 is threatened.

12 ... ♗xf3?!

This turns out badly, since White's pawns become strong and mobile. Better are:

(a) **12 ... ♗d7** 13 ♕d2 ♘c7 14 ♗g5 ♕e8 15 ♔h1 a6 16 a4 b6 17 ♕e1 f6 18 ♗d2 ♘f7 19 ♗d3 b5 20 b3 b4 21 ♘e2 ♕e7 22 ♕g3 ♖ae8 23 ♖ae1 ♘e5 left White with only slightly more freedom in Arkhipov–Belov, Moscow 1987.

(b) **12 ... ♘xf3+** 13 ♗xf3 (13 gf?! ♗h3 14 ♖f2 f5∓) 13 ... ♗xf3 14 ♕xf3. Now Black has no time to bring the knight round to e5 (14 ... ♘b8?! 15 ♗f4 ♕e7 16 ♘b5), but can choose between Arkhipov's **14 ... ♘b4** 15 ♕e2 ♕e7 16 a3 ♘a6 and Belov's **14 ... ♕e7** 15 ♗f4 ♘c7 16 ♖ae1 ♗e5=.

13 gf f5?!

This is Belov's unsuccessful attempt to improve on his original recommendation, 13 ... ♘c7, on which he felt 14 f4 ♘d7 15 ♔h1 ♕h4 16 ♖f3 ♖ae8 17 ♕d2 favoured White.

14	f4	♘f7
15	ef	gf
16	♔h1	♕e7
17	♖f3!	♘h8
18	♕d2	♘g6
19	♖g1	♗f6?

The last chance was 19 ... ♘c7 20 ♖h3 ♘e8 21 ♗d3, though Black's position is unpleasant.

After the text, White's attack crashed through in straightforward fashion: 20 ♖h3 ♗h4 21 ♗h5! ♔g7 22 ♗xg6 hg 23 ♕g2 ♖f6 24 ♗d2 ♖h8 25 ♘b5 ♔f7 26 ♖e3! ♕d8 27 ♗c3 ♖h6 28 ♗xf6 ♗xf6 29 ♖e6 1–0.

Glek–A. Kuzmin
Podolsk 1990

1 d4 ♘f6 2 c4 g6 3 ♘c3 ♗g7 4 e4 d6 5 f4 0–0 6 ♘f3 ♘a6

7	e5	♘d7

7 ... ♘e8?! was seen in Dittmar–Kochiev, Gausdal International

1991, a draw resulting after 8 c5 (after 8 ♗e3!?, Black should try 8 ... f6, since 8 ... ♗g4 9 h3 is just miserable) 8 ... de 9 fe ♗g4 10 ♗e3 c6 11 ♗c4 ♘ec7 12 0–0 b5 13 ♗b3 ♘b4 14 ♕d2 ♘bd5 15 ♗h6 ♕d7 16 ♖ae1 a5, despite White's advantage.

8 ♕e2

8 h4?! is logical, but if it fails to mate Black, it must be dubious: **8 ... c5** 9 e6 (9 d5 de 10 h5) 9 ... fe 10 h5 cd 11 ♘xd4 ♘f6 12 hg hg △ ... e5 (Kuzmin), or **8 ... de!?** 9 de (9 fe c5 10 e6 fe 11 ♘g5 ♘f6∓) 9 ... ♘dc5 10 ♕xd8 ♖xd8 11 ♘d5 ♗g4 (Sokolin).

A better alternative is **8 c5 dc 9 d5**, when it seems that the knight should go to b6:

(a) **9 ... ♘db8** 10 h4! gave White a powerful, though not quite winning, attack in Semkov–Hebden, Villeneuve Tolosane 1989: 10 ... c6 (10 ... ♗g4? 11 h5) 11 h5 ♘b4 (11 ... cd?! 12 hg hg 13 ♘g5) 12 hg hg 13 e6! fe 14 ♘e5 ed (Semkov gives 14 ... ♗xe5 15 fe ed 16 ♕d2! ♕c7 17 ♖h8+! ♔xh8 18 ♕h6+ ♔g8 19 ♕xg6+ ♔h8 20 ♕h5+ ♔g8 21 ♗h6 ♖f7 22 ♕g6+ ♔h8 23 0–0–0 ♕xe5 24 ♕xf7 when White's threats are very potent) 15 ♘xg6 ♗f5! 16 ♕h5!! ♖f6 17 ♕h7+ ♔f7 18 ♘e5+ ♔f8 19 ♕h8+ ♗xh8 20 ♖xh8+ ♔g7 21 ♖xd8 ♘c2+ 22 ♔f2 ♘xa1 23 g4 ♖f8 24 ♖xf8 ♔xf8 25 gf ♘c2 26 ♔g3 ♔e8! 27 ♗h3 ♘d7 with a difficult, though perhaps tenable, ending for Black.

(b) **9 ... ♘b6** 10 a3. Now Semkov gave **10 ... e6** 11 ♗xa6 (11 ♗e3? ed 12 ♗xa6 d4!) 11 ... ba 12 ♗e3 ♘xd5 (12 ... c4!?) 13 ♘xd5 ♕xd5 14 ♕xd5 ed 15 ♗xc5. In Videki–Gallagher, Kecskemet 1990, Black chose instead to preserve his knight and after **10 ... ♘b8** 11 ♗e3 c6 12 dc ♘xc6 13 ♗xc5 ♗g4 14 ♗e2 ♖c8 15 ♕xd8 ♖fxd8 could be very well satisfied. There followed 16 ♖d1 ♖xd1+ 17 ♔xd1 ♗xf3 18 ♗xf3 ♘xe5! 19 ♗xb6 ♘xf3 20 ♗xa7 ♗xc3 21 bc ♖xc3! 22 gf ♖xa3 with a hopeless ending for White.

8 ... c5
9 d5 ♘b6

Black now intends to blow open the centre with ... e6.

10 ♘e4

10 ♗e3 ♗g4 11 0–0–0 de 12 fe ♗xf3 13 gf ♗xe5 14 ♗h6 ♗g7 15 ♗xg7 ♔xg7 16 h4 ♕d6 (Kuzmin) is safe for Black.

10 ... ♗g4

10 ... f5 looks less satisfactory: 11 ♘c3 e6 12 de ♘c7 13 ♗e3 ♗xe6 14 0–0–0 ♕e8 15 ed ♗xc4 16 ♕xc4+ ♘xc4 17 ♗xc4+ ♔h8 18 ♖he1 ♘a6 19 d7 ♕d8 20 ♘g5 ♕a5 21 ♗d2 ♕c7 22 ♖e7 ♕d6 23 ♘f7+ ♖xf7 24 ♖xf7 ♘c7 25 ♖e1 ♕d4 26 ♗d5!++ Zakharevich–Agameliev, Moscow 1991.

11 ♘eg5 f6! (21)

11 ... h6? 12 h3!, is no good since White's centre survives.

12 h3

Kuzmin considered the alternatives 12 ♘xh7?! ♔xh7 13 ♘g5+ fg

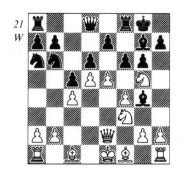

21
W

14 ♕xg4 ♘b4∓ and **12 ef?!** ef 13
♘e6 ♗xe6 14 de ♖e8 15 g4 f5∓.

12	...	♗xf3
13	♘xf3	e6!
14	de	fe
15	fe	♕e7!
16	♗e3?!	

Kuzmin gives instead **16 ♗d2**
de 17 0-0-0 ♕xe6 18 ♘g5 △
♘e4∓, and feels that White's best
is **16 ♗g5!?**.

16	...	de
17	0-0-0	♘c7?!

Instead **17 ... e4** 18 ♘g5 ♘a4
would give Black a powerful
attack.

18	♘g5	♘xe6
19	♘xe6	♕xe6
20	♕g4	♕xg4?!

20 ... ♕c6! 21 ♗d3 e4 22 ♗xe4
♕a4 23 ♔b1 ♕b4∓ was Black's
last chance to preserve any meaningful advantage.

21	hg	♖fd8?!

Correct was **21 ... ♖ac8**.

22	♖xd8+	♖xd8
23	♗xc5	e4
24	b3	

Now Kuzmin gives 24 ... ♗d4

25 ♗xd4 ♖xd4=.

Instead in the game, White
achieved an advantage: **24 ...
♘d7?!** 25 ♗e3 ♘e5 26 ♗e2 a6 27
g5 ♘d3+ 28 ♔c2 ♘b4+ 29 ♔b1
♘c6?! (29 ... ♗d4±) 30 ♗g4
♗d4 31 ♗e6+ ♔g7 32 ♗c1?
(32 ♗xd4+ ♖xd4 33 ♗d5±) 32
... ♖e8 33 ♗d5 e3 34 ♖e1 ♖e5
35 a3 ♖xg5? (35 ... a5!) 36 ♗xe3
♗xe3 37 ♖xe3 h5 38 ♖e6? (38
b4!±) 38 ... ♖g3 39 ♔b2 a5 40
♖d6 ♘e5 41 ♖b6 ♘d3+ 42 ♔b1
♘f4 43 ♖xb7+ ♔f6 44 ♗g8.

Now Black could draw with **44
... ♘xg2!** 45 c5 h4 46 c6 ♖c3 47
♗c4 ♘e3 48 ♔b2 ♖c2+. Instead
after **44 ... ♖xg2?** 45 c5 ♘d3,
White had a chance to win with
46 ♖f7+ ♔e5 47 ♖d7±±, but a
draw was in fact agreed after **46
c6?** in view of the line 46 ... ♖b2+
47 ♔a1 ♖c2 48 c7 ♖c1+ with a
perpetual (½-½).

Cherniakov–Belov
Podolsk 1990

**1 d4 ♘f6 2 c4 g6 3 ♘c3 ♗g7 4 e4
d6 5 f4 0-0 6 ♘f3 ♘a6**

7	♗e2	e5
8	de	

8 0-0 is, naturally, harmless: 8
... ed 9 ♘xd4 ♘c5 10 ♗f3 ♖e8
11 ♖e1 ♗g4! 12 ♗e3 ♗xf3 13
gf ♘h5 left Black at least no worse
in Schön–Fleck, Porz 1988.

A more critical line is **8 fe de**,
and now:

(a) **9 de?!** ♕xd1+ 10 ♗xd1 ♘g4
11 ♗f4 ♘b4∓ (Belov).

(b) **9 ♘xe5 c5.** In Bystriakova–Umanskaya, Stavropol 1989, Black obtained good positional compensation: 10 ♗e3 (10 d5?! ♘xe4) 10 ... cd 11 ♗xd4 ♘g4! 12 ♘f3 ♗xd4 13 ♕xd4 ♘b4 14 0-0-0 ♕xd4 15 ♖xd4 ♘c6 16 ♖d2 ♔g7 17 h3 ♘f6 18 ♖e1 ♗e6 19 ♘g5 ♗c8 20 ♘d5 ♘d7 21 ♘f3 ♖b8 22 ♗d1 ♘de5 23 b3 ♘xf3 24 ♗xf3 ♘e5 25 ♗d1 ♗d7 26 ♔b2 ♖fc8.

(c) **9 d5** and:

(c1) **9 ... ♘c5?!** is too inflexible: **10 ♗g5! h6?!** (10 ... a5 is more solid, but unpromising for Black) **11 ♗xf6! ♕xf6 12 b4!** and now:

(c11) **12 ... ♘xe4?!** 13 ♘xe4 ♕f4 14 ♘fd2 f5 15 g3 ♕e3 16 ♕b3! ♕d4?! 17 ♘c3 e4 18 ♖c1 f4 19 ♘cxe4 ♗f5 20 ♕d3 ♕e5 (D. Ilić–Certić, Belgrade 1989) 21 0-0! fg 22 hg ♖ae8 23 ♗f3++ (Ilić).

(c12) **12 ... ♘a6** 13 a3 ♗g4 14 0-0 ♕e7 15 c5 ♖ad8 16 ♕b3± Berg Hansen–Skodvin, Gausdal International 1990.

(c13) **12 ... ♘d7** 13 c5! a5 14 a3 ab 15 ab ♖xa1 16 ♕xa1 ♕f4 (Hausner–Khalifman, Bundesliga 1990/1) 17 ♕a2! f5 18 g3 ♕e3 19 ♕d2± (Khalifman).

(c2) **9 ... c6** *(22)* is the correct move:

(c21) **10 0-0** cd 11 cd ♕b6+ 12 ♔h1 ♘e8= (Lukin).

(c22) **10 ♗e3** is met most naturally by **10 ... ♘g4** 11 ♗g1 ♗h6. Instead **10 ... cd** 11 cd ♘g4 12 ♗g1 f5 13 ♕b3 fe 14 ♘xe4 ♗f5 15 ♘fd2 ♕a5 16 ♘d6 ♗h6 17

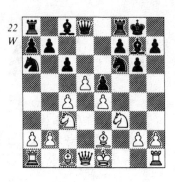

♖d1 was Segal–Piza, Mar del Plata 1990. Black's activity has reached its zenith, and there followed 17 ... ♘c5 18 ♕c4 ♘e3 19 ♗xe3 ♗xe3 20 b4 ♕d8 21 bc b5 22 ♕b3 ♗f2+ 23 ♔xf2 ♗c2+ 24 ♕f3±.

(c23) **10 ♗g5 h6** (10 ... ♕b6?! 11 ♕b3 ♕a5 12 ♘d2 h6 13 ♗h4 g5 14 ♗f2 ♗g4 15 ♕d1 ♗xe2 16 ♕xe2 ♕c7 17 0-0 ♘e8 18 c5 was unsatisfactory for Black in Maksimenko–Martynov, Azov 1991) 11 ♗h4 (11 ♗xf6 ♕xf6 12 0-0=) 11 ... ♕b6 12 ♕d2 (12 ♕c2 ♘g4) 12 ... ♘c5. Now, in Bagaturov–Lukin, Frunze 1989, the tactical possibility 12 ... ♘fxe4 (after 13 ♗f2 or 13 ♕c2) obliged White to exchange, guaranteeing Black a good game: 13 ♗xf6 ♗xf6 14 ♖b1?! (14 ♕xh6 ♕xb2 15 ♖c1 ♗g7 16 ♕e3 is considered unclear by Lukin) 14 ... cd! (14 ... ♗g7 15 b4) 15 cd (15 ♘xd5?! ♘xe4! 16 ♘xf6+ ♘xf6 17 ♕xh6 ♗f5∓) 15 ... ♗g7 16 b4 (16 ♕e3 f5!∓) 16 ... ♘a6 17 ♘a4 ♕d6 18 ♗xa6 (18 0-0 ♗d7 19 ♗xa6

♗xa4) 18 ... ♕xa6 19 ♘c5 ♕d6 20 0-0. The game continued **20 ... f5?!**, when 21 ♖fc1! fe 22 ♘xe4 ♕b6+ 23 ♔h1 ♗f5 24 ♖e1 ♖ad8 25 ♖bd1 would have kept White's disadvantage to a minimum. Lukin recommends instead **20 ... b6** 21 ♘d3 f5 22 ♘f2 ♗b7∓.

8	...	de
9	♕xd8	

9 ♘xe5 ♘c5 10 ♗f3 ♕xd1+ 11 ♔xd1 ♖d8+ 12 ♔c2 (12 ♔e2 ♗e6 13 ♘d5 ♘fd7 14 ♗e3 ♘xe5 15 fe ♘d7 16 ♗g5 ♗xd5 17 cd ♖e8∓ Gorelov-Belov, Moscow 1987) 12 ... ♘fxe4 (This forces a draw; if Black wants more, Belov's 12 ... ♗e6 is worth investigating: 13 ♗e3?! ♘cxe4; 13 ♖e1 ♘fd7; 13 ♘d5 ♘cxe4 14 ♘xc7 ♗f5! 15 g4 ♘xg4 16 ♗xg4 ♗xg4 17 ♘xa8 ♗f5) 13 ♘xe4 ♗f5 14 ♖e1 ♗xe5 15 fe ♖d4 16 ♔c3 ♖d3+ 17 ♔b4 ♘a6+ 18 ♔a5 b6+ 19 ♔xa6 ♗c8+ 20 ♔b5 ♗d7+ 21 ♔a6 ½-½ Ca. Hansen-Berg, Århus 1991.

9	...	♖xd8
10	♘xe5	♘c5
11	♗f3	

11 ♘d5 c6 12 ♘e7+ ♔f8 13 ♘xc8 ♖axc8 14 ♗e3 ♘fxe4 15 0-0 f6 16 ♘f3 f5= Chiburdanidze-Xie Jun, Women's Wch (Manila) 1991.

11	...	♗e6

11 ... ♘fd7 was effective in Vera-Bass, Barcelona 1990: 12 ♘xd7 ♗xc3+ 13 bc ♗xd7 14 0-0 ♗c6 15 ♗e3 ♘xe4 16 ♗xe4 ♗xe4 with a draw in prospect.

12	♘d5

Alternatively:

(a) **12 ♗e3 ♘d3+** 13 ♘xd3 ♖xd3 14 ♔f2 ♗xc4 is equal since 15 ♗e2? fails to 15 ... ♖xc3! 16 bc ♘xe4+ 17 ♔f1 ♗xe2+ 18 ♔xe2 ♘xc3+ (Belov).

(b) **12 0-0 ♘fd7** (12 ... c6 can be met by 13 f5!? gf 14 ef ♗xf5 15 ♗xc6∞ [Belov] or 13 ♗e3 ♘d3 14 ♘xd3 ♖xd3 15 ♔f2 ♘g4+ ½-½ Finegold-Martinović, Dieren 1990) 13 ♘xd7 ♗d4+! 14 ♔h1 ♖xd7 15 ♘d5 is considered in the note to Black's fourteenth move.

12	...	♘fd7! *(23)*

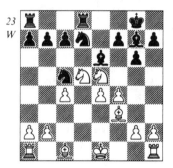

13	♘xd7

The lines following **13 ♘xc7** ♘xe5 14 fe ♗xc4 15 ♗g5 ♘d3+ are playable for Black: **16 ♔f1** ♘xe5+ 17 ♗e2 f6 18 ♘xa8 fg 19 ♘c7 ♖d2 or **16 ♔d2** ♘xe5+ 17 ♗xd8 ♖xd8+ 18 ♘d5 ♘xf3+ 19 gf ♗xd5 20 ed ♗xb2 21 ♖ab1 ♖xd5+ 22 ♔c2 ♗e5 (Belov).

13	...	♖xd7
14	0-0	

14 ♔e2? ♖e8! 15 e5 c6 16 ♗e3 ♘a4∓ Vaiser-Weindl, Mendrisio 1989.

14	...	c6

After **14 ... ♗d4+ 15 ♔h1**
(15 ♗e3? ♖xd5) **15 ... c6**, White
should settle for equality with **16
♗e3** cd **17 ♗xd4** de **18 ♗xc5**
ef (½–½ Solovian–Belov, Podolsk
1990) **19 ♖xf3 ♗xc4**. Instead, in
A. Geller–Belov, USSR 1988,
there followed **16 ♖d1? ♗g7 17
♖b1** (17 ♗e3 ♘a4∓) **17 ... ♖e8
18 b3 ♘xe4! 19 ♗xe4** cd **20 cd**
(20 ♗xd5 ♗f5∓∓) **20 ... ♗g4!
21 ♗f3 ♗f5** with decisive
material gain.

The text is an attempt to keep
more life in the position.

15	♘e3	♗d4
16	♔h1	f5!
17	ef	gf
18	♖d1	

After **18 g4!? ♘d3 19 gf ♗f7**,
Black has plenty of activity.

18	...	♖ad8
19	♘c2	

White remains bottled up after
19 ♖b1 ♘a4 and **19 g4** fg **20 ♗xg4
♗xg4 21 ♘xg4 ♘e4**.

19	...	♗f6
20	♗e3	♘d3
21	♗xa7	♘xb2
22	♖xd7	♖xd7
23	♖e1	♗xc4
24	♘e3	♘d3!

Black has the better chances
in this ending, but Cherniakov
fought well to save the game: **25
♖f1 ♗xa2** (25 ... ♗e6∓) **26 ♘xf5
c5 27 ♗g4 ♔h8 28 ♘g3 ♖e7 29
♗f5 ♗c4 30 ♗xd3 ♗xd3 31
♗xc5 ♖c7 32 ♖c1!? ♔g8?!** (32
... b6 33 ♗a3 ♖xc1+ 34 ♗xc1
♗c3!∓ — Belov) **33 h3 ♗d4 34
♖d1 ♖xc5 35 ♖xd3 ♖c1+ 36
♔h2 ♗g1+ 37 ♔h1 ♗e3+ 38
♔h2 ♗xf4∓ 39 h4 b5 40 ♖b3
♖c4 41 ♔g1 b4 42 ♘e2 ♗e5 43
g3 ♔f7 44 ♔f2 ♔e6 45 ♔e3
♔d5 46 ♔d2 ♖g4 47 ♔c2 ♔c4
48 ♖e3 ♗d6 49 ♔b2 ♗c5 50
♖f3 ♖e4 51 ♖f4 ♖xf4 52 ♘xf4
♗d4+ 53 ♔c2 ♗e5 54 ♘h5!=
b3+ 55 ♔c1 ♔d5 56 g4 ♔e4 57
♔b1** ½–½.

4 Averbakh with 6 ... ♘a6

1 d4 ♘f6 2 c4 g6 3 ♘c3 ♗g7 4 e4 d6

5	♗e2	0–0
6	♗g5	♘a6 *(24)*

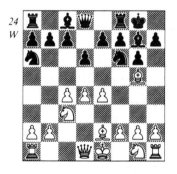

In the Averbakh System, White aims to keep an extremely flexible position. By leaving the king's knight at home for a while, White maintains the option of a kingside advance, which may sometimes lead to a direct attack, but more often aims to block the kingside so White can revert to queenside activity. Only when it is clear where the action will take place, will White's king commit himself to one wing or another. White's sixth move also has a tactical point: 6 ... e5?? loses material after 7 de de 8 ♕xd8 ♖xd8 9 ♘d5.

Black's natural question is 'Can White really achieve so much flexibility for free?' After all, White's king must remain in the centre for at least a few more moves, while the bishop on g5 may become exposed. If Black can find an equally flexible reply, White's position may lose some of its appeal. Such considerations suggest the move 6 ... ♘a6. Black maintains the option of ... c5, while by defending the c7-square, Black not only prepares ... e5, but also frees the queen for action (i.e. after ... ♕e8, White's ♘b5 or ♘d5 would cause no inconvenience). Moreover the queen's bishop is not obstructed (thus White can play g4 less easily).

An extremely important and typical idea for Black is the following pawn sacrifice in response to White's kingside advance *(25)*: 11 g4 (11 h4 is met not by the compromising 11 ... h5, but 11 ... ♕a5 12 g4 h5, transposing) 11 ... ♕a5 12 h4 h5! 13 ♗xf6 ♗xf6 14 gh ♔g7! 15 hg fg 16 h5 ♖h8! 17 h6+ ♔h7 (Ioseliani–Gallagher, Biel 1990) gives Black plenty of

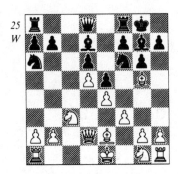

25
W

open lines, while keeping closed most of those White sought to open. In return for this, White has only the h6-pawn which can hardly be maintained in the long term.

In some cases ... ♘a6–c5 causes White some inconvenience, but Black is generally in no hurry to move the knight from a6, especially since after ♗xa6, the opening of the b-file more than outweighs the damage to Black's pawns. A standard method of counterplay is to prepare ... b7–b5, if necessary with ... ♗d7. Petursson–Wojtkiewicz, Bad Wörishofen 1991 is illuminating *(26)*:

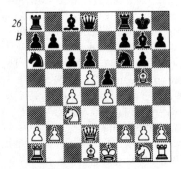

26
B

There followed 9 ... cd 10 cd b5! 11 a3 ♘c5. Now the natural 12 ♗c2 allows 12 ... a5 13 ♘ge2 ♗d7 when White is really being pushed around. Therefore Petursson chose 12 f3 a5! 13 ♘xb5, whereupon 13 ... a4 14 ♘c3 (14 ♖c1 ♕b6∓) 14 ... ♕a5 would have underlined White's slow, and rather uncoordinated development.

Our first illustrative game deals with 7 f4 and other unusual seventh moves. The main line is 7 ♕d2 e5 8 d5; the second and third games consider the replies 8 ... ♕e8 and 8 ... c6 respectively.

Mohr–Miles
Bad Wörishofen 1990

1 d4 ♘f6 2 c4 g6 3 ♘c3 ♗g7 4 e4 d6 5 ♗e2 0–0 6 ♗g5 ♘a6
        7   f4

Instead:

(a) **7 f3** is best met by 7 ... c6 8 ♕d2 e5 9 d5, considered in the game Bykhovsky–Glek.

(b) **7 h4** was tried in Bareev–Kasparov, Linares 1992. After 7 ... h6 8 ♗e3 e5 9 d5 ♘c5, a position known from the line 6 ... h6 7 ♗e3 e5 8 d5 ♘bd7 9 h4 ♘c5 arose. After 10 ♕c2 c6 11 h5 g5 (Kasparov avoids 11 ... cd 12 cd g5?! 13 f3 a5 14 g4 ♗d7 15 ♗b5±, though possible is 11 ... cd 12 cd gh!? 13 ♘f3 ♘g4 14 ♗xc5 dc 15 ♖xh5 a6 16 a4 b6 17 ♘d2 ♕f6∞ Budnikov–Kruppa, USSR Ch (Moscow) 1991) 12 f3 a5 13 g4 ♗d7 14 ♘h3 a4 15 ♕d2 cd 16 cd ♕a5 17 ♘b1!? ♘fxe4!? 18 fe ♘xe4 19 ♕xe5 ♖xa5 Black had reasonable play against White's shattered pawns as compensation for the material deficit.

(c) 7 ♕c1 e5 8 d5 c6 (8 ... ♕e8!?) 9 ♘f3 ♕e8 (Also logical is 9 ... cd 10 cd ♗d7 △ ... ♖c8) 10 0-0 ♘h5 (10 ... c5, blocking the centre and queenside, has its logic now that White's kingside pieces are committed) 11 dc! bc 12 ♖d1 f6 13 ♗e3 f5!? (13 ... ♕e7 14 ♕d2 ♖d8 15 c5 gives White unpleasant pressure, so Black gambits) 14 ♖xd6 f4 15 ♗d2 g5! 16 h3 (16 ♘xg5? ♕e7) 16 ... ♖f6!? 17 ♖xf6 ♗xf6 18 c5! ♘g7 19 b4 ♘c7 20 b5. Now Black should play 20 ... cb 21 ♘xb5 ♘xb5 22 ♕c4+ ♘e6 23 ♕xb5 ♗d7! 24 ♕a5 ♗c6 (Glek), since in Palatnik–Glek, Philadelphia 1990, 20 ... h5?! gave White the possibility 21 bc g4 22 hg hg 23 ♘h2±. Instead there followed 21 ♘h2? cb! 22 ♘xb5 ♘xb5 23 ♕c4+ ♘e6 24 ♕xb5 ♗d7! 25 ♕c4 ♖c8 26 ♗b4 ♔g7, giving Black good attacking chances.

(d) 7 ♘f3 h6! and:

(d1) 8 ♗h4 e5 9 d5 g5 10 ♗g3 transposed to a line of the Petrosian System in Rogers–Mortensen, Vejstrup 1989, whereupon Black introduced a new idea: 10 ... ♘xe4 11 ♘xe4 f5 12 ♘fd2 fe 13 ♘xe4 ♗f5 14 ♗d3 g4∓.

(d2) 8 ♗e3 e5 9 0-0 ♘g4 10 ♗c1 c6! 11 d5 (11 ♖b1!?) 11 ...

f5 12 ♘e1 ♘f6 13 ef gf 14 f4 cd 15 cd (15 ♘xd5 ♗e6) 15 ... ♘g4! 16 ♘d3 ♕b6+ 17 ♔h1 occurred in Farago–Howell, Wildbad 1990. Farago then assesses 17 ... e4!? 18 ♗xg4 ed 19 ♗f3 ♕d4 as unclear.

(d3) 8 ♗f4 e5! 9 de ♘h5 10 ♗e3 de 11 ♕c1 ♔h7 12 0-0 (12 c5 f5 13 ♗xa6 ½-½ Seirawan–Spraggett, Manila IZ 1990) 12 ... c6 13 c5 ♕e7 14 ♘d2 ♘f4 15 ♗xa6 ba 16 ♘c4 ♕e6 (△ 17 ... ♘xg2) 17 ♗xf4 ef 18 ♘d6 ♗e5 19 ♖d1 f3 20 ♕e3 fg 21 f4 ♗g7 22 ♖d2 ♖b8 gave Black reasonable play in Uhlmann–Nunn, Dortmund 1991.

7 ...   ♕e8

This move consistently prepares ... e5, but Black has had some success with other plans:

(a) 7 ... c5 8 d5 ♕a5 (8 ... ♕e8 9 ♘f3 e6 10 de ♕xe6 11 f5 gf 12 ef ♕xf5 13 0-0 gave White dangerous compensation in Moskalenko–A. Kuzmin, Moscow 1991) 9 ♕d2 e6 (9 ... ♖e8?! wastes time: 10 ♘f3 e6 11 de! ♗xe6 12 0-0 ♘b4 13 h3 ♘c6 14 f5!± Savchenko–Shestoperov, Balassagyarmat 1990) 10 de ♗xe6 11 ♘f3 ♗g4 12 0-0 ♘c7 13 f5 ♘d7 14 ♕xd6 ♗xf3 15 ♕xd7 ♗xe2 16 ♘xe2 ♗xb2 17 ♖ad1 ♗e5 18 ♗f4 ♖ae8 19 ♗xe5 ♖xe5 20 ♘f4 g5 21 ♘h5 ♘e8 22 ♕xb7 ♕xa2 23 ♖d5 ♖xe4 24 ♖xc5? ♕e2 25 ♘g3 ♕e3+ 26 ♔h1 ♖h4 0-1 Tukmakov–Barbero, Wijk aan Zee 1991.

(b) 7 ... c6 is Gelfand's imaginative idea, preparing with such moves as ... ♕b6, ... ♘c7–e6 and ... ♘h5, to attack b2, d4, f4 and g5. After **8 ♘f3**:

(b1) **8 ... ♘h5** produces instant chaos: 9 f5! gf (9 ... h6? 10 ♗e3 gf 11 ef ♘f6 12 ♕c1!± ♘g4?! 13 ♗d2 ♗xf5 14 h3 ♘f6 15 ♗xh6 left Black's kingside in a mess in Tukmakov–Nijboer, Wijk aan Zee 1992) 10 ef (10 ♘h4!?) 10 ... ♘f6 11 g4 b5!∞ (Tukmakov).

(b2) **8 ... ♘c7** *(27)*:

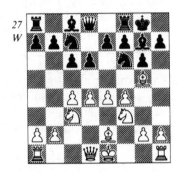

(b21) **9 ♕d2** can be met by **9 ... ♘e6** 10 ♗h4 ♗h6 11 g3 ♘h5 (Seirawan), or **9 ... d5** 10 ♗xf6 ♗xf6 11 cd (11 0–0 ♗g7 12 ♔h1 ♗h6 13 ♖ad1 f6 14 ed cd 15 cd ♔h8 16 ♗c4 ♖b8 Hoeksema–Nijboer, Dutch Ch (Eindhoven) 1991) 11 ... cd 12 e5 ♗g7 13 h4± Moskalenko–Nijboer, Wijk aan Zee 1992.

(b22) **9 d5 ♘h5** 10 f5 (10 ♕d2? f6 11 ♗h4 ♗h6 12 g3 e5) was played in Seirawan–Gelfand, Tilburg 1990. Seirawan then recommends **10 ... cd!** 11 cd (11 fg?! hg 12 ed∓) 11 ... ♘f6! 12 fg hg 13

♕d2 ♘a6! as good for Black. The game continued **10 ... gf?**, when rather than 11 ef ♘f6 12 dc bc 13 g4 ♖b8 14 ♕d2 ♘a6 15 ♘d4 ♕b6 which led to enormous complications, Gelfand proposes 11 ♘d4! h6 12 ♗c1! when none of the lines **12 ... fe** 13 ♗xh5 e5 14 ♘c2 f5 15 0–0± , **12 ... ♘f6** 13 ♘xf5, **12 ... ♗xd4** 13 ♕xd4 e5 (13 ... ♘g7 14 ♗xh6 e5 15 ♕f2 ♘f6 16 ♗xg7 ♔xg7 17 ♖f1 f4 18 g3!) 14 ♕f2 ♘f4 15 ♗xf4 ef 16 ♕xf4±± and **12 ... e5** 13 ♘xf5 ♗xf5 14 ♗xh5 ♗g6 15 0–0± can satisfy Black.

8   ♘f3

This is better than:

(a) **8 e5 ♘d7** △ ... c5.

(b) **8 ♕d2 e5** 9 fe de 10 d5 ♘c5 11 ♕e3 ♘a4 12 ♘b5 ♕e7 13 0–0–0 a6 14 d6 cd 15 ♘xd6 ♕c7 16 ♔b1 ♘c5 17 ♗xf6 (17 ♘f3? ♘fxe4!) 17 ... ♗xf6 18 ♘xc8 ♖fxc8 19 ♗g4 ♘e6! 20 ♗xe6 fe 21 ♖c1 b5 gave Black good play in Tukmakov–Mortensen, Reykjavik 1990. Note the line **22 c5!** ♗e7 23 c6 ♕d6 24 ♘f3 ♖xc6 25 ♖hd1 ♖ac8!=. There in fact followed **22 ♘f3?!** bc 24 ♘d2 (23 ♖c2) 23 ... ♕d8!∓.

8   ...   e5
9   fe

9 de de 10 ♘xe5 ♘c5 offers White nothing at all.

9   ...   de
10   d5

10 ♘xe5 is met by 10 ... c5, whilst on **10 de** ♘g4 11 ♘d5 ♘xe5 Miles notes that neither **12 ♗e7** c6 nor **12 ♘f6+** ♗xf6 13 ♗xf6

♘g4! is desirable for White.

10	...	h6
11	♗xf6	

On 11 ♗h4 Miles planned 11 ... ♘g4 12 ♕d2 f5∞.

11	...	♗xf6
12	a3	♕e7
13	0-0	

13 b4 c5 is a standard way to counter White's queenside ambitions, as White has no real desire to give Black squares with bc or block the queenside with b5.

13	...	♖d8
14	♖b1	c5
15	♕d2	♗g7
16	♖fd1	♗d7
17	b4	♕d6
18	♕e3	♗f8
19	♘b5	♗xb5
20	cb	♘c7
21	♘d2	cb
22	ab	♘e8
23	♘c4	♕e7
24	b6	ab
25	♘xb6	♖ab8 *(28)*

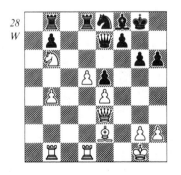

Miles, certainly not a regular King's Indian practitioner, has played very sensibly, keeping to a minimum White's queenside progress, comfortable in the knowledge that White's king is worse in the long term. The game continuation illustrated this well: 26 ♖dc1 ♘d6 27 ♗d3 ♖e8 28 ♖c2 (Black's subsequent bishop manoeuvre shows this to be inaccurate; 28 ♖c3 leaves c2 for the other rook) 28 ... ♕d8 29 ♖bc1 ♗e7! 30 ♕f2 ♗g5 31 ♖f1 ♖f8 32 ♘c4 ♘xc4 33 ♖xc4 h5 34 g3 h4 35 ♗e2 ♖a8 36 ♗g4 ♔g7 37 ♔g2 ♕e7 38 ♕c5 ♖a2+ 39 ♖f2 ♖xf2+ 40 ♔xf2?! ♕f6+ 41 ♔g2 ♖h8 42 ♖c2 (42 ♕f2 h3+ 43 ♔g1 ♕a6) 42 ... hg 43 hg ♗f4!∓ 44 ♕f2 (44 gf ♕xf4∓∓) 44 ... ♕g5 45 ♕f3 ♕h6! 46 ♔f1 ♗xg3! (The bishop is immune due to 47 ... ♕h1+ and 48 ... ♕xe4) 47 ♖c7 ♗f4 48 ♗e6 ♖f8 49 d6 ♕h4 50 d7 ♖d8 51 ♗h3 ♖a8 52 ♔e2 ♖a2+ 53 ♔d3 ♕f6 54 ♔c4 ♕a6+ 0-1.

F. Portisch–Glek
St. Ingbert 1991

1 d4 ♘f6 2 c4 g6 3 ♘c3 ♗g7 4 e4 d6 5 ♗e2 0-0 6 ♗g5 ♘a6

7	♕d2	e5

7 ... c6 8 h4 (8 ♘f3; 8 f3) 8 ... ♘c7 9 h5?! ♘e6 10 ♗e3 c5 11 d5 ♘d4 12 ♗d1 e6 13 ♗h6?! e5 14 ♘h3 ♗g4 15 ♗xg7 ♔xg7 16 ♗xg4 ♘xg4 17 f3?? ♘e3∓∓ Gaprindashvili–Baczinski, Baden Baden 1991.

8	d5	

8 ♘f3 ♕e8 9 d5 (9 de?! de 10

0–0 ♘c5 11 ♗xf6 ♗xf6 12 b4 (12 ♘d5 ♗d8!) 12 ... ♘e6 13 c5 c6 14 ♖fe1 gave White less than nothing in Tukmakov–Gelfand, USSR Ch (Odessa) 1989, but worse still would be 9 0–0? ed 10 ♕xd4 ♘xe4! 11 ♕xe4 ♗xc3∓) 9 ... ♘c5 10 ♗xf6 (10 ♕c2 a5=) 10 ... ♗xf6 11 b4 ♘d7 12 0–0 ♗e7 13 ♖ac1 ♕d8 14 ♖fd1 ♘f6 15 c5 ♘h5 16 g3 f5 17 ♘xe5 de 18 ♗xh5 gh 19 d6 led to sharp play in Van Riemsdijk–Nijboer, Amsterdam 1990.

8 ... ♕e8 *(29)*

For **8 ... c6** see the next game. A third possibility was introduced, though hardly explored, in Schandorff–Høi, Danish Ch (Århus) 1992: **8 ... ♗d7!?** 9 ♗d3 ♘c5 10 ♗c2 a5 ½–½. Black's eighth move is logical and deserves attention.

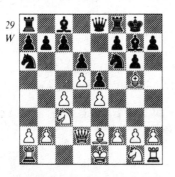

29
W

9 ♗f3

White has a wide choice here:

(a) **9 f3** ♘h5 10 ♗d1 f5 11 ♘ge2 ♕f7 12 ♗c2 ♘c5 13 b4 ♘d7 14 0–0 (△ g4) 14 ... f4 15 ♘b5 ♘b6 was Agrest–Grabarczyk, Bielsko–Biala 1990. Now Agrest gave 16

c5! ♘c4 17 ♕d3 ♘e3 18 cd ♘xf1 19 ♘xc7 ♖b8 20 ♖xf1 △ ♗e7±.

(b) **9 h4** is perhaps best met by 9 ... ♘h5 10 ♗xh5 gh 11 f3 f5 12 ♗h6 ♗xh6 13 ♕xh6 ♘c5 14 0–0–0 fe 15 fe ♗g4, as in Ernst–Pavlović, Bern 1989.

(c) **9 ♘f3** ♘h5 10 g3 f5 11 ♘h4 f4 12 g4 ♘f6 13 f3 h5 14 gh ♘h7 was good for Black in Tisdall–Watson, Oslo Cup 1991.

(d) **9 0–0–0** ♘c5 10 f3 ♘h5 11 ♗h6 a5 12 ♗xg7 ♔xg7 13 ♗d3 f5 14 ♗c2 fe 15 ♘xe4 ♘xe4 16 ♗xe4 ♘f6 17 ♗c2 b5!? initiated play against the white king in Jasnikowski–Piket, Novi Sad OL 1990.

(e) **9 ♗d1** ♘c5 (After 9 ... ♘h5, 10 ♗xh5 transposes to 9 ♗f3 ♘h5 10 ♗xh5, whilst Mirallès gives 10 ♗a4 ♗d7 11 ♗xd7 ♕xd7 12 ♘ge2 f5 13 ef gf 14 ♘g3∞; 9 ... ♗d7 10 h3 ♔h8 11 g4 ♘g8 12 ♗c2± Mirallès–Wiendl, Switzerland 1990) 10 ♗c2 a5 11 ♘ge2. Now, instead of **11 ... ♘h5?!** 12 ♘b5! ♕d7 13 0–0–0 b6 14 f3 a4 (Seirawan–Piket, Wijk aan Zee 1991) 15 ♔b1! △ ♘ec3±, Knaak recommends **11 ... ♗d7** 12 ♘g3 ♘g4! 13 h3 f6 14 hg fg=.

9 ... h5!?

9 ... ♘h5 was Glek's original choice, against Petursson at Belgrade 1988; after 10 ♗xh5 gh 11 ♘ge2 f5 12 ef ♗xf5 13 ♘g3 e4, Petursson's improvement over the game is 14 ♗h6! ♘c5 15 0–0 a5 16 ♗xg7 ♔xg7 17 f3!±, while after Glek's **13 ... ♕g6**, he gives

14 ♘xf5 ♖xf5 15 ♗e3 ♕xg2 16
0-0-0 with quite dangerous compensation.

Also possible is **9 ... c6!?** 10 dc
♕xc6 11 ♖c1 ♗e6 12 b3 ♘c5 13
♘ge2 h6! 14 ♗xf6 ♗xf6 15 ♖d1
♗g5! 16 ♕c2 (16 ♕xd6?! ♖fd8)
16...h5= C. Horvath–Dydyshko,
Harkany 1991.

10 h3

10 ♘ge2 ♘h7 11 ♗h6 f5 gives
Black good play.

10	...	♘h7
11	g4!?	♘xg5
12	♕xg5	f6
13	♕d2	

Black makes good use of the
h-file after 13 ♕h4 hg 14 hg ♔f7.
After the text, Glek decided the
right plan was to close the h-file
and play ... f5; the h3 pawn may
then become a weakness.

| 13 | ... | h4! |
| 14 | ♗g2 | |

14 ♗d1 f5 15 gf gf 16 ♘f3 fe △
... ♖f4 causes White problems.

| 14 | ... | f5 |
| 14 | ♘f3 | |

15 gf gf only opens lines for
Black: 16 ef e4! or 16 ♘f3 fe and
17 ... ♖f4.

| 15 | ... | fg |
| 16 | ♘xh4 | |

After **16 hg** ♗xg4 17 ♘xh4
♖f4!, Black is prepared to sacrifice
the exchange with 18 f3 ♗d7 19
♘e2 ♕f7.

| 16 | ... | ♖f4! |
| 17 | 0-0-0?! | |

Glek gave **17 hg** as best, when
Black has a pleasant choice

between **17 ... ♗f6!?** and **17 ...
♗xg4.**

After the text move, **17 ... gh!** 18
♗xh3 ♖xh4 19 ♗xc8 ♖xh1 20
♗e6+ ♕xe6! 21 de ♗h6 22 ♖xh1
♗xd2+ 23 ♔xd2 c6∓ (Black will
round up the e6-pawn) was Glek's
recommendation.

In the game, **17 ... ♕f7!?** 18 hg
♖xf2 19 ♕g5! ♕f4+ 20 ♕xf4 ef
only gave Black a small advantage
in the ending, but he went on to
win anyway: 21 ♖d2 ♖xd2 22
♔xd2 ♔f7 23 ♘f3?! (23 g5) 23
... ♗xg4 24 ♖h4 ♗h5 25 ♖xf4+
♔e7 26 ♖h4 ♖f8∓ 27 ♖h3 ♘c5
28 ♔e3 ♗h6+ 29 ♔d4 ♗g7+
30 ♔e3 ♗h6+ 31 ♔d4 ♗c1 (31
... a5!?) 32 b4 ♘d7 33 c5 ♗b2!∓∓
34 ♘h4 ♖f2 35 ♗f3 ♘e5! 36 ♔e3
♖xf3+! 37 ♘xf3 ♘xf3 38 ♖xh5
gh 39 ♘d1 ♗d4+ 40 ♔xf3 ♔f6
0-1. The knight is dominated by
the bishop, so the h-pawn is
decisive.

Av. Bykhovsky–Glek
Moscow 1989

1 d4 ♘f6 2 c4 g6 3 ♘c3 ♗g7 4 e4
d6 5 ♗e2 0-0 6 ♗g5 ♘a6 7 ♕d2
e5 8 d5

| 8 | ... | c6 |
| 9 | h4 | |

An interesting idea is **9 ♗d3!?**
♘c5 10 ♗c2. Now Petursson–
Nunn, Reykjavik 1990, continued
10 ... ♕b6?! 11 ♖b1 ♕b4? (11 ...
a5 12 ♘ge2±) 12 ♘ge2! a5 (After
12 ... ♕xc4 13 ♗xf6 ♗xf6 14
b4 ♘a6? 15 ♗d3 the queen is

trapped) 13 a3 ♕xc4 14 ♗xf6
♗xf6 15 b4 ab 16 ab cd 17 bc d4
18 ♘d5 ♗d8 19 ♗b3 ♕a6 20
0–0 dc 21 ♖fc1 ♕d6 22 ♗c4 ♔g7
23 f4! reaching a position where
the piece was stronger than the
pawns. Given that the queen
manoeuvre fails, Black should
clearly investigate Petursson's
suggestion of **10 ... a5** 11 ♘ge2
(11 f3?! cd 12 cd h6=) 11 ... cd 12
cd (12 ed!?) whereupon **12 ... b5!?**
13 ♘xb5 h6 14 ♗xf6 ♗xf6 15
0–0 slightly favours White, whilst
the solid **12 ... ♗d7** is undoubt-
edly the most rational approach.

9 ♘f3 ♘c5 10 ♗xf6 (10 ♕c2
h6 11 ♗d2? cd 12 cd ♘fxe4! 13
♘xe4 ♗f5 14 ♗d3 ♗xe4 15
♗xe4 f5∓ Basin–Ermolinsky,
Simferopol 1988) 10 ... ♕xf6 11
b4 ♘a6 12 a3 c5! 13 ♖b1 ♕e7 14
0–0 f5 15 ♘e1 was Bareev–G.
Kuzmin, USSR Ch (Leningrad)
1990. Bareev analysed 15 ... fe! 16
♘xe4 ♗f5 17 ♗f3 b6 18 ♘d3
♖ac8 19 bc ♗xe4 20 ♗xe4 ♘xc5
as comfortably equal for Black.

9 f3 cd 10 cd ♗d7 generally
transposes to 9 h4 lines after **11
h4** or **11 g4** ♕a5 12 h4 h5. Instead
11 ♗xa6 ba 12 ♘ge2 ♖b8 13
♗e3 ♖b7 14 0–0 ♘e8 15 ♘c1 f5
16 ♘d3 f4 17 ♗f2 g5 18 ♖fc1 g4
merely walked into Black's attack
in Muse–Stangl, Kecskemet 1990.
Another try, **11 ♗b5**, yielded
nothing in Kharlamov–Dyd-
yshko, Harkany 1991: 11 ... ♕a5!
12 ♗xd7 ♘xd7 13 ♘ge2 b5 14
0–0 b4 15 ♘d1 ♖fc8 16 b3

(16 ♘e3 f6 17 ♗h4 ♗h6=
Dydyshko) 16 ... ♘ac5 17 ♘e3
♕b5 18 ♘c4 ♗f8 19 ♕e3 ♘b6!
20 ♖ac1 a5=.

9 ♗f3 cd 10 cd (10 ♘xd5 ♘c5
11 ♘xf6+ ♗xf6 12 ♗xf6 ♕xf6
13 ♘e2 ♖d8 14 0–0 ♘e6 15 ♘c3
♘d4 16 ♗e2 ♗e6 17 ♗d3 ♖ac8
18 b3 g5 was comfortable for
Black in Farago–C. Horvath,
Budapest 1990) 10 ... ♗d7 11
♘ge2 b5 12 a3 ♘c5 13 ♖d1 a5∓
Bilunov–A. Kuzmin, Podolsk
1989.

9	...		cd
10	cd		♗d7
11	f3 *(30)*		

11 ♗xa6 ba 12 h5 (12 f3 ♕a5
13 g4 h5) 12 ... ♕a5 13 ♘ge2
♖ab8 14 f3 ♕b6!∓ Moskalenko–
Glek, Odessa 1989.

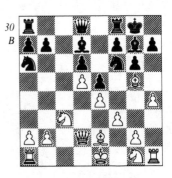

11	...		♕a5

Black has a couple of other
queen moves:

(a) **11 ... ♕e8** 12 g4 h5 13
0–0–0 (13 ♗xf6 ♗xf6 14 gh is
met in the same way as in the
main game) 13 ... hg (Kuzmin felt
that 13 ... ♖c8 and 13 ... ♔h7

14 ♗xf6 ♗xf6 15 gh gh∞ were
better ways to proceed) 14 h5 gave
White quite dangerous play in
Gyurkovics–A. Kuzmin, Budapest 1989, but he failed to make
the most of it: 14 ... ♘xh5 15 fg
♘f4 16 ♗xa6 ba 17 ♕h2 f6 18
♗xf4 ef 19 ♕h7+ ♔f7 20 ♖h6
♖h8 21 ♕xg6+ ♔g8 22 ♖xh8+
♔xh8 23 ♕xe8+ ♖xe8 and Black
won quickly.

(b) **11 ... ♕b6** 12 g4 h5 13
0–0–0 (13 ♗e3 ♘c5 14 g5 ♘h7
15 ♘h3! a5! 16 ♘f2 ♕c7 gave
Black, always able to play ... f6,
enough activity in Budnikov–
Krasenkov, Vienna 1990) 13 ...
♖ac8 (13 ... hg; 13 ... ♔h7) 14
♔b1 ♘c5 15 ♗xf6 ♗xf6 16 gh
♔g7 17 ♘h3 ♖h8 18 hg ♗xh3
19 ♖xh3 fg 20 ♖dh1 ♖h6 21 ♕e1
♖ch8 22 ♕g3 ♕b4 23 ♕g4. White
plans to unpin the h-pawn and
exert pressure on the g-file. In
Schandorff–Berg, Kerteminde
1991, Black's position fell apart:
23 ... a6 24 h5 ♕d4 25 ♖g3 b5 26
♖c1 g5 27 ♖h3 ♖b8 28 ♖hh1 b4
29 ♘a4 b3 30 ab ♖xb3 31 ♖c4
♕e3 32 ♘xc5 dc 33 ♕d7+ ♔g8
34 ♕c8+ ♔h7 35 ♖xc5 ♗d8 36
♕d7+ 1–0.

12 g4

12 ♘h3 ♘h5! (12 ... h5 13 ♘f2;
12 ... ♘c5 13 ♖b1; 12 ... ♖fc8 13
g4 h5 14 ♘f2) 13 g4 (13 ♗e7?
♖fe8 14 ♗xd6 ♘g3∓) 13 ... ♘g3.
Now **14 ♖g1 ♘xe2 15 ♘xe2 ♘b4!?**
(15 ... ♕xd2+ is equal) 16 ♔f1
♗b5 allowed Black good play in
Plotnikov–Golubev, Kramatorsk

1990. Golubev analysed instead **14
♗xa6!** ♕xa6! 15 ♖g1 ♘h5 16 gh
(16 ♗h6 ♘f4!) 16 ... ♗xh3 17
0–0–0! (17 ♗h6 ♖ac8∞) 17 ... b5
when Black has reasonable
counterplay.

12	...	h5
13	♗xf6	♗xf6
14	gh	♔g7
15	♗xa6	

15 hg fg 16 h5 ♖h8 17 h6+
♔h7 18 ♘h3 ♗xh3 19 ♖xh3
♖ac8 20 ♔f1 ♘c5 21 ♖b1 ♕d8
was very playable for Black in
Ioseliani–Gallagher, Biel 1990.

15	...	ba
16	hg	fg
17	h5	

17 ♕g2 ♖h8 18 h5 ♖h6 19 ♘e2
♖b8 20 0–0–0 ♕b4 21 ♖d2 ♖g8
22 ♖c2 ♔f7 23 hg+ ♖gxg6 24
♕f1 ♕b6 25 ♔b1 ♕e3=
Gaprindashvili–Ioseliani, Tbilisi
1991.

17	...	♖h8
18	h6+	♔h7 *(31)*

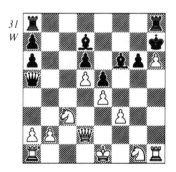

31
W

Black's pawn sacrifice is now a
standard idea. Black's king is safe
and he has good play, especially

on the f-file.

19	♘h3	♛d8
20	♛g2	♗h4+
21	♔e2	♖b8!
22	b3	♖c8
23	♖ac1	♖f8
24	♖hg1	♛f6
25	♘f2	

Glek now recommends **25 ...
♖c7!∓** since 26 ♘g4 ♛g5! 27 ♘e3
♛xg2+ favours Black after **28
♘xg2 ♗g5** and **28 ♖xg2 ♗b5+!**.
In the game **25 ... ♗g5?** 26
♛xg5! ♖xf3+ 27 ♔d2 ♛xf2+ 28
♘e2 ♛f6 29 ♛xf6 ♖xf6 30 ♖gf1!
♖xf1 31 ♖xf1 ♗e8 32 ♖f6 ♖d8
33 ♘g3! ♖d7 34 ♖e6! ♗f7 35 ♖f6
gave Black nothing better than
repeating with **35 ... ♗e8**. Instead
35 ... ♔xh6?! 36 ♘f5+ ♔g5 37
♖xd6 ♗e8 38 ♖xd7 ♗xd7 39

♘d6! ♔f4 40 ♘b7 g5 41 ♘c5 ♗c8
42 ♔e2 only gave White chances,
since the d-pawn is at least as
dangerous as the g-pawn. 42 ...
a5! 43 d6 g4 44 ♔f2 g3+ 45 ♔g2
♗g4 46 d7 ♗xd7 47 ♘xd7 ♔xe4
48 ♔xg3 followed, whereupon **48
... ♔d3!** would have been
sufficient, e.g. 49 ♘c5+ ♔c3 50
♔f3 ♔b4! 51 ♘a4 ♔a3= (Glek).
Instead, some less accurate play
by both sides led to a draw anyway: **48 ... ♔d4?** 49 ♔f3 e4+ 50
♔f4! e3 51 ♔f3 ♔d3 52 ♘e5+
♔d4 53 ♘g4 ♔c3 54 ♔xe3 ♔b2
55 ♔d3 ♔xa2 56 ♔c3? (56 ♔c2!
a4 57 b4 ♔a3 58 ♔c3 a6 59 ♘f2
♔a2 60 ♔c2 ♔a3 61 ♘d3 ♔a2
62 ♘c5±±) 56 ... a4! 57 b4 ♔b1
58 ♘e3 a3 59 ♘c2 a2 60 ♘a1
♔xa1 61 ♔c2 a6 ½-½.

5 Classical with 7 ... ♘a6

1 d4 ♘f6 2 c4 g6 3 ♘c3 ♗g7 4 e4
d6

	5	♘f3	0–0
	6	♗e2	e5
	7	0–0	♘a6 (32)

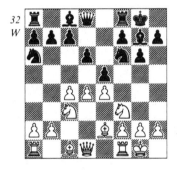

7 ... ♘a6 is by no means an
obvious or natural move, which
perhaps explains why it has only
appeared very recently on the
tournament scene. It is not that
the move tended to be rejected
because of any presumed defect (it
only takes a little analysis to see
that White cannot win the e5-
pawn), but rather the move was
not even considered.

Having made this conceptual
leap, one naturally compares 7
... ♘bd7. Several

advantages over the older move
are apparent:

(a) The c8-bishop is not
obstructed, and so may venture to
g4, increasing the pressure on d4.
Also, if the king's knight should
move to g4, lines with ♕xg4 are
ruled out. A further point is that
if a later ... f5 is met by ef, the
possibility of recapturing with the
bishop is sometimes useful.

(b) The c7-square is defended,
so the queen is free to move to
e8, increasing the pressure on e4
(access to squares on the a4–e8
diagonal is sometimes useful too).

(c) The knight does not interfere
with the queen defending d6, so
d5 can be met by ... c5 or ... c6
without Black needing to fear the
reply dc bc, ♕xd6.

(d) Since the knight covers b4,
White's standard queenside
advance is slower. Even after suit-
able preparation, b4 may be well
met by ... c5, when it is difficult
for White to open lines in any
useful way. Alternatively, Black
may choose to play ... c5 before
White plays b4.

(e) After ... c7–c6, the knight

will often find the c7 square useful
sometimes as a more convenient
route to e6 than (following 7 ...
♘bd7) via f8 since the rook does
not have to move.

(f) ... ♘b4 may be an annoying
reply to ♕c2.

Does 7 ... ♘a6 have any disad-
vantages?

(a) Occasionally, the fact that e5
is less well covered is a problem.

(b) Opening the centre with ...
ed cannot be followed by placing
the queen's knight on e5.

(c) Black must reckon with the
possibility of ♗xa6, though often
use of the b-file is more important
than the shattering of the queenside pawns.

(d) Following White's d4–d5,
Black often wishes to play ... ♘c5.
With the knight on a6, Black does
not have the option of first securing this square with ... a5; thus,
if White already has e4 securely
defended, ... ♘c5 may be met by
b4.

(e) White's eventual queenside
advance threatens to leave the
knight rather stranded on a6.

Dreev–Glek, Frunze 1988, one
of the earliest games with 7 ...
♘a6, illustrates a number of these
points *(33)*:

Black now played 9 ... ♗g4,
intending to meet 10 ♘xe5 with
10 ... ♘b4! 11 ♕d1 ♕xd1 12 ♗xd1
♗xd1 13 ♖xd1 ♘xe4= and 10
♖d1 with 10 ... ♕e8 11 b3 ♗xf3
12 ♗xf3 ♕e6= (Black's position
is rock solid). There followed 10

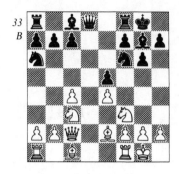

♗e3 ♗xf3 11 ♗xf3 c6 12 b4!?,
when 12 ... ♘c7 would be fine for
Black, but Glek decided the pawn
could be taken: 12 ... ♘xb4! 13
♕b3 ♕a5! 14 ♗d2 ♘d3 15 ♘b1
(15 ♕xb7? ♖ab8 followed by ...
♖b2 is good for Black) 15 ... ♕d8
16 ♗e3! ♘f4 17 ♕xb7 ♕d3 (17 ...
♕d7=) 18 ♘d2 ♖fc8 19 ♖ab1 and
then Black should have played 19
... ♘e6! followed by 20 ... ♘d4.

The rôle of the queen's knight
is exemplified by Berg Hansen–
Schandorff, Danish Ch (Århus)
1992 *(34)*:

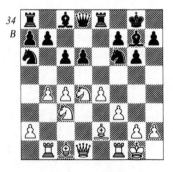

Black could now try 11 ... ♘xb4
12 ♖xb4 c5, but instead preferred
11 ... ♘c7. From this square, the

knight supports a possible ... d5 (which would be the answer to 12 ♗e3), while eyeing the e6-square. Play continued 12 ♔h1 ♘h5 13 g4 (White cannot afford to allow ... ♕h4 and ... ♗e5, while 13 ♗e3 gives Black the option of 13 ... f5) 13 ... ♕f6! 14 gh (14 ♗e3 ♘f4 15 ♕d2 ♘ce6) 14 ... ♕xd4 with a slight edge for Black.

Steingrimsson–Kochiev, Gausdal 1991, illustrates another way to organise Black's knights *(35)*:

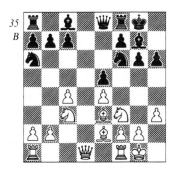

Play now continued 13 ... ♘d7 (The alternative is 13 ... ♘h5 14 c5 ♘f4, allowing ♗xa6 in return for open lines and activity) 14 a3 ♘ac5 (Having provoked the tempo-losing a3, the knight heads for greener pastures before b4 comes. Black avoids ... c6 for as long as possible, to deny White use of the d6-square) 15 b4 ♘e6 16 c5 ♘f4 17 ♗c4 (White may have an edge here, but clearly Black's game is very playable) 17 ... g5 18 ♘b5 ♕d8 19 a4 a6 20 ♘c3 c6 21 ♘d2 ♕e7 22 ♘b3 ♖e8. White is not making progress very

quickly, and Black went on to win with the inevitable kingside attack.

Other aspects of the knight's position on a6 were demonstrated in Shirov–J. Polgar, Brno 1991 *(36)*:

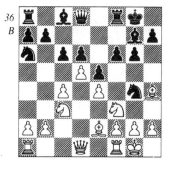

Were the knight on d7, Black would need to take measures to secure the d6-pawn. Here, Judit was able to adopt an active approach: 11 ... ♘h6 12 ♘d2 g5 13 ♗g3 f5 14 ef ♘xf5 15 ♘de4 ♘d4 16 ♗g4 h6 17 h3 ♗f5 (Now we see also the benefit of the knight not obstructing the queen's bishop) 18 ♖e1 ♕d7 19 ♘e2 ♗xg4 20 hg ♕xg4 21 ♘xd4 ♕xd1 22 ♖axd1 ed 23 ♗xd6 ♖f7 24 dc bc 25 ♘c5 ♖d8 and an endgame was reached in which Black was active enough not to be in serious danger.

Finally, we consider a typical situation in which, following White's d4–d5, Black effectively manages to play ... a7–a5 despite the knight being on a6. A miracle? Witness Kiselëv–Krasenkov, Moscow Ch 1989 *(37)*:

Black played 9 ... ♗g4 10 d5

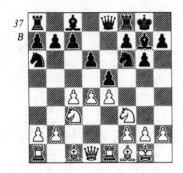

37
B

♘b4!? threatening 11 ... ♗xf3 when White would have to recapture with the pawn, since 12 ♕xf3 lets the knight into c2. 11 a3?! ♗xf3 12 gf ♘a6 13 f4 ef 14 ♗xf4 ♘h5 is clearly promising for Black, so White chose 11 ♗e2 a5 12 ♗e3 b6 13 a3 ♘a6. Black's queen's knight has lost two tempi, but so has White's king's bishop. Meanwhile, Black has provoked d4–d5 without (as often necessary in the 7 ... ♘bd7 line) misplacing the rook on e8, and managed to keep White's queenside expansion in check by playing ... a5. After 14 b3, Krasenkov recommends 14 ... ♘h5 15 g3 f5∞, rather than the game's 14 ... ♘c5?! 15 h3!±.

8 ♖e1 and others

Guseinov–Glek
Azov (USSR Teams) 1991

1 d4 ♘f6 2 c4 g6 3 ♘c3 ♗g7 4 e4 d6 5 ♘f3 0–0 6 ♗e2 e5 7 0–0 ♘a6

8   ♖b1
More common moves are **8 ♖e1**

(see next game), and **8 ♗e3**, considered in the next section. White has a number of even rarer ideas:

(a) **8 b3** ed 9 ♘xd4 ♖e8 10 f3 c6 11 ♗b2. Now 11 ... d5 12 ed cd 13 ♕d2 dc 14 ♗xc4 ♗e6 was not bad for Black in Blees–J. Piket, Dutch Ch (Hilversum) 1989, but Piket afterwards preferred 11 ... h5!? △ ... h4, ... ♘h5.

(b) **8 ♕c2** is only useful as a drawing attempt, or to repeat moves (useful for time-trouble addicts), since after 8 ... ♘b4, White has nothing better than 9 ♕d1 (other queen moves are well met by 9 ... ♘c6). Then **9 ... ♘a6** repeats, while in Dautov–Savchenko, Tbilisi 1989, **9 ... ♗g4** was tried, but after 10 d5 a5 11 ♗e3 b6 12 a3 ♘a6 13 h3 ♗d7 14 ♘d2 ♘e8 15 ♖c1 f5 16 ef gf 17 f4 ♘f6 18 ♗d3 ef 19 ♗xf4 White had some advantage.

(c) **8 de de** is a very insipid form of exchange variation:

(c1) **9 ♕xd8** ♖xd8 10 ♗e3 (10 h3 ♘c5 11 ♗g5 c6 12 ♖fd1 ♖e8 13 ♗d3 ♗e6 was already promising for Black in Martin–Mestel, British Ch (Eastbourne) 1990) 10 ... ♘g4 11 ♗g5 f6 12 ♗c1 c6 13 h3 ♘h6 14 a3 ♘c5 15 ♗e3 ♘e6 16 ♖fd1 ♖e8 17 c5 ♘f7 18 b4 f5 19 ♗c4 ♗f6 20 ♖a2 ♔g7 21 ef gf 22 ♖e2 was Kamsky–Benjamin, US Ch (Los Angeles) 1991; 22 ... ♘f8!? would then have been pleasant for Black.

(c2) **9 ♕c2** ♗g4 (9 ... ♘b4!?) 10 ♗e3 (10 ♘xe5 ♘b4!; 10 ♖d1 ♕e8

11 b3 ♗xf3 12 ♗xf3 ♕e6=) 10 ... ♗xf3 11 ♗xf3 c6 gave Black full equality in Dreev–Glek, Frunze 1988.

(d) **8 ♗g5 h6 9 ♗h4** is a reasonable idea, which has not become popular. A couple of rapid games, Kožul–Damljanović, Belgrade 1992 saw **9 ... ed** 10 ♘xd4 ♘c5 11 f3 ♘e6 12 ♘xe6 ♗xe6 13 ♖c1 c6 14 ♗f2 ♘h5 15 ♕d2 g5 16 ♖fd1 ♘f4 17 ♗f1 ♗e5 18 c5 which very marginally favoured White, and **9 ... ♕e8** 10 d5!? (10 ♖e1 ed 11 ♕xd4 g5 12 ♗g3 ♘h5 13 ♕d2 ♘c5 14 ♗f1 ♗g4 15 ♘d4 ♘xg3 16 hg c6 was fine for Black in Savchenko–Yurtaev, Simferopol 1988) 10 ... ♗d7 (10 ... ♘h7 and 10 ... ♘h5 come into consideration) 11 ♘d2 ♘c5 12 ♗xf6 ♗xf6 13 b4 ♘a4 14 ♕b3 a5 15 a3 ♗g5 16 ♘f3 ♘xc3 17 ♕xc3 ♗g4 18 ba ♗xf3 19 ♗xf3 ♕a4 20 ♖fb1 ♖fb8 21 ♖b5! c6 22 dc bc 23 ♖xb8+ ♖xb8 24 ♗d1 1–0.

8 ... ed

Black is not actually obliged to exchange:

(a) **8 ... c6** can be met by **9 ♖e1** (see 8 ♖e1 c6 9 ♖b1); instead **9 de** de 10 ♕xd8 ♖xd8 11 b4 ♘c7 12 ♘xe5 ♘xe4 13 ♘xe4 ♗xe5 14 ♗g5 ♖e8 15 ♗d3 ♗f5 gave White less than nothing in Petran–Timoshchenko, Budapest 1989. White's most consistent is **9 b4**, when 9 ... ed 10 ♘xd4 ♖e8 11 f3 transposes to the main line below.

(b) **8 ... ♖e8** 9 de de 10 b4 c6

11 ♕xd8 ♖xd8. Black is a whole tempo down on the previous line, but still has no problems. Korchnoi–Gelfand, Manila IZ 1990 concluded 12 ♗e3 ♘g4 13 ♗g5 f6 14 ♗h4 ♗e6 15 a3 ♘h6 16 ♖fd1 ♘f7 17 ♘d2 ♘c7 18 ♘b3 b6 19 a4 g5 20 ♗g3 ♘d6 21 ♘d2 ½–½.

9 ♘xd4 ♖e8
10 f3 c6
11 b4 *(38)*

11 ♔h1 can be met by **11 ... ♘d7!?** or **11 ... ♘h5** 12 g4 ♘f6 (12 ... ♕f6 13 ♗e3 ♘f4 14 ♕d2±) 13 ♗f4 (13 ♗g5!?) 13 ... h5 14 g5 ♘d7 15 ♕d2 (15 ♗xd6 ♘dc5 16 ♘b3 ♘xb3 17 ab ♕xg5∞ Neverov) 15 ... ♘e5 16 ♖bd1 ♕e7 17 ♖g1 (Epishin–Neverov, Tbilisi 1989) when 17 ... ♗d7!? 18 ♘c2 ♗e6 19 b3 ♖ad8 20 ♘e3 ♗c8 21 ♗g3 would have left things unclear.

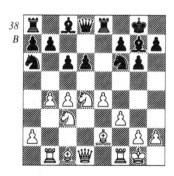

38
B

11 ... ♘h5

The alternatives seem preferable:

(a) **11 ... ♘xb4!?** 12 ♖xb4 c5∞ 13 ♖b3 cd 14 ♘b5 ♗d7 (14 ... ♘d7) 15 ♗b2 ♗xb5 16 ♖xb5 ♘d7 17 ♗xd4 ♘c5 18 ♖b2 ♗e5

19 g3 ♕a5 gave Black quite good prospects in Simonenko–Sokolin, Azov 1991.

(b) 11 ... ♘c7!? 12 ♔h1 ♘h5 13 g4 ♕f6 14 gh ♕xd4 15 ♗b2 ♗h3 16 hg hg 17 ♕xd4 ♗xd4 18 ♖fd1 ♗e5 19 ♗f1 ♗xf1 20 ♖xf1 ♘e6 21 ♘e2 a5 22 b5 ♖ec8 23 ♖fc1 ♔f8 ½ – ½ Berg Hansen–Schandorff, Danish Ch (Århus) 1992.

12 ♗e3!

12 g4?! ♕f6! 13 ♗e3 ♘f4 14 ♔h1 was played in Neverov–Asanov, Barnaul 1988, whereupon the natural 14 ... h5! would have given Black excellent chances.

12 ... ♘c7

The most natural follow-up to Black's last move is 12 ... f5, exploiting the undefended bishop on e3, but White would simply ignore this, with 13 b5±. This suggests that Black's ... ♘h5 was premature; Schandorff's 11 ... ♘c7 may well be the correct method.

13 ♕d2 f5
14 ef gf
15 ♗d3! ♕f6

White's grip on the centre is very apparent after 15 ... f4 16 ♗f2 ♕f6 17 ♘e4 ♕h6 18 c5±.

16 ♘de2 f4
17 ♗d4 ♕h6
18 ♗xg7 ♕xg7
19 ♘e4 d5
20 ♘d6 ♖d8?!

Better would have been 20 ... ♖f8 21 c5 when Glek considers that White is only a little better,

though 21 b5!? could be tried instead.

After the text move, White obtained a very firm grip on the position: 21 c5± ♖f8 22 ♖f2 ♔h8 23 ♖e1 b6!? 24 ♗c2 bc 25 bc ♘e6 26 ♗f5! ♘g5!? 27 ♘d4 ♗a6 28 ♗g4 ♘g3!? 29 hg fg 30 ♖fe2 ♗xe2 31 ♖xe2 (31 ♘4f5! is immediately decisive) 31 ... ♕h6 32 ♕e3 ♖ab8 33 ♕e5+ ♔g8 34 ♕xg3 ♖b1+ 35 ♔f2 ♕f6 36 ♗e6+ ♔h8 37 ♕e5 ♘e4+ 38 ♖xe4 1–0.

Black lost on time, but there is no hope anyway: 38 ... de 39 ♕xf6+ ♖xf6 40 ♘xe4±±.

Aseev–Glek
Krumbach 1991

1 d4 ♘f6 2 c4 g6 3 ♘c3 ♗g7 4 e4 d6 5 ♘f3 0–0 6 ♗e2 e5 7 0–0 ♘a6

8 ♖e1 c6

Instead, 8 ... ed 9 ♘xd4 ♖e8 10 ♗f1 leaves Black struggling to avoid transpositions (after ... ♘c5) to inferior lines of the 7 ... ♘bd7 system. In Malaniuk–Kovalëv, Simferopol 1988, Black suffered a total disaster: 10 ... c6 11 ♘b3!? d5? 12 cd cd 13 ♗g5 h6 14 ♗xf6 ♕xf6 15 ♕xd5 ♘b4 16 ♕b5 ♘c6 17 ♖ad1 ♖b8 18 ♖e3 ♗e6 19 ♘c5 ♘d4 20 ♕a4 ♗g4 21 e5 ♗xd1 22 ♕xe8+ ♖xe8 23 ef 1–0.

Instead 8 ... ♕e8 9 ♗f1 (9 de de 10 b3 ♘d7 11 ♗a3 ♘dc5 12 ♕c2 ♗g4 13 ♖ad1 ♕c8= L. Hansen–Douven, Lugano 1989) 9

Classical with 7 ... ♘a6 55

... ♗g4 is playable, but has failed to gain much popularity. Then **10 ♗e3** is met by 10 ... ♗xf3 11 ♕xf3 ♘g4 12 d5 ♘xe3 13 ♕xe3, as in Neverov–Asanov, Azov 1991, when Wahls suggests 13 ... c5!? 14 a3 ♗f6 14 ♖ab1 ♗d8 15 b4 ♗b6. The main line is **10 d5** *(39)*:

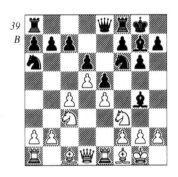

(a) **10 ... ♘b4** 11 ♗e2 (11 a3?! ♗xf3; 11 ♕b3!? a5 12 ♘d2 ♘d7 13 ♘a4 ♘a6!? Eingorn–Asanov, Beijing 1991) 11 ... a5 12 ♗e3 b6 13 a3 ♘a6 14 b3. Krasenkov now gave **14 ... ♘h5** 15 g3 f5 as unclear; instead of Kiselëv–Krasenkov, Moscow Ch 1989, **14 ... ♘c5?!** 15 h3! ♗d7 (15 ... ♗xf3 16 ♗xf3 ♘fd7 17 b4± ab 18 ab ♖xa1 19 ♕xa1 ♘b3 20 ♕a7! ♕b8? 21 ♕a4!±±) 16 ♘d2 ♕e7 17 b4 ♘b7 left White somewhat better.

(b) **10 ... ♘h5** 11 h3 ♗xf3 (11 ... ♗d7?! 12 ♖b1 ♘c5 13 ♘b5! gave White a solid edge in Vanheste–Douven, Dutch Ch (Hilversum) 1989) 12 ♕xf3 f5 13 ♕d1 ♕f7 14 a3 (Krasenkov suggests that this may be unnecessary since after 14 ♕c2!?, 14 ... ♘b4 15

♕b1 is not a major inconvenience) 14 ... ♘c5 15 ♕c2 permits Black equality after the simple **15 ... ♘xe4** 16 ♘xe4 fe (Krasenkov) or **15 ... a5** 16 ♗e3 f4 (16 ... ♘xe4!?) 17 ♗xc5 dc 18 ♗e2 ♘f6= Krasenkov–Kochiev, Gausdal International 1991.

9 ♗f1

A number of other moves come into consideration:

(a) **9 de** de 10 ♕xd8 ♖xd8 11 ♘xe5 ♘b4 (11 ... ♘c5 12 ♗f1 ♖e8 13 f4 ♘fxe4= Baikov–Smirin, USSR 1988) 12 ♗d1 ♘h5 13 ♘f3 ♘d3∓ (Riemersma).

(b) **9 d5** c5 (9 ... ♘c5 transposes to an old line considered satisfactory for Black) 10 ♗g5 (10 a3 ♘e8 11 ♖b1 f5) 10 ... h6 11 ♗h4 ♕d7! 12 ♘d2 ♘h7 13 ♗g3 h5 14 a3 ♕e7 15 h3 h4 16 ♗h2 f5 17 ef gf 18 f4 e4 19 ♔h1 ♔h8 20 ♘f1 ♖g8 gave Black good play on the g-file in M. Gurevich–Glek, Belgrade 1988.

(c) **9 ♗g5** h6 10 ♗h4 ♕e8 11 de de 12 ♕d6 ♕e6 13 ♕a3 ♖e8 14 c5 ♘c7 15 ♖ad1 ♕e7 16 ♖d6 g5 17 ♗g3 ♘d7 18 ♗c4 ♘f8 19 ♖ed1 ♗g4 gave Black a reasonable position in Lutz–Poldauf, German Ch 1991.

(d) **9 ♗e3** ♘g4 10 ♗g5 ♕c7 (10 ... ♕e8!?) 11 ♗h4!? f5? (11 ... ♔h8) 12 ef gf 13 c5! smashed Black's pawn centre in Lobron–Kovalëv, FRG Cup 1991. Korchnoi recommends **13 ... dc** as the most stubborn, whilst **13 ... d5?** fails to 14 de ♘xe5 (14 ... ♘xc5

15 ♘xd5 cd 16 ♖c1) 15 ♘xe5
♗xe5 16 ♗xa6 ba 17 ♘xd5
♗xh2+ 18 ♔h1 cd 19 ♕xd5+
♔h8 20 ♖e8!±±. The game continued **13 ... e4?!** 14 cd ♕xd6 15
♗g3 ♕e7?! 16 h3 ♘f6 17 ♗xa6!±
ba 18 ♘e5 ♕e8 (18 ... ♗e6!?) 19
♕a4 when Black had no real hope.

(e) **9 h3**, preventing ... ♘g4 and
... ♗g4, is best met by exchanging
on d4:

(e1) **9 ... ♘h5** 10 ♗e3 ♘f4 11
♗f1 c5 12 de de 13 ♗xf4 ef 14
e5± Aseev–Ubilava, Daugavpils
1989.

(e2) **9 ... ♕e7** 10 ♗f1 ♘d7 11
a3 ed 12 ♘xd4 ♘dc5 13 ♖b1 ♘c7
14 b4 ♘5e6 15 ♗e3 ♘xd4 16
♗xd4 ♗e5 17 ♕d2 ♕f6 18 ♘e2
♘e6 19 ♗e3 g5 20 g3! (Aseev–
Volke, Kecskemet 1989) 20 ... ♕g6
21 ♗g2 ♔h8± (Aseev).

(e3) **9 ... ♖e8** 10 d5 (The move
h3 is not a useful extra tempo after
the exchange of queens) 10 ... ♘h5
(10 ... c5 11 ♗g5 h6 12 ♗h4 ♕d7
13 ♘h2 ♘h7 14 ♕d2± Burgess–
Boros, Ålborg 1991) 11 ♗g5 ♕d7
12 ♕d2 c5 13 ♘h2 and now 13 ...
♘f4 14 ♗xf4 ef 15 ♕xf4 did not
give Black compensation in Cu.
Hansen–I. Sokolov, Wijk aan Zee
1991, since by preparing e5, White
soon forced ... f6.

(e4) **9 ... ed** 10 ♘xd4 ♖e8 11
♗f3 (Of course, 11 f3 leaves the
kingside weak, but White argues
that the bishop is OK on f3, since
... ♘e5 is not possible) 11 ... ♕b6!
(With c4 undefended, raids by the
queen are more justified) 12 ♖e2

(12 ♘c2 ♗e6 13 ♗e3 ♕c7 14
♘a3?! ♘d7 15 ♕d2 ♘dc5 16 ♖ad1
♗e5 17 b3 f5∓ Burgess–Schandorff, Bellinge Kro 1991; 14 b3!?
is better, whilst Black may try 13
... ♕xb2!?) 12 ... ♘d7 13 ♗e3
♘ac5 14 ♖d2 ♕c7 15 ♕c2 a5 16
b3 ♘b6 17 ♖ad1 ♕e7 18 ♘de2
♗e5 19 ♗d4 h5 20 a3 ♕f6 21
♗xe5 de 22 b4 ab 23 ab ♘e6 24
c5 ♘c4 25 ♖d3 ♘f4 gave Black
a good position in Cu. Hansen–
Schandorff, Odense 1991. 26 ♘xf4
ef 27 ♗e2 ♘e5 28 ♖d6 ♕h4 29
♕d2 ♗xh3! 30 gh ♕xh3 31 f3
♕g3+ 32 ♔h1 ♕h3+ 33 ♔g1 g5
34 ♖f1 ♕g3+ 35 ♔h1 ♖a3!? 36
♖d8 ♕h3+ 37 ♔g1 ♕g3+ 38
♔h1 ♖xd8 39 ♕xd8+ ♔h7 40
♕f6 followed, with Black winning
eventually.

(f) **9 ♖b1** and now:

(f1) **9 ... ♘g4** 10 h3 ed 11 ♘xd4
♕f6 12 hg ♕xd4 13 ♗f4 ♕xd1 14
♖exd1 ♗e5 15 ♗h6 ♖e8 16 ♘a4
c5 17 ♗e3 ♘b4 18 f4 ♗g7 19
♖xd6 ♗f8 20 ♖d2 ♖xe4 21
♔f2± ♗e6? 22 ♘c3 Guseinov–
Nikitin, Azov 1991.

(f2) **9 ... ♕e7** can be met by **10
♗f1 ♗g4** 11 d5 ♘b4 12 ♗e2 a5
13 ♗e3 c5 14 a3 ♘a6 15 ♘d2
♗c8 16 ♘b3 b6 17 ♘c1 ♘d7 18
♘d3 f5 19 b4± Ionov–Smirin,
Klaipeda 1988, or **10 d5 ♘c5** 11
♘d2 (11 ♗f1!?; note that 11 ♕c2?
♘fxe4 12 ♘xe4 ♘xe4 13 ♕xe4
♗f5∓∓ is a standard drawback
to playing ♖b1) 11 ... a5 12 b3
♗h6! 13 ♕c2 ♗d7 14 a3 ♖fc8 15
b4 ab 16 ab ♘a6 17 b5?! (17 ♕b3!

c5 18 b5 ♘b4 19 ♖d1 ♖a7! 20
♗a3 ♘c2 21 ♕xc2= Timosh-
chenko) 17 ... ♘c5∓ Ftačnik–
Timoshchenko, Palma GMA
1989.

(f3) **9 ... ed 10 ♘xd4 ♖e8** *(40)*
gives White three options:

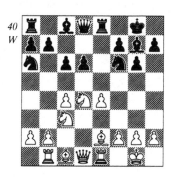

(f31) **11 ♗f3** seems rather
harmless after **11 ... ♘c5** 12 b4
♘e6 13 ♗e3 (13 ♘de2 ♘d7!) 13
... ♘xd4 14 ♗xd4 ♗e6 15 ♗e2
♕e7 16 ♕c2 d5! 17 cd cd 18 ♗b5
♖ec8 19 ed ½-½ Neverov–Glek,
corres 1988, or **11 ... h6!?** 12 h3?!
(12 ♗f4 g5 13 ♗g3 g4 14 ♗e2
♘c5 15 f3∞ Khalifman) 12... ♘h7
13 ♘c2 when instead of **13 ...
♕h4?!** 14 ♕xd6 ♗e5 15 ♕d1 ♘c5
which led to approximate equality
in J. Piket–Khalifman, Wijk aan
Zee 1991, Khalifman recommends
13 ... ♘g5∓.

(f32) **11 ♗f1 ♘g4** (After 11 ...
♘c5 12 f3, Glek suggests 12 ...
d5!? or 12 ... ♘h5!?) 12 h3 ♕b6
13 hg ♕xd4 14 ♕f3 was tried in
Pinter–Sinkovics, Hungary 1991.
It is not clear precisely how
dangerous this is, because Black

played badly: 14 ... ♘c5? 15 ♗f4!
♘e6 16 ♖bd1 ♕b6 17 ♗xd6 ♘g5?
18 ♕g3 ♗xc3 19 bc ♘xe4 20
♖xe4 ♖xe4 21 ♗c7! ♕b2 22
♖d8+ ♔g7 23 g5 1-0.

(f33) **11 f3 ♘h5** (11 ... ♘c7 is
well met by Ribli's 12 ♗f4 or 12
♗f1 d5 13 cd ♘fxd5 14 ♘de2
♘b6 (Pinter–Szekely, Hungary
1991) 15 b4!±) 12 ♗e3 (12 f4?!
and 12 g4?! are both met by 12
... ♕f6!) 12 ... f5 was played in
Utemov–Glek, Moscow 1989.
White played weakly: 13 ♗f1 f4
14 ♗f2 ♗e5 15 b4 ♕f6 16 ♕d2
♔h8 17 ♖ec1 ♘c7 18 ♖d1 (18 b5
c5!) 18 ... g5! 19 c5 (19 h3 ♘g3!)
19 ... dc 20 bc g4∓ with a strong
attack for Black.

9 ... ♗g4

Or 9 ... ed 10 ♘xd4 ♘g4 11 h3
♕b6 12 hg ♕xd4 *(41)* and now:

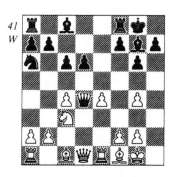

(a) **13 ♗e3 ♕e5** 14 g5 ♕e7 (14
... ♘c5 15 f4 ♕e7 16 ♗xc5 dc 17
e5 h6 18 gh ♗xh6 19 g3 f6! 20
♕c2 ♗f5 21 ♗d3 ♗xd3 22 ♕xd3
f5 allowed White a comfortable
edge in Eingorn–Dydyshko, Azov
1991) 15 ♕d2 ♘c5 16 ♖ad1 ♗e5

17 b4 ♘d7 18 f4 ♗g7 19 f5 f6 20 fg ♘e5 21 gh+ ♚h8 22 ♛xd6 ♛xd6 23 ♖xd6 fg gave Black active play for the sacrificed pawn in Beliavsky–Gelfand, Paris (Immopar) 1991. After 24 ♘a4 ♗g4 25 ♘c5 b6 26 ♘d3 ♘xc4 27 ♘f2 ♖xf2 28 ♗xc4 ♖ff8 29 ♖xc6 ♖ae8 30 ♗d5 ♗d7 31 ♖c7 ♗e6 32 ♗xe6 ♖xe6 33 ♗f2 ♗e5, Black's threats were sufficient to secure a perpetual.

(b) **13 g5** ♘c5 (13 ... ♛e5 14 ♗e3 is considered above, under 13 ♗e3) 14 ♛f3 ♛e5 15 ♗f4 ♛e7 16 ♛g3 ♗e5 17 ♖ad1. Now, instead of **17 ... ♘e6?!** 18 ♗xe5 de 19 ♛xe5 ♛xg5 20 ♛xg5 ♘xg5± Krasenkov–Kaula, Poland 1991, Krasenkov recommends **17 ... ♖e8** 18 b4 ♘d7 19 ♖d2±.

(c) **13 ♛e2** ♛e5 (13 ... ♛c5 14 ♗e3 ♛b4 15 ♖ad1 ♖e8 16 a3 ♛a5 17 ♖xd6 ♘c5 18 ♗d4 ♗xd4 19 ♖xd4 ♘b3 20 ♖dd1 ♛e5 21 f3 left Black with no real compensation in Levitt–I. Rogers, London [Lloyds Bank] 1990) 14 ♗e3 ♘c5 15 f3 (15 f4?! ♛e7 16 ♗xc5 dc 17 e5 fails here due to White's insufficient control over f6: 17 ... f6! 18 e6 f5) 15 ... ♛e7 16 ♛d2 (16 ♖ad1) 16 ... ♗e5 17 ♗g5 (Else 17 ... ♛h4 with a strong grip on the dark squares) 17 ... ♛c7 18 b4 (18 ♖ad1 a5) 18 ... ♘e6 19 ♗e3 was W. Schmidt–P. Cramling, Novi Sad OL 1990. Now **19 ... f5** proved reasonable, but Cramling and Bellón indicate **19 ... a5!** 20 a3 ab (20 ... f5) 21 ab ♖xa1 22 ♖xa1 ♛e7 as best, with ideas of ... ♛f6 or ... ♛h4, while 23 f4 ♗xc3 24 ♛xc3 ♘g7 is unclear.

10   d5

The main alternative is **10 ♗e3**, when Black should probably choose between the following:

(a) **10 ... ♘h5** 11 d5 ♘b4 12 ♗e2∞ is untested.

(b) **10 ... ed** 11 ♗xd4 ♘c7 (11 ... ♘b4 12 ♖c1 c5 13 ♗e3 ♘d7 14 ♗e2 ♗xf3 15 ♗xf3 ♗e5 16 ♘e2 ♘c6 17 ♖c2 ♘f6 18 ♗f1 a6 ½–½ P. Schlosser–Topalov, Altensteig 1990) 12 h3 (12 ♗e2 ♘e6 13 ♗e3 ♛e7 14 h3 ♗xf3 15 ♗xf3 ♘d7∞ Gurevich) 12 ... ♗xf3 13 ♛xf3 ♘e6 14 ♗e3 ♘d7 15 ♖ad1 (15 ♛g3 ♘dc5!?) 15 ... ♗e5 16 g3 ♖e8 17 ♛e2!? ♘ec5 18 ♛d2 ♛a5!? 19 ♗d4 ♖e6 20 ♗xe5 ♘xe5 21 ♖e3! (M. Gurevich–Damljanović, Belgrade 1991) 21 ... ♛b6! 22 ♛e2 f6 23 h4 ♘f7 24 ♗h3 ♖e7∞ (Gurevich).

(c) **10 ... ♗xf3** 11 ♛xf3 ♘g4 12 d5 (12 ♛xg4 ed 13 ♗g5 f6 14 ♗d2 dc 15 ♗xc3 f5 16 ♛h3 ♗xc3 17 ♛xc3 fe 18 ♖xe4 ♛b6 19 ♛d4 ½–½ Bernard–Sharif, France 1991) 12 ... ♘xe3 13 ♛xe3 f5 14 a3 ♘c5 15 ♖ad1 ♘b3 16 ef ½–½ Karolyi–P. Schlosser, Kecskemet 1990.

10   ...   ♘b4

This is probably better than **10 ... c5** 11 ♗g5 ♛d7 12 ♗e2 ♗xf3 13 ♗xf3 ♚h8 14 a3 ♘g8 15 ♗g4 f5 16 ef gf 17 ♗h3 ♛f7 18 f4± Shirov–Epishin, Tbilisi 1989.

11   ♗e2   a5

12 h3!? *(42)*

Other moves give Black less problems:

(a) **12 ♗e3** c5 13 g3!? ♘e8 14 a3 ♘a6 15 ♕d2 ♖b8 16 ♘h4 ♗d7 (16 ... ♗xe2?! 17 ♕xe2 f5 18 ef gf 19 f4±) 17 ♘g2 ♘ac7 18 a4 f5 19 f4 b6 20 fe. Now **20 ... ♗xe5** 21 ♖f1 ♘g7 is roughly level, while in Bareev–Glek, Moscow Ch 1989, **20 ... de** 21 ef gf 22 ♗g5 ♗f6 23 ♗h6 ♘d6!? 24 ♗xf8 ♕xf8 gave Black adequate compensation.

(b) **12 ♗g5** h6 13 ♗e3 ♘h5 (13 ... c5) 14 a3 ♘a6 15 g3 ♘f6 16 ♕d2?! h5 17 ♖ad1?! cd 18 cd ♗d7 19 ♗h6 ♘c5 20 ♗xg7 ♔xg7 21 ♘g5 ♕e7 22 ♗c4 h4 gave Black good kingside play in Eingorn–Christiansen, Reykjavik (Summit) 1990.

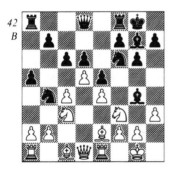

12 ...   ♗d7

12 ... ♗xf3 13 ♗xf3 gives White an edge, while the alternative retreat for the bishop has the drawback that after **12 ... ♗c8** 13 a3 ♘a6, 14 b4± is possible due to the undefended rook on a8. The text leaves d6 unprotected, so

Black has to negotiate a permanent static weakness.

13 dc   ♗xc6
14 ♗f1?!

Aseev recommends **14 ♗d3!±**, keeping e4 firmly guarded. Note that 14 ... ♘xd3 would just reduce Black's counterchances, while the weakness of d6 remains.

14 ...   ♘a6
15 ♗g5   h6
16 ♗h4

16 ♗d2 ♘c5 17 ♕c2 ♘fd7 followed by ... f5 gives Black counterplay.

16 ...   g5

Not **16 ... ♘c5?** 17 ♘d2±, when the queen covers h5.

17 ♗g3   ♘h5
18 ♘d5   ♘c5
19 ♘d2   ♘xg3
20 fg   ♗xd5
21 cd   f5

The worst is now over for Black, whose active pieces compensate for the slight weakness of the light squares.

22 ef   ♖xf5
23 ♕c2

Black emerges unscathed after the pawn grab 23 ♘e4 ♘xe4 24 ♖xe4 ♕b6+ 25 ♔h2 ♕xb2 26 ♖b1 ♕xa2 27 ♗c4 ♕f2∓.

23 ...   ♖f7?!

Aseev considers 23 ... e4, activating the King's Indian bishop, to be fully equal.

24 ♘e4   ♖c8?

Black could keep a respectable game with **24 ... ♕b6**. Instead, White is given time to establish complete hegemony over the light squares leading to the black king.

25 ♔h2   ♛b6
26 ♖ad1   ♖ff8

26 ... ♖cc7 27 ♘xc5 ♛xc5 28 ♛g6 ♖f6 29 ♛e8+ ♖f8 30 ♛e6+ followed by ♝d3, is terminal.

27 b3!   ♘xe4
28 ♛xe4   ♛b4?

Relatively best was **28 ...** ♛c7 29 ♝d3 ♝f6±.

After the text move, Black's king lacks defenders. Despite serious time trouble, White finished off neatly: 29 ♝c4! ♖f2 (29 ... b5 30 a3 wins after either 30 ... ♛xa3 31 ♝d3 or 30 ... ♖xc4 31 ab) 30 a3 ♛xa3 31 ♝d3 ♖c7 32 ♛h7+ ♔f8 33 ♖f1 ♖cf7 34 ♖c1 ♖xf1 35 ♖c8+ ♔e7 36 ♝xf1 (36 ♝b5!?) 36 ... ♛xb3 37 ♖c7+ ♔f8 (37 ... ♔f6 38 ♝d3!) 38 ♖c8+ ♔e7 39 ♝d3 e4 40 ♛xe4+ ♝e5 41 ♛g4 ♛xd5 42 ♝c4 1–0.

Main Line: 8 ♝e3

8 ♝e3 has emerged as White's most popular option against 7 ... ♘a6. This line is especially important, as it often arises via the move order 7 ♝e3 ♘a6 8 0–0.

Black's most frequent choice, 8 ... ♘g4, is considered in the third and fourth games below. The subject of the second game is the important alternative 8 ... c6, which originates from the 1990 World Championship.

First we deal with the nowadays less common 8 ... ♛e8, which may

be better than its reputation.

Miles–Anand
Rome 1990

1 d4 ♘f6 2 c4 g6 3 ♘c3 ♝g7 4 e4 d6 5 ♘f3 0–0 6 ♝e2 e5 7 0–0 ♘a6

8 ♝e3 *(43)*

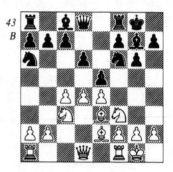

8 ...   ♛e8
9 h3!?

White prevents 9 ... ♘g4 and challenges Black to justify the queen's position on e8. Two other moves are less convincing:

(a) **9 ♖e1** ♘g4 10 ♝c1 (Gelfand analysed 10 ♝g5 f6 11 ♝h4 f5 12 ef gf 13 de de 14 ♛d5+ ♔h8 15 h3 c6 16 ♛d6 ♘h6 as fine for Black) 10 ... f5 11 ef gf 12 de de 13 h3 ♘f6 14 c5 e4 15 ♝xa6 ba 16 ♘d4 (16 ♝f4!? ♝e6! 17 ♘d4 ♖f7= Gelfand) 16 ... ♛e5!? gave Black reasonable prospects in Van Wely–Gelfand, Arnhem 1988/9. The continuation illustrates the dangers in this deceptive position: 17 ♘b3 ♔h8 18 ♝e3 f4 19 ♝d4 ♛g5 20 ♘xe4? ♘xe4 21 ♖xe4

♗b7!∓∓.

(b) **9 de** de (9 ... ♘g4 is rather over-ambitious: 10 ed ♘xe3 11 fe cd 12 ♘d4! ♘c5 13 ♕c2! ♕e5 14 ♖ad1 a5 occurred in Garcia Palermo–Ermolinsky, Forli 1989, whereupon the players considered 15 ♘db5! advantageous for White: 15 ... ♖a6 16 ♗f3± or 15 ... ♕g5 16 ♘d5 ♗e5 17 ♘xd6!±) 10 ♘d2 ♘d7 (10 ... c6; 10 ... b6 11 a3 ♘c5 12 b4 ♘e6 13 ♘b3 ♗b7 14 ♕c2 ♖d8 15 ♖ad1 ♘d4 16 ♘xd4 ed 17 ♖xd4 ♖xd4 18 ♗xd4 ♗xe4 19 ♕b2 ♘h5 20 ♗xg7 ♘xg7 21 ♖e1 ♗c6 22 ♕a1 ♕d8 ½–½ Browne–Tal, San Francisco 1991) 11 a3 (11 ♘b3∞ Borik–Hölzl, Randers Z 1982; 11 ♘b5 ♕e7 12 a3 b6 13 b4 c6 14 ♘c3 ♘c7 15 ♘b3 ♗b7 16 ♕c2 ♖ac8= Winants–Bosboom, Wijk aan Zee 1991) 11 ... f5 12 f3 (12 ef gf 13 f4 e4 allows Black the useful regrouping ... ♘ac5–e6) 12 ... f4 13 ♗f2 ♘ac5 14 b4 ♘e6 15 c5 g5 16 ♖a2 ♖f6 17 ♗c4. Now, in J. Piket–Kožul, Wijk aan Zee 1991, **17 ... ♘f8** 18 ♘d5! ♖f7 19 b5 ♔h8 20 ♘b3 c6 21 ♘c3 ♖f6 22 bc bc 23 ♖d2 ♘g6 24 ♘a5 ♗f8 gave Black reasonable kingside counterplay, but Kožul later preferred the more direct **17 ... ♔h8!** 18 ♗xe6 (18 ♘d5 ♖g6) 18 ... ♖xe6 19 ♘d5 ♕d8 intending ... ♖g6 and a kingside attack.

9 ...   ed?!

Since the e4-pawn is poisoned, Black should investigate alternatives:

(a) **9 ... c6** 10 ♖e1 h6?! 11 ♖b1 ♕e7?! 12 c5 ♘d7 13 cd ♕xd6 14 ♗xa6 ba 15 de ♕xd1 16 ♖exd1 ♖e8 17 ♖bc1± Bareev–Mohr, Bled/Rogaška Slatina 1991.

(b) **9 ... ♘d7** 10 ♖e1 f5 11 ef gf 12 de de 13 c5 c6 14 ♗xa6 ba 15 ♗f4 ♕e7 16 ♕b3+ ♔h8 17 ♕c4 ♖g8 18 ♖e2 ♗f6 19 ♗h2 e4 gave Black counterchances in Fishbein–Tseitlin, Beersheva 1991. White came up with an interesting exchange sacrifice: 20 ♗d6 ♕g7 21 ♘e1 ♘e5 22 ♗xe5 ♗xe5 23 ♖d1 ♕h6 24 ♖ed2 ♗e6 25 ♖d6 ♗h2+ 26 ♔h1 ♗xd6 27 ♕d4+ ♕g7 28 ♕xg7+ ♖xg7 29 ♖xd6.

10   ♗xd4   ♘xe4? (44)

This move seems to lose by force, but it is difficult for Black to organise this position, e.g. 10 ... ♘c5 11 e5!.

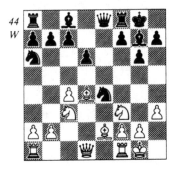

11	♗xg7	♔xg7
12	♕d4+	♘f6
13	♘d5	♕d8
14	♘g5	♖e8

The rook steps out of a possible fork: 14 ... c6 15 ♘xf6 ♕xf6 16 ♕xf6+ ♔xf6 17 ♘xh7+. However, it is already too late to avoid disaster on the long diagonal.

15	♘xh7!	♖e4
16	♕c3	♖xe2
17	♘hxf6	♕h8

17 ... ♖e5 18 f4 does not help.

| 18 | ♘e4+ | 1-0 |

In view of 18 ... ♔h7 19 ♘g5+ ♔g8 20 ♕f3.

Karpov–Kasparov
New York Wch (5) 1990

1 d4 ♘f6 2 c4 g6 3 ♘c3 ♗g7 4 e4 d6 5 ♘f3 0-0 6 ♗e2 e5 7 ♗e3 ♘a6 8 0-0

| 8 | ... | c6 |
| 9 | de | |

More critical is **9 d5 ♘g4 10 ♗g5 f6** *(45)* and now:

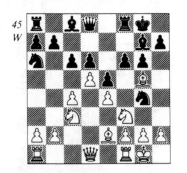

(a) **11 ♗d2** c5 (11 ... f5 12 ♘e1 ♘f6 13 f3 fe!? 14 fe cd 15 cd ♘c5 16 ♕c2 a5 17 ♗f3 was tried in De Boer–Yedidia, Groningen 1990; Wahls suggests that 17 ... ♗d7= would have justified Black's play) 12 ♘e1 f5 13 ♗xg4 fg 14 ♘d3 ♗d7 15 a3 ♗f6 16 b4 b6 yielded approximate equality in Brunner–Chiburdanidze, Geneva 1990.

(b) **11 ♗h4!?**. It is not clear how Black should equalise:

(b1) **11 ... h5** 12 ♘d2 ♘h6 13 h3 g5 14 ♗g3 g4 15 hg hg 16 ♖b1 ♘c7 17 b4 cd 18 cd ♖f7 19 ♘c4 ♗f8; now 20 b5! would have favoured White in Van Wely–Nijboer, Dutch Ch (Eindhoven) 1991.

(b2) **11 ... c5** allowed White an edge in Ruban–Lingnau, Berlin 1991 after 12 ♘d2 (12 ♘e1!? is more ambitious) 12 ... ♘h6 13 a3 ♘f7 14 ♖b1 ♗h6 15 b4 ♗g5 16 ♗xg5 ♘xg5 17 ♕c2.

(b3) **11 ... ♘h6** 12 ♘d2 ♘f7 (12 ... g5!? 13 ♗g3 f5 14 ef ♘xf5 15 ♘de4 ♘d4 16 ♗g4 h6 17 h3 ♗f5 18 ♖e1± Shirov–J. Polgar, Brno 1991) 13 ♖b1 c5 (13 ... ♗h6!?) 14 f3 (14 a3 is Ruban–Lingnau) 14 ... ♗h6 15 ♗f2 f5 16 a3 ♗g5 17 ♕e1 b6 18 b4 h5 19 ♗d3 f4 20 ♗c2 ♗f6 21 ♗a4 g5 22 ♗c6 ♖b8 23 ♕d1 g4 24 ♕a4 was played in Cebalo–Berg, Ålborg 1991. Black tried **24 ... ♗h4** 25 b5 ♗xf2+ 26 ♔xf2 ♕h4+ 27 ♔e2 ♕xh2 28 ♔d3 ♕xg2 29 ba g3 30 ♗e8 h4 31 ♗xf7+ ♔xf7 32 ♕c6 which gave insufficient compensation. Instead **24 ... cb** 25 ab ♗h4, with similar ideas, but more open lines, was a better try.

| 9 | ... | de |
| 10 | ♕xd8 | |

Karpov considered **10 ♘d2 ♕e7!** very comfortable for Black.

10 h3 ♕e7 11 ♕c2 ♘h5 12 ♖fe1

♘c5 13 ♖ad1 ♘e6 14 c5 ♘hf4 15
b4 ♘xe2+ 16 ♘xe2 ♘c7 17 ♘c3
a5 18 a3 ab 19 ab f6 20 b5 ♘xb5
21 ♘xb5 cb 22 ♕b3+ ♗e6 23
♕xb5 ♖fd8 24 ♖xd8+ ♖xd8 25
♖b1 ♖d7 gave Black a perfectly
defensible position in Lobron–
Kasparov, Germany (simul) 1991.

| 10 | ... | ♖xd8 |
| 11 | ♖fd1 |

11 ♘xe5 ♘xe4 12 ♘xe4 ♗xe5
14 ♗g5 ♖e8 gives White nothing.

| 11 | ... | ♖e8! |

Instead 11 ... ♖xd1+?! 12 ♖xd1
♗e6 (12 ... ♗g4!?) 13 ♘xe5 ♘xe4
14 ♘xe4 ♗xe5 15 ♗g5 would give
White a useful edge.

| 12 | h3 | ♗f8 |

12 ... ♘h5 (Premature; it is more
important to secure the queenside)
13 c5 ♘f4 14 ♗f1 ♗e6 15 ♘g5
h6 16 ♘xe6 ♘xe6 17 ♗xa6 ba 18
♖ac1± ♖ab8 19 b3 f5 20 f3 ♗f8
21 g4!? ♘d4 22 ef gf 23 gf ♗xc5
24 ♘e4! led to a clear endgame
advantage for White in Cifuentes–
McDonald, Andorra 1991.

| 13 | ♘d2 | b6!? |

Other moves allow White more
play on the queenside: 13 ... ♗b4
14 ♖ac1 ♘c5 15 f3± (Karpov); 13
... ♗c5 14 ♗xc5 ♘xc5 15 b4 ♘e6
16 ♘b3 ♗d7 17 ♖d6!? ♖ed8 18
♖ad1 ♗e8 19 ♘a5 (Zaitsev); 13
... ♘c5 14 b4 ♘e6 15 c5 (Wahls).

14	a3	♘c5
15	b4	♘e6
16	♘b3

16 ♘f3!? ♘h5 17 ♖ac1 (17
♖ab1!?) 17 ... f6 18 ♖b1 ♔f7 19
♗f1 ♖b8 20 a4 ♖b7 21 b5 c5 (21

... ♖c7 22 bc ♖xc6 23 c5±) 22
♘d5 ♘hf4 23 a5 gave White a
useful queenside initiative in Cifuentes–Visser, Groningen 1990.
Since the knight achieved little on
h5, Wahls proposed 16 ... ♘d7,
intending 17 ... f5, and meeting 17
♖ac1 with 17 ... a5; he suggested
in reply 17 b5∞.

| 16 | ... | ♗a6!? |
| 17 | f3 |

The more forcing 17 b5 cb 18
cb ♗b7 19 f3 ♖ac8 gives Black no
problems. After the text move, however, Black's knights can threaten
to invade White's kingside.

17	...	♘h5
18	♗f2	♖ed8
19	♗f1	♘hf4

Black invests a tempo to loosen
White's kingside pawn structure.

| 20 | g3 | ♘h5 |
| 21 | ♔g2 |

Prophylaxis is necessary; after
21 ♘a4 ♘g5 22 ♔g2 ♖xd1 23
♖xd1 ♗c8 24 g4 ♘f4+ 25 ♔g3
h5 Black would have serious
counterplay.

| 21 | ... | f5 |

The standard thrust is executed
only after the pieces have done all
they can to provide targets for it.

| 22 | ♖ab1 | ♖ac8 |
| 23 | ♖xd8 |

Karpov considered 23 ef gf 24
♘a4 ♖xd1 25 ♖xd1 ♖c7 26 c5
♗xf1+ 27 ♔xf1 ♖g7 28 g4 b5
29 ♘c3 ♘hf4 to be unclear, so
instead exchanged off into a level
ending.

The remaining moves were: 23

... ♖xd8 24 ♖d1 ♖xd1 25 ♘xd1
fe 26 fe c5= 27 bc (27 b5 ♗b7 28
♘c3 ♘d4) 27 ... ♘xc5 28 ♘xc5
♗xc5 29 ♗xc5 bc 30 ♘c3 ♘f6
31 ♔f3 ♗b7 32 ♗d3 ♔f8 33 h4
h6 34 ♗c2 (34 ♘a4 ♘d7 35 ♗f1
♗c6 achieves nothing) 34 ... ♔e7
35 ♗a4 a6 36 ♔e3 ½–½. Apparently an uneventful draw, but
observe how actively Black had to
play to deny White an edge.

Cu. Hansen–Schandorff
Kerteminde 1991

1 d4 ♘f6 2 c4 g6 3 ♘c3 ♗g7 4 e4
d6 5 ♘f3 0–0 6 ♗e2 e5 7 0–0
♘a6 8 ♗e3

8	...	♘g4
9	♗g5	♕e8

9 ... f6 is less popular, though
certainly playable. After 10 ♗c1
(46), Black has tried four moves:

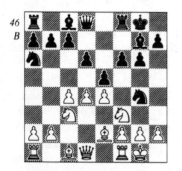

(a) 10 ... ♕e8 11 h3 ♘h6 12 de
(12 ♖b1± Karpov) 12 ... de 13 b3
♗e6 14 ♗a3 ♖f7 15 ♕c2 ♗f8
16 ♗xf8 ♕xf8 17 a3 ♖d7 18 ♖fd1
(18 b4!? Zaitsev) 18 ... ♖xd1+ 19
♘xd1 ♘f7 20 ♘e3 c6 21 b4 ♘c7

22 c5 ♖d8 23 a4 ♗c8 24 ♗c4
♘e6 25 ♗xe6 ♗xe6= Cebalo–I.
Sokolov, Yugoslavia 1989.

(b) 10 ... ♘h6 11 ♖b1! ♘f7 (11
... ed 12 ♘xd4 f5 fails to 13 ♗xh6
♗xh6 14 ef±) 12 de (Avoiding 12
b4 ed 13 ♘xd4 ♘xb4!) 12 ... de
13 b4 c6 14 b5 ♘c7 (14 ... ♕xd1
15 ♗xd1! cb 16 cb ♘c7 17 ♗b3
♗e6 18 ♗e3± Benjamin) 15
♗a3 ♖e8 16 bc bc 17 ♕a4 ♗d7
18 ♖fd1 ♕c8 19 c5!? (19 ♖d2 is
also strong) 19 ... f5 20 ♗c4 ♗e6
21 ♘d2 ♗h6 22 ♗f1 ♗d7 23
♘b3 ♗g7 gave White a strong
position in Benjamin–Kindermann, Novi Sad OL 1990. Now
24 ♖xd7! ♕xd7 25 ♖d1 ♕e7 26
♕xc6 ♖ed8 27 ♘d5 ♘xd5 28 ed
would have been a powerful
exchange sacrifice.

(c) 10 ... ♔h8 11 h3 ♘h6 12
de!? fe (12 ... de 13 ♕xd8 ♖xd8
14 ♗e3 ♗e6 15 ♖fd1 ♘f7 16
a3±) 13 ♗e3 ♘f7 14 ♕d2 ♘c5
15 ♘g5 ♘xg5 16 ♗xg5 ♗f6 17
♗e3 ♘e6 18 ♗g4! gave White a
pleasant advantage in Karpov–
Kasparov, New York Wch (7)
1990. After 18 ... ♘d4, Wahls gives
19 ♗xc8 ♕xc8 20 f4! c5 21 ♘d5!
♗g7 22 ♗xd4±, whilst Zaitsev
analysed 18 ... ♘f4 19 ♘d5 g5 20
c5 and 18 ... ♗g5 19 ♗xe6 ♗xe3
20 ♕xe3 ♗xe6 21 c5 as promising
for White. The game continued 18
... h5 19 ♗xe6 ♗xe6 20 ♘d5
(This knight cannot be removed
without exposing a serious weakness in Black's camp) 20 ... ♗h4
21 ♖ac1 ♔h7 22 ♖c3 ♖f7 23 b3

c6 24 ♘b4 ♖d7 (24 ... ♕d7!?) 25 ♖cc1 ♗f6 26 f4! ef (26 ... d5!? 27 cd cd 28 ed gives White the advantage after 28 ... ♗xd5 29 f5! and 28 ... a5 29 ♕e2 ♗xd5 30 ♘xd5 ♖xd5 31 f5± — Zaitsev) 27 ♗xf4 whereupon Kasparov blundered with 27... ♕a5?, allowing 28 ♘d5! ♕c5+ when 29 ♗e3! ♗g5 30 ♘f6+! would have been immediately decisive.

(d) **10 ... c6** 11 h3 ♘h6 12 ♗e3 ♘f7 13 de de 14 c5 ♘c7 15 ♗c4 ♗e6 16 ♕e2 ♕e7 17 b4 ♗h6 18 ♗xh6 ♘xh6 19 ♘d2 ♘f7 20 ♘b3 ♖fd8 21 ♖fd1 ½-½ Khalifman–P. Cramling, Hamburg 1991.

10   de

(a) **10 d5** h6 11 ♗h4 f5 12 ♘d2 ♘f6 13 f3 g5 14 ♗f2 f4 15 g4 fg 16 hg ♕g6 17 g4 h5 18 ♔g2 led to sharp play in Fyllingen–Chekhov, Gausdal International 1991.

(b) **10 h3 h6** gives White two possibilities, neither especially promising:

(b1) **11 ♗h4 ♘f6!** (11 ... ed 12 ♘xd4 ♘f6 13 ♗f3 ♕e5 14 ♗g3 ♕c5 15 ♘a4 ♕a5 16 a3 ♘d7 17 ♘b5 ♘b6 18 ♘xb6 ♕xb6 19 ♕e2 ♗e5 also worked out well for Black in Peshina–Ryskin, Minsk 1988) 12 de (12 d5!?) 12 ... de 13 ♘d2 c6 gave Black excellent prospects in Chekhov–Yurtaev, Riga 1988: 14 ♗g3 ♘h7 15 a3 ♘c5 16 b4 ♘e6 17 c5 ♕e7 18 ♘c4 ♖d8 19 ♕b1 ♘f4 20 ♖d1 ♗e6 21 ♕c2 h5, though White managed to draw in the end.

(b2) **11 ♗c1 ed!** (11 ... ♘f6 12 de de 13 ♗e3 transposes to the next game, Vladimirov–Kochiev) **12 ♘xd4 ♘f6 13 ♗f3 ♘h7!** *(47)* (13 ... ♘c5 14 ♖e1± Chekhov) and now:

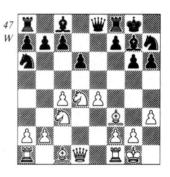

(b21) After **14 ♖e1, 14 ... ♘c5?!** 15 ♗e3 ♕d8?! (15 ... ♘g5 — b22) 16 ♘b3!± ♘e6 17 ♗e2 ♕h4 18 ♗f1 f5 19 ef gf 20 g3 ♕f6 (20 ... ♕d8 21 f4!±) 21 ♘d5 ♕f7 22 ♘d4!± gave Black rather a depressing position in I. Sokolov–Gelfand, Belgrade 1991. Instead Sokolov analyses **14 ... ♘g5!** 15 ♗g4 (15 ♗e3 is (b22)) 15 ... ♗xg4 16 hg ♕e5 17 ♘c2 ♕e6! 18 f4 ♘h7 19 ♘d5 c6 20 f5 ♕d7 21 ♘f4 g5 22 ♘h5 ♗e5 23 ♘d4 ♘f6 24 ♘f3 ♕e7∞.

(b22) **14 ♗e3 ♘g5** 15 ♖e1 c6 (Sokolov suggests that 15 ... ♘c5 16 ♘db5 ♕d8 17 ♗xc5 dc 18 ♕xd8 ♖xd8 19 ♘xc7 ♘xf3+ 20 gf ♖b8 gives adequate compensation) 16 ♖c1 ♘c5 17 ♖c2 ♕e7 18 ♘b3 ♘xf3+ 19 ♕xf3 ♘d3 (19 ... f5!? 20 ♗xc5 dc 21 e5 ♗e6)

20 ♖d1 ♞xb2 (20 ... ♞e5!? 21 ♕e2
♝e6) 21 ♖xb2 ♝xc3 22 ♖c2
♝e5 23 ♝xh6 ♖e8 24 c5 led to
a draw in J. Piket–Gelfand, Wijk
aan Zee 1992.

10   ...   de

If Black wishes to avoid the
lines following 11 ♞d2, the move
order **10 ... h6** may be investi-
gated. Then **11 ♝c1** de 12 h3 (12
♞e1) 12 ... ♞f6 13 ♝e3 transposes
to Vladimirov–Kochiev below,
whilst Glek suggests **11 ♝d2**
♞xe5!?. Bönsch–Glek, Budapest
1989 continued **11 ♝h4** de 12 ♞e1
(12 ♝g3!?) 12 ... ♞f6 13 ♞d3 c6
14 b4 ♞c7∞.

11   ♞d2!?

Less effective is **11 ♞e1** h6 12
♝d2 (12 ♝h4 f5!? 13 ef gf 14
♝xg4 fg 15 ♕e2 c6 16 ♞e4 ♕g6
Chekhov) 12 ... f5!? (12 ... ♞f6 13
♞d3 c6 14 ♝e3 ♞d7 15 b4 was
A. Shneider–Glek, Budapest 1989;
Glek considered 15 ... ♞c7 16 c5
♕e7 17 ♞b2 ♖d8 18 ♞c4 ♞f6 19
♕c1 ♔h7 20 ♞d6 ♞e6 unclear)
13 ef?! (Chekhov analysed 13 f3
♞f6 14 ♞d3 c6 15 c5 f4 16 b4 g5
and 13 ♝xg4 fg 14 ♞c2 c6 15
♝e3 ♞c7 16 ♕d2 ♔h7 17 ♖fd1
♞e6 as unclear) 13 ... gf 14 ♝xg4?!
fg 15 ♞c2 ♝e6 16 ♕e2 ♕g6, as
in Bönsch–Chekhov, Berlin 1989.
It turns out that White cannot use
the e4-square. After 17 ♝e3 (17
♞e3 c6∓) 17 ... ♝f5 18 ♞e1 c6
19 ♖d1 ♞c7 20 ♝c5 ♖fe8 21 ♞d3
b6!? 22 ♝a3 ♖ad8 23 ♞xe5 ♖xd1
24 ♞xg6 ♖xe2 25 ♖xd1 ♝xc3,
Black won material.

For **11 h3** see the next game.

11   ...   h6

Two other moves look
insufficient:

(a) **11 ... ♝f6?!** 12 h4!? (12
♝xf6 ♞xf6 13 a3 c6 14 b4 ♞c7
15 c5 ♝e6 16 ♞c4 ♝xc4 17 ♝xc4
♖d8 18 ♕b3±) 12 ... h6 13 ♝xg4
hg 14 ♞d5 ♝d8 15 ♝xc8 ♖xc8
and now **16 h5±** is given by Chekhov, but **16 hg!** is stronger: **16 ...
♝xg5** 17 ♕g4 ♕d8 18 ♞f3; **16 ...
c6?** 17 ♕g4 ♖a8 18 ♞f6+ ♝xf6
19 gf ♞c5 20 ♞f3 ♕e6 21 ♕h4±±
Wells–Moss, Hastings Challengers 1991/2.

(b) **11 ... ♞f6?!** 12 ♞d5 ♕e6?!
13 b4 c6 14 b6 cd 15 cd ♞xd5 16
ed ♕f5 17 ♝e7 ♖e8 18 d6 ♞c5
19 ♖c1 b6 20 ♝f3 ♖b8 21 ♝c6
♝d7 22 ♞b3 ♝f8 23 ♞xc5 bc 24
♝xf8 ♔xf8 25 ♖xc5 ♖bd8 26
f4 1–0 Cu. Hansen–Ca. Hansen,
Kerteminde-Søndersø 1991.

12   ♝h4   ♞f6

Chekhov analysed **12 ... f5?!** 13
ef gf 14 ♝xg4 fg 15 ♞de4± but
an interesting alternative is **12 ...
h5** 13 h3 ♞h6 14 ♝g5 c6 15 ♝e3
♕e7 16 ♕c1!? ♔h7 (16 ... ♞c5?
17 ♞b3!) 17 c5 f5 (17 ... ♞xc5 18
♞d5 cd 19 ♝xc5 ♕g5 20 h4!
♕xh4 21 ♞f3±) 18 ef gf 19 ♝xa6
ba 20 f4 ef 21 ♝xf4 ♕xc5+ 22
♔h1 which Hansen and Schandorff considered to favour White
slightly, due to the untidy nature
of Black's position.

13   ♞d5   g5

13 ... ♞xd5 14 cd gives White
a very pleasant position, as do **13**

... ♛d8 14 f4! (14 ... ef 15 e5) and
13 ... ♛e6 14 ♗xf6! ♗xf6 15 c5
♗d8 16 ♗c4 ♛d7 17 ♗xa6 ba
18 ♞c4± (Hutters).

14	♗g3	c6
15	♞xf6+	♗xf6
16	♗g4	*(48)*

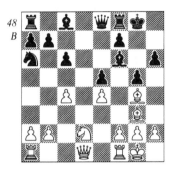

White now appears to have a
substantial positional advantage,
but Schandorff pointed out that
16 ... ♗d8! intending ... f6, followed by placing the bishop on b6
and the knight on e6, would have
given Black a satisfactory game.
His actual choice was rather care-
less and left Black with a prospect-
less position.

16	...	♗e6?
17	♛f3	♔g7
18	♖fd1	♖d8
19	♞f1	♗xg4

19 ... ♗xc4 20 ♞e3 ♗e6 (20 ...
♖xd1+ 21 ♖xd1 ♗e6 22 ♗xe6
♛xe6 23 ♖d6!±±) 21 ♖xd8 ♛xd8
22 ♗xe6 fe 23 ♞g4 △ ♖d1 and
♛c3 is very dangerous for Black.

20	♛xg4	♛e6
21	♛e2	♖xd1
22	♖xd1	♖d8

| 23 | ♞e3 | |

23 ♖xd8 ♗xd8 24 ♞e3 is perhaps a little more accurate, since
Black could now try **23 ... ♖xd1+**
24 ♛xd1 ♞c5.

23	...	♔h7
24	♖xd8	♗xd8
25	♞f5	♗f6
26	♛h5	

White has a decisive attack. The
game finished: 26 ... ♗h8 27 h4
gh 28 ♗xh4 ♞c5 29 ♛e2 ♛g6?!
30 ♞e7! ♛xe4?! (30 ... ♛e6 31 ♛f3
is rather miserable, but does not
lose immediately) 31 ♛h5 ♛xc4
(31 ... ♛f4 32 g3 ♛c1+ 33 ♔h2
does not help) 32 ♛f5+ ♔g7 33
♗f6+ 1-0.

Vladimirov–Kochiev
Gausdal International 1991

1 d4 ♞f6 2 c4 g6 3 ♞c3 ♗g7 4 e4
d6 5 ♞f3 0-0 6 ♗e2 e5 7 0-0
♞a6 8 ♗e3 ♞g4 9 ♗g5 ♛e8 10
de de

| 11 | h3 | h6 |

11 ... ♞f6 12 ♗e3 leads to a
similar position, except that
Black's pawn is still on h7. In
Illescas–Epishin, Spain 1992,
Black embarked on some strange
manoeuvres: 12 ... ♛e7 13 ♞d5
♛d8 14 ♞xf6+ ♗xf6 15 a3 ♛e7
16 ♛c2 c5 17 ♞d2 ♗g5 18 ♞b1
f5 19 ♞c3 f4 20 ♞d5 ♛d8 21 ♗d2.
Black's e5-pawn turned out to be
a serious problem.

12	♗c1	♞f6
13	♗e3	

13 b3 does not look like a critical

move, but White was successful in Kaplun–Danailov, Warsaw 1989: 13 ... ♛e6 14 ♗a3 ♖e8 15 ♛c2 ♘h5 16 ♖fd1 ♘f4 17 ♗f1 ♛f6?! 18 ♘d5 ♛e6 19 ♖d2 c6 20 ♘xf4 ef 21 ♖e1 c5 22 e5 ♛b6 23 ♗d3±.

13 ... ♘d7

Black has three other choices, only the last of which merits serious consideration:

(a) **13 ... c6** 14 c5 ♘c7 15 ♛d6! ♘e6 16 ♘xe5 ♘g5 17 ♗xg5 hg 18 ♗c4± Chekhov.

(b) **13 ... b6** 14 a3 ♗b7 15 ♘d2 ♖d8 16 ♛c2 ♘h7 17 b4 ♘g5 18 c5 f5 19 ♗xg5 hg 20 c6 ♗c8 21 ♘d5 ♘b8 22 b5 ♖f7 23 ♗c4 led to disaster for Black in Malaniuk–Chekhov, Kecskemet 1989.

(c) **13 ... ♘h5 14 c5 ♘f4** *(49)* has been Glek's preference:

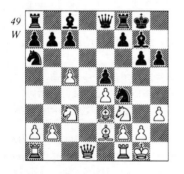

(c1) **15 ♗b5!?** ♛e6! (15 ... c6 16 ♗xa6 ba 17 ♗xf4 ef 18 e5±) 16 ♖e1! (Certainly not 16 ♛a4?? ♘xg2! 17 ♔xg2 ♛xh3+ 18 ♔g1 ♛g4+! 19 ♔h2 ♛xf3∓∓ Shirov–Glek, Moscow 1991). Now Glek gave **16 ... g5** as unclear, whilst a calm option for Black is **16 ...**

c6 17 ♗xa6 ba 18 ♗xf4?! (18 ♛d6!?± Kovalëv) 18 ... ef 19 ♘d4 ♛c4!∞. In Shirov–Kovalëv, Bundesliga 1991/2, Black opted for a violent method: **16 ... ♘xg2?!** (16 ... ♔h8!?) 17 ♔xg2 ♛xh3+ 18 ♔g1 ♗g4, though White's accurate play managed to repulse the attack: 19 ♗f1! ♛h5 20 ♗e2 ♖ad8 21 ♘d2 f5 22 ef! gf 23 ♗xg4 ♛g6! 24 ♘ce4! h5! 25 ♗g5! fe 26 ♗xd8 ♖xd8 27 ♛b3+ ♔h8 28 ♘xe4! ♛xg4+ 29 ♛g3 ♛f5 30 ♛g5! with a won ending for White.

(c2) **15 ♗xa6** ba 16 ♘d5 ♘xd5 17 ♛xd5 ♖b8 (17 ... ♗e6 18 ♛d2 ♖d8 19 ♛c3 ♛c6 20 ♖fe1 f6 21 ♘d2 ♖f7 22 ♘b3 ♛xe4 23 ♗xh6 ♛c4 24 ♛xc4 ♗xc4 25 ♗xg7 ♔xg7 26 ♘a5 gave White a substantial advantage in Miles–Timoshchenko, Moscow [GMA] 1989) 18 ♛d2 ♔h7 19 ♛c3 ♛b5 20 b3 ♗b7 21 ♘xe5 ♛e8! (21 ... ♗xe4? 22 ♗d4! ♖bd8 23 ♖fe1 f5 24 ♖ad1 ♖fe8 25 a4! ♛b8 26 c6 ♖xd4 27 ♖xd4 ♗xe5 28 ♖d7+ ♔h8 29 ♛c4, rather surprisingly, gave White a devastating attack in Novikov–Glek, Odessa 1989) 22 ♗d4 ♖d8 23 f4 (23 ♘f3? ♖xd4 24 ♘xd4 ♛xe4∓∓) 23 ... ♗xe4 24 ♖ae1 ½-½ Neverov–Glek, Odessa 1989.

14 ♘b5!?

White has tried three other moves:

(a) **14 ♛c1** ♔h7 15 ♛b1 (15 ♘b5 ♛e7 16 ♖d1 ♘dc5 17 ♘d2 c6= Lein) 15 ... c6 16 ♘d2 ♛e7 17 ♖e1 f5 18 ef gf 19 f4 e4 20 ♘b3

♘dc5 21 ♘xc5 ♘xc5 22 ♕c2 ♗e6
gave Black good play in Barlov–
Kochiev, Palma (GMA) 1989. In
particular, Black has good control
over d4.

(b) **14 ♕d2** ♔h7 15 ♖ad1 f5 16
ef gf 17 ♘b5 f4 18 ♗xa7 e4 19
♖fe1 ♕g6 20 ♗d4 ♘f6 21 ♘e5
♕g5 22 ♘g4 ♗f5 ½–½ Tisdall–
Chekhov, Gausdal [Peer Gynt]
1990. Clearly there is scope for
further investigation!

(c) **14 a3**. Now:

(c1) **14 ... ♘ac5 15 b4 ♘e6 16
c5** (16 ♘b5?! b6 17 ♕d5 ♖b8 18
♘xa7? ♗b7 19 ♕d3 ♘f4∓). It
seems that Black may not quite
equalise here:

(c11) **16 ... f5!?** is a suggestion
of Zsuzsa Polgar's.

(c12) **16 ... c6** 17 ♗c4! ♕e7 18
♕d2 ♔h7 19 ♖fd1 ♖e8 20 ♕c2!
♘df8 21 ♖d6 ♘f4 should be met
by the immediate **22 b5!**. However,
in Zsu. Polgar–Kindermann,
Munich 1991, **22 ♖ad1** ♘8e6 23
♔h2?! (23 b5!) 23 ... ♕f6 (23 ...
♘g5!? 24 ♘g1) 24 b5! ♗f8 25 bc
was also effective.

(c13) **16 ... ♘f4!?** 17 ♗c4 is
assessed ± by Chekhov, but
Black's game is playable. Steingrimsson–Kochiev, Gausdal International 1991 continued 17 ... g5
18 ♘b5 ♕d8 19 a4 a6 20 ♘c3
c6 21 ♘d2 ♕e7 22 ♘b3 ♖e8 23
b5 ♗f8 24 bc bc 25 a5 ♘f6 26
♕c2 ♘6h5 27 f3 ♕f6 28 ♔h2 ♘g7
29 ♘a4 ♗e6 30 ♘d2 h5 31 ♖ab1
♕g6 32 ♖b6 g4 33 ♗xe6 ♖xe6
34 ♖fb1 ♘xg2! and White's king

was obliged to take a walk.

(c2) **14 ... f5** (14 ... c6 15 b4 f5
16 c5 f4 17 ♗c1 transposes) 15 b4
f4 16 ♗c1 c6 17 c5 ♔h7! (not 17
... ♘c7 18 ♕d6! ♘e6 19 ♗c4±;
if 17 ... g5, then 18 ♘d2!? ♘c7 19
♘c4 gives White some advantage,
e.g. Van Wely–M. Piket, Amsterdam 1990 continued 19 ... ♘f6 20
♗b2 ♗e6 21 ♘xe5 ♗xh3 22
♘c4 ♗e6 23 e5 ♘fd5 24 ♘e4 ♕d7
25 ♘ed6 g4 26 ♗d3 ♘e7 27 ♖e1
♘cd5 28 ♗c2±) 18 ♘d2?! (This
is not so effective here; better is 18
♗xa6 ba 19 ♕a4 ♖f6 20 ♗b2
g5, when Black seeks counterplay
with a kingside pawn storm) 18 ...
♘c7 19 ♘c4 ♘e6 20 ♘d6 ♕e7 21
♗g4 (Chekhov suggests 21 ♗c4!?
♘d4 22 ♗b2) 21 ... ♘f6!∓ 22
♘xc8 ♖axc8 23 ♗xe6 ♕xe6 gave
Black the better prospects in Barkhagen–Chekhov, Gausdal International 1991.

| 14 | ... | f5 |
| 15 | ♖e1 | f4 |

15 ... ♘f6 16 ef gf 17 ♘h4±
(Vladimirov).

16	♗c1	♕e7
17	b3	♘dc5
18	♗a3	♔h7
19	♕c2	c6
20	♖ad1	♗e6!
21	♘c3	♗f7! *(50)*

Instead **21 ... ♖fd8** 22 b4 ♘d7
23 c5 allows White a small advantage. After the text, 22 b4 would
be met by 22 ... ♘e6.

22	♘a4	♖fd8
23	♘b2	♖xd1
24	♖xd1	♖d8

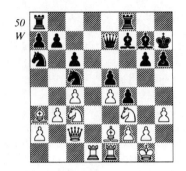

| 25 | ♘d3 | b6 |
| 26 | ♘fe1 | |

Vladimirov analyses **26 ♘xc5** ♘xc5 27 ♗xc5 bc with equality, and **26 ♘dxe5?** ♖xd1+ 27 ♗xd1 ♗xe5 28 ♘xe5 ♕xe5 29 ♗b2 ♕e8 30 ♕c3 which fails to the simple defence 30 ... ♕g8∓.

| 26 | ... | ♕c7 |
| 27 | ♗b2 | ♘xd3?! |

After **27 ... ♘xe4** 28 ♘xf4 (28 ♘f3 ♖e8∞) 28 ... ♖xd1 29 ♗xd1 ♘xf2 30 ♕xf2 ef 31 ♗xg7 ♔xg7 32 ♕d4+ ♔g8 33 ♘d3, White has compensation for the pawn.

| 28 | ♘xd3 | ♕e7 |
| 29 | ♗c3 | ♖e8? |

This is a serious mistake, since White can now exert considerable pressure on the long diagonal. Vladimirov considers that **29 ... ♘c5** 30 ♘xc5 ♖xd1+ 31 ♕xd1 bc allows White only a small advantage.

The game concluded as follows: 30 ♕b2 ♗g8 31 c5! ♘b8 (31 ... ♘xc5 32 ♘xc5 bc 33 ♕a3 △ ♗g4 leaves White well in control) 32 a4! (Instead 32 b4! b5 33 ♖a1 would give White a clear superiority) 32 ... bc 33 ♖c1 ♘d7 (33 ... c4? 34 bc ♗xc4 35 ♘xf4+; the next few moves were played in mutual time-trouble) 34 ♗g4 ♘f6 35 ♗f3 ♘d7 36 ♗g4 ♘f6 37 ♗xe5 ♘xg4 38 ♗xg7 ♔xf2? (38 ... ♕xg7 39 ♕xg7+ ♔xg7 40 hg c4! 41 bc ♖xe4 42 ♖b1=) 39 ♕xf2 ♕xg7 40 ♘xc5 g5 41 ♖d1 (Now White is again in full charge of the game) 41 ... ♖e7 42 ♕d2 ♗f7 (42 ... ♕e5 43 ♘d7+ +) 43 ♕d8 ♗e8 44 b4! ♕e5 45 ♕d6 h5 46 a5 ♔g7 47 ♕xe5+ ♖xe5 48 ♖d6 g4 49 h4!+ + ♗g6 50 ♖xc6 ♔f7 51 ♖c7+ ♖e7 52 ♖xe7+ ♔xe7 53 b5 ♔d6 54 b6 ab 55 ab ♗f7 56 e5+ ♔c6 57 b7 ♔c7 58 e6 ♗e8 59 e7 1–0.

6 Averbakh with ... h6 and ... c5

1 d4 ♘f6 2 c4 g6 3 ♘c3 ♗g7 4 e4 d6 5 ♗e2 0–0 6 ♗g5 h6 7 ♗e3 c5

This is a closely related idea to the pawn sacrifice in the Sämisch Variation which is considered in the next two chapters. White is invited to exchange queens and win a pawn, in return for apparently nebulous compensation: Black has a slight development advantage, and has opened some lines (in particular for the g7-bishop). However, detailed analysis has provided firm support for Black's idea, as White seems unable to maintain his queenside pawns intact without his/her king coming under direct fire. A simple illustration of this is the game Sofieva–Matveeva, USSR Women's Ch (Alma Ata) 1988 *(51)*:

Now 17 ♗a3? would give Black tremendous play after 17 ... ♘e4 or 17 ... ♘h5, so there followed 17 ♗xf6 ♗xf6 18 b3 ♗h4+ 19 ♔f1 ♗g3 when Black regained her pawn with a slight edge.

Naturally White may meet 7 ...

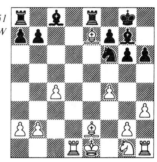

51
W

c5 with 8 d5, but this has much less bite than the older line 6 ... c5 7 d5, since then White can meet 7 ... h6 with 8 ♗f4 (attacking d6) and 7 ... e6 with 8 ♕d2, when Black finds it difficult to obtain counterplay.

White's sharpest treatment is 8 dc ♕a5 9 ♕d2!?, which may be recommended to those who wish to stake everything on a violent attack.

Bareev–Yurtaev
European Club Cup 1990

1 d4 ♘f6 2 c4 g6 3 ♘c3 ♗g7 4 e4 d6

    5   ♗e2   0–0

6 ♗g5 h6 *(52)*

7 ♗e3

The alternative retreats are less promising:

(a) 7 ♗f4 is met most logically by 7 ... ♘c6 8 d5 (8 ♘f3 ♘xd4=) 8 ... e5 9 ♗e3 ♘d4 10 ♗xd4 ed 11 ♕xd4 ♖e8 12 ♕d3 ♘d7 which gave Black good compensation in Brinck Claussen–Andersson, Copenhagen 1965.

(b) 7 ♗h4 c5 is likely to lead to a minor variation of the Benoni which is comfortable for Black.

7 ... c5

It is also well worth considering Lanka's idea 7 ... ♘bd7 8 ♕d2 c5 9 d5 ♕a5!. Clearly unpromising for White is 10 ♗xh6 ♗xh6 11 ♕xh6 ♘xe4 12 ♖c1 ♘df6, but 10 ♘f3 and 10 a4 may be considered. Practice has seen 10 f3 ♔h7 11 ♘h3 a6! 12 ♘f2 b5 13 cb (13 f4!? Knaak) 13 ... ♘b6 *(53)*, with a Benko-type position. Black intends ... ♘fd7–e5, followed by ... ab and ... ♗a6, fighting for the c4- and d3-squares. As we shall see in the following examples, a

kingside advance is also a possibility.

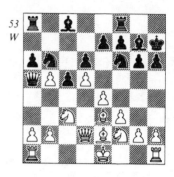

(a) 14 ♘fd1 ♘fd7 15 a4?! ♘e5 16 b3 ab 17 ♗xb5 f5!. White has endeavoured to secure the queenside, but Black finds other targets, e.g. 18 0–0 fe 19 fe ♖xf1+ 20 ♗xf1 ♘g4∓ (Shirov). Moskalenko–Shirov, Moscow 1991, continued 18 ef ♗xf5 (18 ... ♖xf5!? 19 0–0 c4! 20 f4 ♘g4 21 bc ♗a6!) 19 h3, when Shirov gives 19 ... c4! 20 ♗xb6 ♕xb6 21 bc ♘d3+ 22 ♔f1 ♕d4∓ as Black's best.

(b) 14 0–0 ♘fd7 15 ♘fd1! ♘e5 16 b3 ab 17 ♗xb5 f5! (After 17 ... ♗a6?! 18 ♗xa6 ♕xa6 19 ♘f2! White has all the vital light squares covered and is ready to advance in the centre) 18 ♖c1 g5!? (Lanka and Bologan analyse 18 ... fe 19 fe ♖xf1+ 20 ♗xf1 ♘g4 21 ♗f4 g5 22 ♗g3 ♗d4+ 23 ♔h1 ♗a6 also with good play) 19 ef (Else there follows a standard pawn storm) 19 ... ♗xf5 20 ♗e2 c4! (Now d5 is a target) 21 g4!? (21 ♘f2∓) 21 ... ♗g6 22 h4!? gh 23 f4 ♘d3 25 f5 ♗f7 25 ♗xd3 cd 26

♕xd3 ♗f6! 27 ♗d4! ♘xd5 28 ♗xf6 ♘xf6 29 ♘f2 ♖g8 30 ♖ce1! ♖a7! gave Black a strong attack in Yakovich–Bologan, Gausdal International 1991. The game concluded 31 ♔h2 ♖c7 32 ♘b5 ♕xa2! 33 ♔h3 ♖b7 34 ♖e3 ♕a5 35 ♘d4 ♕b4 36 ♖fe1? ♘d5 37 ♔xh4 ♘xe3 38 ♖xe3 ♕c5∓∓ 39 ♘e4 ♕e5 40 g5? ♕h2+ 0-1.

8 e5

This has traditionally deterred Black from the logical plan with ... h6 and ... c5. However, games by Chekhov and Yurtaev have shown that Black can now sacrifice a pawn for good compensation. White has two reasonable alternatives:

(a) **8 d5** is the most obvious. After **8 ... e6**, rather harmless are **9 ♘f3** ed 10 ed ♘g4 11 ♗d2 f5 12 0-0 ♘d7 13 ♖b1 b6 14 b4 ♘de5 15 bc bc 16 ♕c1 g5 which gave Black good kingside play in Uhlmann–Visser, Amsterdam 1990, and **9 de** ♗xe6 10 ♕d2 ♔h7 11 h3 ♘c6 12 ♘f3 ♕a5 13 ♖ad1 ♘d7 14 ♕xd6 ♖ad8 with full compensation (Portisch–Nunn, Brussels 1988). More critical alternatives are:

(a1) **9 h3** ed 10 ed. Now after **10 ... ♗f5!?** 11 g4!? ♗c8 12 ♕d2 b5 13 ♗xh6 b4 14 ♗xg7 ♔xg7 15 ♘d1 ♘e4 16 ♕f4 ♖e8 17 h4 (Hort analyses 17 ♘e3!? g5! 18 ♕h2! b3! 19 ab ♘a6 with compensation for Black) 17 ... ♕f6! Black's queenside initiative provided counterplay in Hort–J. Polgar, Munich

1991, while the solid approach is **10 ... ♖e8**, e.g. **11 ♗d3** b5!, **11 ♘f3 ♗f5** 12 g4 ♗e4 13 0-0 ♗xf3 14 ♗xf3 ♘bd7 15 ♕d2 (Agzamov–G. Kuzmin, Erevan 1981) 15 ... h5!, or **11 ♕d2 ♔h7** 12 ♗d3 b5! 13 ♘xb5 ♘e4 14 ♗xe4 ♖xe4 15 ♖c1 a6 16 ♘a3 f5 17 ♘e2 g5 18 f3 ♖e8 19 ♔f2 ♖a7! 20 f4 ♖ae7∓ Frog–Bagaturov, Moscow 1991.

(a2) **9 ♕d2 ed 10 cd ♖e8 11 f3 h5! 12 a4** (12 ♗g5!?) **12 ... a6** and now:

(a21) Seirawan mentions **13 h4** ♘h7! 14 g3 b6!.

(a22) **13 a5?!** ♘h7! 14 ♗d1 ♘d7 15 ♘ge2 ♘e5 16 b3 ♕h4+?! (16 ... f5 is good for Black according to Seirawan) 17 ♗f2 ♕f6 led to a sharp struggle in Seirawan–Kasparov, Skellefteå 1989.

(a23) **13 ♗g5** ♕c7 (13 ... ♕a5!? 14 ♗f4!? — Budnikov) 14 ♖c1 ♘h7 intending ... f5 was OK for Black in Budnikov–W. Schmidt, Katowice 1990.

(b) **8 dc!?** ♕a5 *(54)* gives White two possibilities:

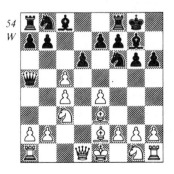

54
W

(b1) **9 ♗d2** leads to relatively quiet play after **9 ... ♕xc5** 10 ♗e3 (10 ♘f3 ♗g4) 10 ... ♕a5 11 ♕d2 ♘c6 12 h3 ♔h7 13 ♘f3 ♗e6 14 0–0 ♘d7 15 ♖fd1 ♖ac8 16 ♖ac1 ♘de5 17 b3 ♘xf3+ 18 ♗xf3 f5 19 ef ♗xf5 20 ♗e2 g5= Dokhoian–Balashov, Sverdlovsk 1987, or Yurtaev's more interesting approach **9 ... dc** 10 e5 ♘h7 11 f4 ♘c6 12 ♘f3 ♗f5 (12 ... f6 13 ef ♘xf6 14 0–0 ♗f5 15 ♘d5 ♕d8∞) 13 0–0 (13 ♘h4) 13 ... ♖ad8 14 ♘d5 ♕a6 15 ♕b3 ♖d7 16 ♖fd1 e6 17 ♘e3 ♗e4 18 ♗c3 ♖fd8 which left Black fine in Segalchik–Kovalëv, USSR 1987.

(b2) **9 ♕d2** is more ambitious. 9 ... dc 10 ♗xh6 ♖d8 11 ♕e3 ♗xh6 12 ♕xh6 ♘xe4 13 ♖c1 ♘c6! 14 ♘f3 ♘d4 15 h4 ♘xe2 yielded an extremely sharp position in Seirawan–Timman, Tilburg 1990. White now lost his way with **16 ♘g5?** ♘f6 17 ♔xe2 (17 h5 ♘f4 18 hg ♘xg6) 17 ... ♗f5! 18 f3 ♕b4 19 b3 ♕a3 20 ♔f2 ♖d2+ 21 ♔g3 ♖xg2+! 22 ♔xg2 ♕b2+ 23 ♔g3 ♘h5+ and suffered a decisive material loss. Instead Seirawan analysed **16 h5!** g5! (16 ... ♘2xc3? 17 hg±±) 17 ♘xg5 ♘f6 18 ♔xe2 without coming to any conclusion, suggesting that Black investigate 18 ... ♗f5, 18 ... ♕a6, 18 ... ♕b4 19 b3 ♕a3∞ and 18 ... ♕b6 19 b3 ♖d2+ 20 ♔f1!? ♖xf2+ 21 ♔g1.

8	**...**	**de**
9	**de**	**♕xd1+**
10	**♖xd1**	**♘g4**

11	**♗xc5**	**♘xe5** *(55)*

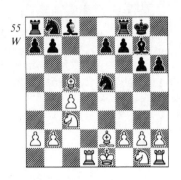

12 ♘d5

Alternatively:

(a) **12 ♘f3** ♘bc6 13 0–0 ♗f5 14 ♘h4 ♗e6 15 ♘d5 ♖ac8 16 ♗xe7 ♖fe8 17 ♘f6+ ♗xf6 18 ♗xf6 ♘xc4 19 ♘f3 ♘b6 20 a3 ♘d5 21 ♗d4 ♗g4 was very pleasant for Black in Borisenko–Yurtaev, Tashkent 1988.

(b) **12 ♗xe7** ♖e8 13 ♘d5 ♘a6 transposes to the note to Black's 12th move, below, while avoiding 12 ... ♘bc6.

12 ... ♘bc6

The other idea is **12 ... ♘a6 13 ♗xe7** (13 ♘xe7+?! ♔h7 14 ♗a3 ♖e8!? 15 ♘xc8 ♖axc8 16 b3 ♘c6∓) **13 ... ♖e8**:

(a) **14 ♗a3 ♗e6 15 ♔f1 ♖ad8 16 b3** was played in Petursson–Nunn, Reykjavik 1988. Petursson's analysis shows that **16 ... ♘c6!** *(56)* would have brought equality:

(a1) **17 ♘f3 ♖d7.** Now **18 h3** ♖ed8∓ is simple enough, but Petursson gives **18 b4 ♘cxb4!** 19 ♘xb4 ♖xd1+ 20 ♗xd1 ♗xc4+

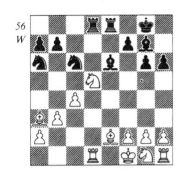

21 ⌯g1 ⯰d8 22 ♝c2 ♘c7! (△ …
a5) 23 ♘e1 ♝c3 24 ♘bd3 ⯰e8 as
winning for Black despite White's
extra piece.

(a2) **17 f4** ♘d4 18 ♝f3 ♘c2 19
♝c1 ♘ab4 20 ♘e2 ♘xa2 21 ♝d2
♘ab4 22 ♝xb4 ♘xb4 23 ⌯f2∓.

(a3) **17 ♝f3** ♘d4 (17 … ♘e5!?)
18 ♘e7+ ⌯h7 19 ♝xb7 ♘c2! 20
⯰xd8 ⯰xd8 21 ♘d5 ♘xa3 22
♝xa6 ♝xd5 23 cd ⯰xd5 24
⌯e2=.

(b) **14 b3** ♝f5 15 ⌯f1 (Lputian
noted the line 15 ♘f3 ♘c6 16
♘f6+ ♝xf6 17 ♝xf6 ⯰e6 18
♝c3 ⯰ae8 19 ⯰d2 ♘c5∓, whilst
15 ♘h3 ♘c6 16 ♘f6+ ♝xf6 17
♝xf6, as in Lputian–Chekhov,
USSR 1986, allowed Black the
strong possibility 17 … ⯰e6!, e.g.
18 ♝c3 ♝xh3 19 gh ⯰ae8 20 ⯰d2
♘c5 21 f3 ♘d3+! — Chekhov) 15
… ♘c6 16 ♝a3 (16 ♝f6 ♘cb4
(Agzamov–Yurtaev, Frunze 1985)
17 ♝xg7 ⌯xg7 18 ♘f3 ♘xa2∓)
16 … ⯰e6?! 17 b4 ♝f8 18 c5±
was Ruzhale–Glek, Blagoveshchensk 1988. Glek suggests instead
the more natural **16 … ⯰ad8!?**.

13 f4

Again White has a couple of
alternatives:

(a) **13 ♘f3** ♝e6 14 b3 ⯰fd8 15
0–0 ⯰d7 16 ♘f4 ♝f5 17 ♘xe5
♝xe5 18 ⯰xd7 ♝xd7 19 ⯰d1
⯰d8 20 ♘d5 ⌯f8 21 ⯰d3 b6 22
♝a3 ⌯e8 23 f4 ♝d4+ 24 ⌯f1
♝f5 25 ⯰d1 ♝c2 26 ⯰d2 ♝e4
27 ♝d3 ♝xd3+ 28 ⯰xd3 ♝c5
led to a draw in Petursson–Piket,
Wijk aan Zee 1990.

(b) **13 b3** ♝e6 14 ♘c7 ⯰ad8 15
♘xe6 fe 16 ♘f3 b6 17 ♝e3 ♘xf3+
18 ♝xf3 ♝c3+ 19 ⌯e2 ♘d4+
20 ♝xd4 ⯰xd4= Khalifman–
Yurtaev, Riga 1988.

13 … ♘g4
14 ♝f3

An important move order is **14
h3** ♘f6 15 ♝f3 (15 ♘xe7+ ♘xe7
16 ♝xe7 ⯰e8 17 ♝xf6 ♝xf6 18
b3 ♝h4+ 19 ⌯f1 ♝g3 20 ♝f3
♝xf4 21 ♘e2 ♝e5 22 ⌯f2 h5 23
⯰he1 h4 24 ⌯f1 ⯰b8 25 ♘c3
♝f5 26 ♘b5 ♝c2 27 ⯰d7 ♝g3
⯰c1 ♝e4 29 ♘d4 ⯰bd8 ½–½
Sofieva–Matveeva, Alma Ata 1988)
15 … ♝f5 16 ♘e2 (16 g4 ♝c2!
was given as equal by Rashkovsky;
17 ⯰d2 ♘e4 18 ♝xe4 ♝xe4 19
⯰hh2 ⯰fd8 20 ⯰he2 ♝b1 21
♘c3 ♝d3∓ was Bai Min–Chen
De, China 1987) and Black's best
is now **16 … ⯰fd8** transposing
to the main line. Instead **16 …
♝c2?!** 17 ⯰d2! ♘e4 18 ♝xe7
♘xd2 19 ⌯xd2 ⯰fe8 20 ⌯xc2
♘xe7 21 ♘c7± (A. Kuzmin) and **16
… ♘e4?!** 17 ♝a3± (17 … g5?! 18
g4) cannot be recommended.

14	…	♗f5
15	♘e2	♖fd8
16	h3	

Yurtaev analysed **16 0–0** ♗xb2 17 h3 ♘f6 18 ♖d2 ♘xd5 19 cd ♗g7 20 dc ♖xd2 21 cb ♖b8 22 ♗xa7 ♖xb7 23 ♗xb7 ♖xa2∓.

16	…	♘f6
17	♘g3	

17 ♘xe7+ ♘xe7 was analysed by Lepeshkin:

(a) **18 ♖xd8+** ♖xd8 19 ♗xe7 ♖e8 20 ♗xf6 (20 ♗c5 ♘e4; 20 ♗a3 ♗d3 △ … ♘e4) 20 … ♗xf6 21 b3 (21 g4 ♗e4; 21 ♔f2 ♗xb2 22 ♗xb7 ♗d3∓) and now **21 … ♗b1** 22 ♔d2 ♗xa2 23 ♘c1 ♗b1 24 ♗xb7 ♖d8+ 25 ♔e2 ♖e8+ or **21 … ♗h4+** 22 ♔d2 (22 ♔f1 ♗d3) 22 … ♖d8+ 23 ♔c1 ♗e7! 24 ♗d5 ♗a3+ 25 ♔d1 ♗e4 26 ♘c3 ♗xg2 27 ♖g1 ♗xd5=.

(b) **18 ♗xe7** ♖xd1+ 19 ♔xd1 ♖e8 (19 … ♘e4 20 g4 ♘f2+ 21 ♔d2 ♘xh1 22 gf ♘f2∞) 20 ♗a3 ♘e4 21 ♖f1 ♖d8+ 22 ♔c1 ♖c8 23 b3 b5 24 g4 bc! leaves White with problems.

17	…	♗c2! *(57)*

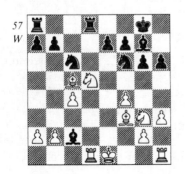

57
W

The bishop turns out to have just enough squares! Instead, rather dismal would be 17 … e6 18 ♘xf5 gf 19 ♘e7+ ♘xe7 20 ♗xe7±.

18	♖d2	♗b1
19	b3	♘xd5
20	cd	♗c3
21	♔e2!	

The only move, since **21 0–0** ♘b4! and **21 dc** ♖xd2 22 0–0 b6! both leave Black on top.

21	…	♗xd2
22	♖xb1	

22 dc ♗xa2 23 c7 ♗xf4 gives Black plenty of pawns for the piece and play against the white king.

22	…	♗b4

Now White was able to restore the material balance: 23 dc ♗xc5 24 c7 ♖f8 25 ♗xb7 ♗d6 26 ♗xa8 ♖xa8 27 ♖c1 ♖c8 28 ♔f3 ♖xc7 29 ♖xc7 ♗xc7 30 ♘f1 f5. In this knight versus bishop ending White must be very careful since there are pawns on both sides; Yurtaev gave **31 b4** ♔f7 32 a4 ♔e6 33 ♘e3 as sufficient to hold the balance. Instead the game continued **31 ♘d2?** ♔f7 32 ♔e3 g5 33 fg hg 34 ♘f3 ♗f4+!∓ and Black was able to win: 35 ♔f2 ♔f6 36 ♘d4 ♗d6 37 ♔e2 ♗c5 38 ♘c6 ♔e6 39 ♘d8+ ♔e5 40 ♔f3 ♗b6 41 ♘c6+ ♔d6 42 ♘b4 e5 43 ♔e2 e4∓∓ 44 ♘a6 ♔e5 45 ♘b4 ♗c5 46 ♘c6+ ♔d5 47 ♘a5 f4 48 ♘c4 ♔d4 49 ♘a5 ♔d5 50 ♘c4 ♗b4 51 ♔f2 ♔d4 52 ♔e2 ♔c3 53 ♘d2 ♔d4 54 ♘c4 e3! (*Zugzwang*) 55 a3 ♗c5 56 ♘a5 ♗b6 57 ♘c6+ ♔c3 0–1.

7 Sämisch Gambit: 6 ... c5

1 d4 ♘f6 2 c4 g6 3 ♘c3 ♗g7 4 e4 d6

| 5 | f3 | 0-0 |
| 6 | ♗e3 | c5 *(58)* |

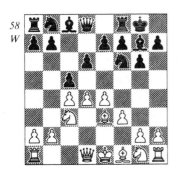

58
W

Although not an entirely new variation, this pawn sacrifice only became popular around the end of the 1980s. It is easy to understand why players may have been sceptical about the line: Black loses a pawn and allows the queens to be exchanged! The game Karpov–Barle, Ljubljana/Portorož 1975 seemed to confirm the gambit's dubious status. Only Chekhov continued to refine Black's methods of counterplay, but his games received little coverage.

However, in 1985 Sax and Glek played some interesting games with Black, and in subsequent years a new generation of Soviets, most notably Khalifman, Gelfand and Shirov, enthusiastically demonstrated the merits of Black's position. Currently it is one of the most topical lines in the King's Indian.

So what does Black obtain for the pawn? Firstly, a significant development advantage, a wonderful open diagonal for the g7-bishop and some excellent squares for knights (c5, b4, e5 and ideally d3). Furthermore, White's kingside development, as often in the Sämisch, is rather ponderous, so the king can find itself a little embarrassed on the dark squares. A purely positional device is to double White's pawns by exchanging on c3, after which the play takes on a Nimzo-Indian flavour.

It is natural for White to try to dissipate Black's initiative by exchanging pieces, but the following example, Beliavsky–Nunn, Amsterdam 1990, shows that this may have the opposite effect *(59)*: 16 ... ♗e6 17 ♖xd8+ ♖xd8 now

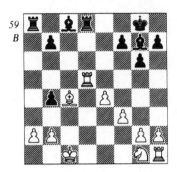

left White in great difficulties, since 18 &xe6 &h6+! 19 &c2 &d2+ 20 &b3 fe is a disaster. Beliavsky decided his best chance was an ending a pawn down: 18 &d5 &h6+ 19 f4 &xf4+ 20 &b1 &xd5 21 ed &xd5 22 &f3∓.

Black's compensation is of a highly amorphous nature. White can certainly prevent invasions on d3, and has little trouble clearing the a1–h8 diagonal of targets, so the alert gambiteer must seek out the weakest link in White's position according to the specific circumstances. In some cases this is the other long diagonal *(60)*:

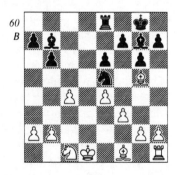

Arlandi–Khalifman, Groningen

1985/6 continued 18 ... f5! 19 ef &xf3! 20 f6 &xg5 21 fg &h3! after which White never really had a chance.

Sometimes the way in which Black's position hangs together verges on the miraculous *(61)*:

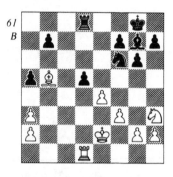

In Andrianov–Glek, corres 1986–8, Black spotted the weakness of a3 and h2(!): 21 ... &f8! 22 a4 &d6!. By breaking the pin, Black threatens 23 ... de, so White now has no choice: 23 ed &xh2 24 f4 g5! 25 fg &xd5. The threat of 26 ... &c3+ now gave Black time to defend his rook, and a draw was agreed shortly.

Razuvaev–Shirov
Bundesliga 1991/2

1 d4 &f6 2 c4 g6 3 &c3 &g7 4 e4 d6 5 f3 0–0 6 &e3 c5

	7	dc		dc
	8	&xd8		

Retaining the queens does not help White: after **8 &xc5 &c6 9 &e3 &d7!**, Black's straightforward plan ... &a5, ... &d8 gave

White some problems in Dlugy–Gelfand, Palma (GMA) 1989. After **10 ♖c1 ♕a5 11 ♘h3 ♖d8 12 ♘f2** (12 ♕c2 ♘c5 13 ♘f2 ♘b4 14 ♕b1 ♘xa2!; best is 12 ♘f4!∞) **12 ... ♘c5 13 ♗d2 ♗xc3! 14 bc** (14 ♖xc3 ♕xa2 15 b3 ♘xb3 16 ♖xb3 ♖xd2!) **14 ... ♗e6∓** (14 ... ♕xa2!?) **15 ♕c2 ♘e5 16 ♗f4 ♘xc4 17 ♗e2 g5!! 18 ♗xg5 ♘d3+ 19 ♗xd3 ♕xg5** Black went on to score a comfortable victory. Dlugy later improved with **10 ♘ge2 ♘de5 11 ♘f4 ♘a5 12 ♕a4** (Dlugy–Lein, New York 1990) when 12 ... ♗d7! 13 ♕b4 ♖c8 would have secured good counterplay.

8 ...   ♖xd8
9 ♗xc5

9 e5 is less effective than 8 e5 (considered in the next chapter); after 9 ... ♘fd7 10 f4 ♘c6 11 0-0-0 b6 12 ♘f3 ♗b7 13 ♗e2 ♗h6!, Black threatens the e-pawn.

9 ...   ♘c6
10 ♖d1

The main lines, **10 ♗a3** and **10 ♘d5**, are dealt with in the next two illustrative games. Rarer options for White:

(a) **10 ♗e2 ♘d7** (10 ... b6 11 ♗a3 — see 10 ♗a3 b6 11 ♗e2) 11 ♗a3 (11 ♗e3 ♘de5) 11 ... ♗xc3+ 12 bc ♘de5 13 ♖d1 was successful in Christiansen–Wilder, US Ch 1986, but only because Black allowed a strong exchange sacrifice: **13 ... ♗e6?!** 14 ♖d5!. Instead **13 ... ♖xd1+ 14 ♔xd1 ♗e6** would have been fine for Black.

(b) **10 ♗e3 ♘b4** (Black may try 10 ... ♘d7 intending ... ♗xc3 and ... ♘de5; if 11 ♘ge2 then 11 ... ♘de5 12 ♘f4 e6 13 ♖c1 b6 14 ♔f2 ♗a6 15 b3 ♘b4 gave White some problems in Shvedchikov–Perelshtein, Moscow 1989) 11 ♖c1 ♗e6 12 b3 ♘e8 13 ♔f2 (13 ♗c5!?) 13 ... ♗xc3 14 ♖xc3 ♘xa2 15 ♖c2 ♘b4 16 ♖b2 ♖d1 17 ♗c5 ♖xf1+ 18 ♔xf1 ♘d3 19 ♗a3 ♘xb2 20 ♗xb2 ♖d8 21 ♔e2 b5∓ Tataev–Chekhov, Moscow 1975.

(c) **10 ♘ge2 ♘d7** (10 ... b6 11 ♗a3 — see 10 ♗a3 b6 11 ♘ge2) **11 ♗e3** (11 ♗a3 ♘de5; 11 ♗f2 ♘de5 12 ♘f4 ♘a5) **11 ... ♘de5 12 ♘f4 ♘b4** *(62)* (12 ... ♘a5!?) and now:

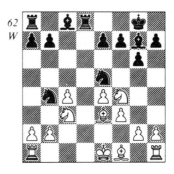

(c1) **13 ♔f2 ♗e6!** 14 ♘cd5 ♗xd5 15 ♘xd5 (15 cd ♖dc8 16 ♗e2 ♖c2 and 15 ed ♖ac8 16 a3 ♘c2 are both promising for Black) 15 ... ♘c2 16 ♖c1 ♘xe3 17 ♔xe3 e6 18 ♘c3 ♗h6+ 19 f4 g5!∓ Gunawan–Gelfand, Minsk 1986.

(c2) **13 ♖d1** fails to 13 ... ♘xf3+! 14 gf ♗xc3+ 15 bc ♘c2+ 16 ♔e2 ♖xd1∓.

(c3) **13 ♖c1 ♗e6!**? 14 b3 (14 ♗c5 a5 transposes to Novikov–Wojtkiewicz (7 ♘ge2 ♘c6 8 ♕d2 a6 9 dc dc 10 ♕xd8 ♖xd8 11 ♗xc5 ♘d7 12 ♗e3 ♘de5 13 ♘f4 ♘b4 14 ♖c1 ♗e6 15 ♗c5 a5); 14 ♘xe6 ♘ed3+ 15 ♗xd3 ♘xd3+ 16 ♔f1 fe 17 ♖c2 ♘xb2=) 14 ... ♖ac8 15 ♗e2 ♘ed3+ 16 ♗xd3 ♘xd3+ 17 ♘xd3 ♖xd3 18 ♗d2 ♗xc3 19 ♗xc3 b5 was analysed by Chekhov and Dvoretsky. Black regains the pawn with equality.

(c4) **13 ♖b1** ♘c2+ 14 ♔f2 ♘xe3 15 ♔xe3 ♘c6 16 ♘d3 ♘a5 17 ♘b4 ♗d4+ 18 ♔d2 ♗c5+ 19 ♘bd5 ♘c6 20 ♘a4 ♗d4∓ Zaid–Ubilava, USSR 1974.

10 ... ♖xd1+

Also worth consideration is **10 ... ♘d7** 11 ♗a3 b6 (11 ... ♗xc3+ 12 bc b6) 12 ♘ge2?! (12 ♘d5) 12 ... ♗b7 13 ♘d5 ♘de5 14 ♘c1 e6 15 ♘e7+ ♘xe7 and now White should play **16 ♖xd8+** ♖xd8 17 ♗xe7 ♖e8 18 ♗d6 ♘xc4 19 ♗xc4 ♖c8 20 b3 b5 with only a small disadvantage. Instead in Arlandi–Khalifman, Groningen 1985/6 there followed **16 ♗xe7?** ♖xd1+ 17 ♔xd1 ♖e8 18 ♗g5 f5 19 ef ♗xf3! 20 f6 ♘xg5 21 fg ♘h3! and Black won impressively: 22 ♘d3 ♔xg7 23 ♔e1 ♖d8 24 ♘e5 g5 25 ♘g4 h5 26 ♘e3 g4 27 ♗e2 ♘f4 28 ♖g1 ♖d4 29 ♗f1 ♘g6 30 ♗e2 ♘f4 31 ♗f1 ♗e4! 32 a3 e5 33 g3 ♘d3+ 34 ♗xd3 ♖xd3 35 ♘d1 ♗f3 36 ♘c3 e4 37 ♘d5 e3 0-1.

11 ♘xd1

11 ♔xd1 ♘d7 12 ♗a3 ♗xc3 13 bc ♘de5 is comfortable for Black: 14 ♘e2 ♘xc4 15 ♗c1 e5 16 ♘d4 ♘4a5 17 ♘xc6 ♘xc6 18 ♗c4 ♗e6 ½-½ Dlugy–Van der Wiel, Wijk aan Zee 1990.

11 ... ♘d7!

An improvement over 11 ... ♗e6 12 ♘e3 ♘d7 13 ♗a3 a5 (Belov suggests 13 ... ♘b6!? △ ... ♘a4) 14 ♘e2 ♘b4 15 ♘c3 ♗d4 16 ♔d2 ♖d8 17 ♘ed5 ♗xd5 18 cd ♘b6 19 ♗b5 e6 20 de fe (Murey–Belov, Moscow 1989) 21 ♔e2 ♖c8 22 ♗xb4! ab 23 ♘a4 ♘xa4 24 ♗xa4 ♗xb2 25 ♗b3 ♔f7 26 ♖d1 ♔e7 27 f4± (Belov).

Shirov's move gives White no time for ♘e2-c3.

12	♗a3	a5
13	♘e3	♘b4
14	♘h3	♘c5 *(63)*

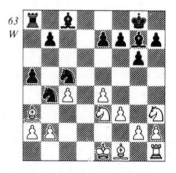

White already has problems. His queenside faces demolition while his kingside is hibernating.

15	♘f2	e6
16	♗e2	b6
17	♘fd1	♘xa2
18	♘c2	♗a6

19	♗xc5	bc
20	♘a3	♘c1!

White now makes a desperate attempt to cover the weaknesses of b2 and c4, but finds his king in trouble.

21	♘b5	♖b8
22	♗f1	a4
23	♔d2	♘b3+
24	♔c2	♖d8
25	♘bc3	♖d2+
26	♔b1	♘a5
27	g3	a3
28	ba	♗xc4
29	f4	♗b3

0–1

Gheorghiu–Gelfand
Palma 1989

1 d4 ♘f6 2 c4 g6 3 ♘c3 ♗g7 4 e4 d6 5 f3 0–0 6 ♗e3 c5 7 dc dc 8 ♕xd8 ♖xd8 9 ♗xc5 ♘c6
10   ♘d5   ♘d7! *(64)*

Black should avoid 10 ... ♘xd5?! 11 cd b6 (11 ... ♗xb2?! 12 ♖b1 ♗c3+ 13 ♔f2 b6 14 ♗a3± Karpov–Barle, Ljubljana/ Portorož 1975) 12 ♗a3 ♘d4 13 0–0–0 e6 14 ♘e2 ♘b5 15 ♗e7 ♖d7 16 ♗h4± Bronstein–Dvoretsky, Vilnius 1975, **10 ... e6?!** 11 ♘e7+ ♘xe7 12 ♗xe7 ♖d7 13 ♗a3 b6 14 ♘h3! ♗a6 15 ♘f2 ♖c8 16 ♖c1 ♗h6 17 ♖c2± Moiseev–Chekhov, USSR 1975 and **10 ... ♖d7?!** 11 0–0–0 e6 12 ♘xf6+ ♗xf6 13 ♗d6 b6 (Christiansen–B. Ivanović, Lucerne 1989) 14 ♘e2!? ♗a6 15 f4 ♖ad8 (15 ... ♗xc4 16 e5 ♗e7 17 ♘c3 ♗xf1

18 ♖hxf1 ♗xd6 19 ♘e4!±) 16 e5 ♘xe5 17 fe ♗xe5 18 c5! bc 19 ♘c3± (Knaak).

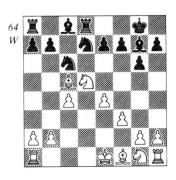

64
W

11   ♗xe7

The most fashionable move. Alternatively:

(a) **11 ♘xe7+** ♘xe7 12 ♗xe7 ♗xb2 13 ♖b1 (13 ♗xd8 ♗xa1 14 ♗e7 ♘e5 15 f4 ♘c6 16 ♗d6 ♗e6 Rodrigues–Chekhov, Algarve 1975) 13 ... ♗c3+ 14 ♔f2 (14 ♔d1 ♖e8 15 ♘e2 ♗e5 16 ♗b4 ♘b6 17 ♘c3 a5 18 ♗a3 ♗xc3 19 ♖xb6 ♗b4! was good for Black in Gunawan–Khalifman, Minsk 1986) 14 ... ♗d4+ 15 ♔g3 (After 15 ♔e1 Black can play for a win with 15 ... ♖e8 followed by 16 ... f5) 15 ... ♖e8. Black is playing for mate!: **16 ♗a3** ♘f6 17 ♗b2 ♘h5+ 18 ♔h4 ♗c5! or **16 ♗g5** ♘f6 17 ♘h3 (17 ♘e2 ♘h5+ 18 ♔h4 ♗f2+ 19 g3 f6 20 ♗h6 ♘g7) 17 ... ♘h5+ 18 ♔h4 ♔g7! 19 g4 h6 20 ♗xh6+ ♔xh6 21 gh f5 22 ♔g3 fe 23 ♗g2? (23 hg ef 24 ♘f2 ♔xg6∓) 23 ... gh 24 f4 ♖g8+ 25 ♘g5 h4+ 0–1 Gil-Howell, World Junior (Gausdal) 1986.

(b) **11 ♗a3 e6 12 ♘c7** (12
♘c3?! ♗xc3+ 13 bc b6) **12 ...
♖b8 13 0-0-0** is perhaps most
critical:

(b1) **13 ... ♗h6+?!** 14 ♔b1 b6
15 ♘e2 ♗b7 16 ♘c3 ♘c5 17
♗e2 ♗f4 18 ♘7b5 a6 19 b4!±
Beliavsky–Chekhov, USSR Ch
1980.

(b2) **13 ... b6** 14 ♘e2 (14 ♘h3?!
a6!∓ 15 ♗d6?! ♗b7 16 f4 ♖bc8
17 e5 ♘c5∓ Babula–Rašik,
Prague 1990; 14 ♘b5 ♗a6 15 ♘e2
♘de5 16 ♘ec3 ♗h6+ 17 ♔c2
♖xd1 18 ♘xd1 ♖d8 19 ♘d6 ♗f8
20 c5 ♗xf1 21 ♖xf1 bc 22 ♘b7
♘d4+ gave Black good play in
Ward–Hassapis, British Ch (Eastbourne) 1990) 14 ... ♗b7 15 ♗d6
♘c5 16 ♘b5 ♖bc8 17 ♘ec3 a6 18
♘a3 f5 19 ef gf 20 ♔b1 ♘d4 gave
Black reasonable compensation in
Petursson–Sax, Biel IZ 1985.

(b3) **13 ... a6** 14 f4 ♗f8 15
♗xf8 ♔xf8 16 ♘f3. Now, instead
of **16 ... ♔e7** 17 ♖e1 ♘a7 18 b4
♔d6 19 ♘d5! ed 20 ed which
gave Black serious problems in
Petursson–Mortensen, Espoo Z
1989, Hazai suggests **16 ... ♘c5**.

11	...	**♘xe7**
12	**♘xe7+**	**♔f8**
13	**♘d5**	

13 ♘xc8?! ♗xb2 14 ♖b1
♗xc3+ 15 ♔f2 is good for Black
after either **15 ... ♗d4+!?** 16 ♔e1
♖axc8 or **15 ... ♖axc8**, e.g. 16
♖xb7 ♘c5 17 ♖xa7? ♘xe4+!.

13	...	**♗xb2**
14	**♖b1**	**♗g7** *(65)*

Black varied unsuccessfully

with **14 ... ♗a3** in a blitz game
Karpov–J. Polgar, Monaco 1992:
15 ♘h3 b6 16 ♗e2 ♘e5 17 ♘f2
♗b7 18 f4 ♘c6 19 h4 ♘d4 20
♖h3 ♖ac8 21 h5 ♗xd5 22 cd ♖c2
(Keene recommends 22 ... ♗b4+
23 ♔f1 ♘xe2 24 ♔xe2 ♖c2+ 25
♔f1 ♗c5, but White can try 24
hg!?) 23 ♗d3 ♖xa2 24 ♗c4 ♖c2
25 ♖xa3 ♖xc4 26 ♖xa7±.

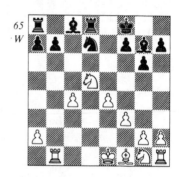

15 ♘e2

This position is critical for the
whole variation and has seen num-
erous other ideas for White.

(a) **15 g4** b6 16 g5 ♗b7 17 h4
♖ac8 18 f4 ♘c5 19 e5 ♗xd5 20 cd
♖xd5∓ Levitt–Watson, London
(WFW) 1990.

(b) **15 h4** ♘c5 16 h5 g5∞ (Vogt).

(c) After **15 ♘h3**, a simultaneous
game Karpov–Gallati, Zurich
1988, continued **15 ... ♘c5** 16 ♘f2
(16 ♘hf4 ♗e6), whereupon Hazai
recommends 16 ... ♗e6! 17 ♗e2
♖ac8 18 0-0 ♖d6 19 ♘d3 ♖a6 as
the way to obtain counterplay. An
alternative approach is **15 ... b6**
16 ♗e2 ♗b7 17 0-0 ♖ac8 18
♖bc1 ♗h6!= 19 ♖c2 ♗xd5 20

ed b5 21 ♖b1 bc 22 ♖xc4 ♘b6 23 ♖xc8 ♖xc8 24 d6 ♖c2 25 ♔f1! ♖d2 ½-½ P. Jakobsen–Burgess, Danish Ch (Århus) 1992.

(d) **15 ♗d3** b6 16 ♘e2 ♘e5 17 ♔d2 ♗a6 18 ♖hc1 ♖ac8 19 ♖b4 ♗h6+ 20 f4 f5 21 ♘d4 fe! 22 ♘e6+ ♔f7 23 ♘xd8+ ♖xd8 24 ♖a4 ♘xd3 25 ♖xa6 ♗xf4+ 26 ♘xf4 ♘c5+ gave Black the advantage in Bogdanović–Belov, Moscow 1985.

| 15 | ... | ♘c5! |
| 16 | ♘c1 | |

Gelfand gave **16 ♘ef4 ♗d7** 17 ♗e2 ♖ac8, with compensation for Black, while on his suggestion **16 ♘ec3**, Hazai recommends 16 ... ♗e6 17 ♗e2 ♗xc3+ 18 ♘xc3 ♘d3+ with equality.

| 16 | ... | ♗e6 |
| 17 | ♘d3 | |

17 ♘b3 ♖ac8! 18 ♗e2 ♘a4! gives White problems over c3.

| 17 | ... | ♖ac8! |

17 ... ♘a4 18 ♖xb7 ♖ab8 19 ♖b3! would not be adequate for Black.

| 18 | ♗e2?! | |

Now White starts to go astray. Gelfand recommends **18 ♘xc5** ♖xc5 19 ♖b3! (19 ♖xb7 ♖a5!) 19 ... b5 20 ♖xb5 ♖xb5 21 cb ♗xd5 22 ed ♖xd5 with equality.

| 18 | ... | ♘a4! |
| 19 | ♘3f4 | |

After **19 ♖xb7** ♖xc4 20 ♖xa7 ♘c3! White has serious problems.

19	...	g5!
20	♘h5	♗c3+!
21	♔f1	

Dlugy suggests that instead **21 ♘xc3** ♘xc3 22 ♖xb7 gives reasonable chances of survival.

| 21 | ... | ♗d4 |
| 22 | h4 | ♗xd5 |

Instead, **22 ... h6** would allow counterplay after 23 hg hg 24 ♘hf6. After the text, Gelfand gives **23 cd** ♘c3 24 ♖b4! ♗e5 (24 ... ♗b6 25 ♖xb6!) 25 hg ♘xa2 26 ♖b1 ♘c3 27 ♖e1 ♘xe2 28 ♖xe2 ♖c1+ 29 ♖e1 ♖dc8 30 ♔f2 ♖8c2+ 31 ♔e3 ♖c3+ 32 ♔f2 ♖xe1 33 ♖xe1 a5 34 ♖d1! as White's best chance.

23	ed?	♘c3
24	♖xb7	♖b8
25	♖b3	

25 ♖xb8 ♖xb8 26 ♗d3 ♖b2∓∓.

| 25 | ... | ♘xa2 |
| 26 | ♖d3 | |

After **26 ♖xb8** ♖xb8 27 g4 ♘c3, the a-pawn will advance with decisive effect.

26	...	♖b1+
27	♗d1	♗b6!
28	♘f6	♘b4
29	♔e2	

The simple plan of pushing the a-pawn is also effective after **29 ♖d2** ♗e3 30 ♔e2 ♗xd2 31 ♔xd2 a5 32 hg a4 33 ♖xh7 a3.

The game finished: **29 ... ♘xd3** 30 ♔xd3 a5 31 hg a4 32 ♘e4 a3 33 ♘c3 ♖a1 (33 ... ♗a5! is more elegant) 34 ♔c2 ♗d4 35 ♘b5 a2 36 ♔b3 ♖a8 0-1.

Van der Sterren–Shirov
Kerteminde 1991

1 d4 ⏃f6 2 c4 g6 3 ⏃c3 ⏃g7 4 e4 d6 5 f3 0–0 6 ⏃e3 c5 7 dc dc 8 ⏁xd8 ⏅xd8 9 ⏃xc5 ⏃c6
10   ⏃a3   a5

10 ... b6 is also playable:

(a) **11 ⏃e2 ⏃b7 12 ⏃h3 ⏃d7 13 0–0–0 ⏃xc3 14 bc ⏃a6 15** ⏃f4 e6 16 c5 led to mass exchanges and a level ending in Knaak–Hazai, Camaguey 1987.

(b) **11 ⏅d1 ⏃d7 12 ⏃d5 e6 13** ⏃e7+ ⏃xe7 14 ⏃xe7 ⏅e8 15 ⏃a3 ⏃c5 16 ⏃h3 (16 b3 ⏃b7 17 ⏃h3 f5) 16 ... f5 17 ⏃e2 (17 ⏃f2 ⏃b7 18 ef ef+) 17 ... fe 18 fe ⏃b7 19 0–0 ⏃xe4 20 ⏃g5 (Vilela–Hazai, Camaguey 1987) 20 ... ⏃c2! 21 ⏅d2 ⏃e4 22 ⏅xc2 ⏃d4+ 23 ⏇h1 ⏃xg5= Hazai.

(c) **11 ⏃ge2 e6** *(66)* and now:

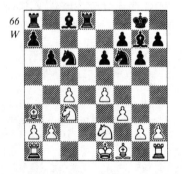

66
W

(c1) **12 ⏅d1 ⏃d7 13 b3 (13 ⏃f4** ⏃xc3+ 14 bc ⏃a6 15 c5=) 13 ... ⏃b7 14 g3?! ⏃de5 15 ⏃g2 ⏃d3+ 16 ⏇f1 a6!? 17 f4 b5 18 ⏃c1 bc 19 bc f6!? (19 ... ⏃a5 20 e5=) should, in Brenninkmeijer–Gelfand, Arnhem 1987/8, have

been met by **20 f5!** e5 21 ⏃d5∞. Instead, after **20 ⏃e3?** ⏃a5!, Black was well in control.

(c2) **12 ⏃b5 a6** (12 ... ⏃e8 13 ⏃c1 ⏃b7 14 ⏃b3 a5 15 ⏃e2 ⏃b4 16 ⏇f2 ⏃c2 gave Black reasonable prospects in Arbakov–Glek, Belgorod 1989) 13 ⏃d6 ⏃d7 14 0–0–0 ⏃c5. Here Zak recommended **15 g3** ⏃e5 16 ⏃xc5 bc 17 ⏃g2 ⏅b8 18 b3! ⏃c6, when Black has compensation, as an improvement over **15 f4?** e5! 16 f5 gf 17 ef ⏃h6+ 18 ⏇c2 ⏃d4+!, as in Zaid–Chekhov, Sochi 1975. After 19 ⏃xd4 ⏅xd6 20 ⏃xc5 bc 21 ⏃b3 ⏃xf5+ 22 ⏃d3 e4 23 ⏃e2 e3+ 24 ⏇c1 ⏅d2! 25 ⏃xd2 ed+ 26 ⏅xd2 ⏅d8 27 ⏅d1 ⏅d4∓∓ the unbreakable pin left White in a comical mess.

(c3) **12 ⏃a4** has the point that **12 ... ⏃a6?!** is comfortably met by 13 ⏃ec3 ⏃d4 14 0–0–0!∓. Therefore in Ivanchuk–Gelfand, Reggio Emilia 1991/2, Black targeted instead the more sensitive points in White's camp: **12 ... ⏃h6!** 13 ⏅d1 (13 ⏇f2 ⏃e5!? exposes White's king after 14 g4 ⏃exg4+!? or 14 ⏃e7 ⏃d3+ ⏇g3 ⏃h5+ 16 ⏇h4 ⏅e8) 13 ... ⏃a6 14 ⏃ec3 (14 b3!? ⏅xd1+ 15 ⏇xd1 ⏅d8+ 16 ⏇c2 ⏅d2+ 17 ⏇b1 ⏅d1+ 18 ⏃c1 ⏃d4 19 ⏃b2 ⏃xe2 20 ⏅xd1 ⏃xc1∞ is Gelfand's analysis) 14 ... ⏃d4! 15 ⏃d3 (Not 15 ⏃e7?! ⏃c2+ 16 ⏇f2 ⏃e3+ 17 ⏇g3 ⏃h5+ 18 ⏇h4 ⏅e8) 15 ... ⏃h5!. Black has full compensation, so White wisely returned

the pawn: 16 ♔f2 ♘f4 17 ♗b1!
♗xc4 18 ♗e7 ♖d7 19 ♗f6 ♗g7
20 ♗xg7 ♔xg7 21 b3 ♗a6 22 g3
♘h5 23 ♘d5 ♘c6 24 ♘e3 ½-½.
Like many games in this variation,
a short draw, but full of tactical
nuances.

Another possible move is 10 ...
e6, which after 11 ♘ge2 b6 (as in
Ivanchuk–Gelfand) transposes to
the line 10 ... b6 11 ♘ge2 e6.

11 ♖d1
This is White's most natural-
looking move here. Alternatively:

11 ♘d5 ♘xd5 12 cd ♘b4 13
0-0-0 (13 ♔f2 e6 14 ♗c4 ed 15
ed ♘xd5∓ Beliavsky; 13 ♖d1 e6
14 ♗c4 ed 15 ed ♘c2+ 16 ♔f2
♘xa3 17 ba ♗d7∓ Timosh-
chenko–Khalifman, Tashkent
1987) 13 ... e6!? 14 ♗c4?! (14 d6!?
can be met by 14 ... ♘xa2+ 15
♔b1 ♘b4 16 f4 e5 or 14 ... ♗e5)
14 ... ed (14 ... b5!?) 15 ♗xb4 ab
16 ♖xd5 ♗e6! 17 ♖xd8+ ♖xd8
18 ♗d5 ♗h6+ gave Black a clear
advantage in Beliavsky–Nunn,
Amsterdam 1990.

11 ♗c5 is rather paraxodical,
but White is arguing that ... a5
has weakened Black's position. 11
... ♘d7 12 ♗e3 (12 ♗f2!?) 12 ...
a4 (12 ... ♗xc3+ 13 bc b6 14
0-0-0± Knaak) 13 0-0-0 a3 14
♘ge2 ab+ 15 ♔xb2 b6 16 ♔b1
(16 ♘d4? ♘c5) 16 ... ♗a6 17
♘d4 ♘a5!? (Nowak suggests 17 ...
♘xd4 18 ♗xd4 ♗xd4! 19 ♖xd4
♘e5=) 18 ♘d5 was Knaak–
Wojtkiewicz, Stara Zagora Z
1990. Now Black's best was 18 ...

♘c5∞; the game continued **18 ...**
♗xc4 19 ♗xc4 ♘xc4 20 ♘c6
♖f8! 21 ♘dxe7+ (21 ♗g5!?) 21
... ♔h8 22 ♖xd7!? (22 ♗d4 ♘c5)
22 ... ♘xe3, whereupon Knaak
recommended 23 g3 ♘c4 (Nowak
gave 23 ... ♖a3 24 ♘a7!? ♖a8 25
♘ec6 as unclear) 24 f4 ♘a3+ 25
♔c1 ♘b5 (25 ... ♘c4 26 ♔c2!)
26 ♖d2 ♘c3 27 e5±.

11 ... ♗e6!
In Nenashev–Nunn, Manila
OL 1992, Black failed to achieve
compensation with 11 ... ♖xd1+
12 ♔xd1 ♘b4 13 ♘ge2 b6 14 ♘c1
e6 15 ♘a4 ♘d7 16 b3 ♗a6 17
♗b2!±.

12 ♘d5 ♗xd5
13 cd ♘b4
14 ♗b5
14 ♗d3 ♘xd3+ 15 ♗xd3 e6=
Dragomaretsky–Glek, Moscow
1989.

14 ... ♘c2+ (67)

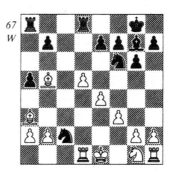

67
W

15 ♔f2!?
A new idea in this game. Previously played was **15 ♔e2 ♘xa3**
16 ba ♖ac8 17 ♘h3 ♖c2+ (17 ...
♗h6?! only gave Black problems

after the strong reply 18 g4! in Knaak–J. Piket, Novi Sad OL 1990) 18 ♖d2 ♖xd2+ 19 ♔xd2 e6 20 ♔e2 ed 21 ♖d1 ♗f8 22 a4 ♗d6!= 23 ed ♗xh2 24 f4 g5 25 fg ♘xd5 26 ♔f3 ♗c7 27 ♗c4 ♘c3 28 ♖xd8+ ♗xd8 29 ♗b3 b5 30 ab ♘xb5 31 ♔g4 ♘d4 ½-½ Andrianov–Glek, corres 1986-8.

| 15 | ... | ♘xa3 |
| 16 | ba | e6?! |

Knaak prefers **16 … ♖ac8** 17 ♘e2 ♖c2 18 ♖c1 ♖xa2 19 ♖c7 ♗f8!? 20 a4∞.

17 d6!?

17 ♘e2 ed 18 e5 ♘d7 19 f4 ♘c5∞.

17	...	e5
18	♘e2	♗f8
19	d7	♗xa3?!

Kramnik recommends that Black prevent the g2–g4 idea with **19 … ♗c5+** 20 ♔g3 ♗xa3 21 ♖d3 ♗c5 22 a4 b6 23 ♖hd1 ♖a7 24 ♔h3 h5!.

20 ♖d3?!

After this, Black seems in no real danger.

A much more forceful approach

was successful in Kramnik–Nunn, Manila OL 1992: 20 g4! h6 21 h4 a4!? 22 ♖d3 ♗b2! 23 g5! hg 24 hg ♘h7 25 f4! ♖a5?! (25 … ef 26 ♖d5!±) 26 ♖d5 f6 27 ♖xh7±±.

20	...	♗c5+
21	♔g3	♔f8
22	♖c1	b6
23	a4	♔e7
24	♖cd1	♖a7
25	♔h3	♗b4

Black has enough play to secure a draw. He now threatens to occupy the c-file; after White prevents this, he threatens to win the d7-pawn. White can only prevent this by forcing the exchange of knights, whereupon Black manoeuvres his bishop to d4 and can happily sacrifice the exchange for the passed pawn and play against a4. Play continued: 26 ♖c1 ♗d6 27 ♘c3 ♖c7 28 ♖cd1 ♗b4 29 ♘d5+ ♘xd5 30 ♖xd5 f6 31 g3 ♖c2 32 ♖5d3 ♗c3 33 f4 ♗d4 34 fe fe 35 ♖1d2 ♖c5 36 ♔g2 ♖xd7 37 ♗xd7 ♔xd7 38 ♖xd4+ ed 39 ♖xd4+ ♔e6 40 ♔f3 ♔e5 ½-½.

8 Sämisch Gambit Declined

1 d4 ♘f6 2 c4 g6 3 ♘c3 ♗g7 4 e4 d6 5 f3 0–0 6 ♗e3 c5

In view of White's difficulties in finding any advantage by accepting the pawn, it is understandable that methods of declining the gambit have come under scrutiny. While hardly testing the soundness of Black's idea, these lines lead to rich middlegames, with plenty of scope for innovation.

Portisch's 7 dc dc 8 e5 enjoyed a good reputation for a couple of years, but Black has found a number of promising replies, as we see in the first game below.

The second game covers the Benoni situations arising after 7 ♘ge2 ♘c6 8 d5, and includes a brief survey of the consequences of Black meeting 6 ♗g5 and 6 ♘ge2 with 6 ... c5. An important point to note in this type of Benoni is the rôle of Black's h-pawn. A well-timed thrust by this pawn disrupts White's position, while securing some space for Black on the kingside. Christiansen–Benjamin, USA Ch (Jacksonville) 1990, is a good example *(68)*:

There followed 12 ... h5! 13

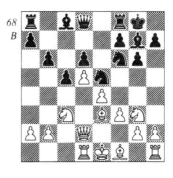

♗e2 h4 14 ♘f1 ♘h7 (Prevents ♗g5 and prepares ... f5, after which ef would be met by ... gf, controlling e4 and opening the g-file) 15 f4 ♘g4 16 h3 ♘xe3 17 ♘xe3. Then the logical continuation was De Firmian's suggestion 17 ... g5! 18 0–0 gf 19 ♖xf4 ♗e5 20 ♖f1 ♖e8 followed by ... ♘f8–g6 which gives Black a firm grip on the dark squares around White's king. Note that Black will ideally wait for White to play either 0–0 or ♕d2 before driving the knight from g3, since then the manoeuvre ♘f1–d2 is ruled out.

After 7 ♘ge2 ♘c6 8 ♕d2, one idea is to clarify matters with 8 ... cd, leading to Maroczy positions, but generally Black prefers to wait, with 8 ... e6 or 8 ... a6. This still leaves White the choice between accepting the gambit, and a Benoni position. If White delays this decision too long, Black may take over the centre, as in Gheorghiu–Shirov, Moscow 1989 *(69)*:

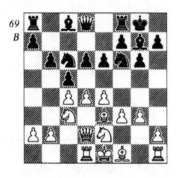

69
B

10 ... ♗a6! 11 b3 ♖e8 12 ♔f2?! (12 dc) 12 ... d5! 13 e5 cd 14 ♗xd4 ♘d7 15 cd ♘cxe5 16 ♘f4 ♗b7!. Black has torn open lines, exposing White's backward development.

Kohlweyer–Kindermann
Bundesliga 1991/2

1 d4 ♘f6 2 c4 g6 3 ♘c3 ♗g7 4 e4 d6 5 f3 0–0 6 ♗e3 c5

	7	dc		dc
	8	e5		♘fd7
	9	f4		f6

9 ... ♘c6 10 ♘f3 f6 (Hazai suggests that 10 ... ♕a5 11 ♗e2 ♖d8 12 ♕a4 ♕xa4 13 ♘xa4 b6 brings equality) 11 ef ♘xf6 12 ♕xd8 ♖xd8 13 ♗xc5 was the move order used in L. Hansen–Fishbein (note to White's fifteenth move).

10   ef *(70)*

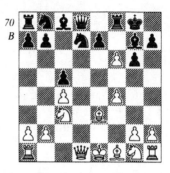

70
B

10 ...   ♘xf6
Black's other recaptures are also interesting:

(a) **10 ... ♖xf6**. After this idea of Shirov's, White must beware of the rook's considerable nuisance value. An illustration of this is Gavrikov–Shirov, Biel 1991: **11 ♗xc5?!** ♕a5 12 ♗f2 (12 ♗e3) 12 ... ♖d6! 13 ♕c1 ♘c5 14 ♘f3, when 14 ... ♗g4! 15 ♗e2 ♗xf3 16 gf ♘c6 17 0–0 ♘d4 would have given Black the upper hand. Shirov gave instead the interesting line **11 ♘f3!** ♖e6! 12 ♕d5 ♕b6! 13 0–0–0! ♗xc3 14 bc ♘f6 15 ♕d8+ ♔g7 16 ♕xc8 ♖xe3 17 ♖d3! ♖xd3 18 ♗xd3 ♕c6 19 ♕xc6! (19 ♕d8 ♕b6=) 19 ... ♘xc6 20 ♖e1, judging White's chances as slightly preferable.

(b) **10 ... ef** has been Black's standard choice, but may not quite equalise:

(b1) **11 ♗e2** ♕e8! (Gelfand's

improvement over 11 ... ♘c6 12 ♘f3 ♖e8 13 ♗f2 ♘b6?! 14 ♕xd8 ♘xd8 15 ♗xc5 ♘xc4 16 0-0-0! ♗e6 17 ♘d4 ♗f7 18 ♘db5 ♖c8 19 ♗xc4 ♖xc5 20 ♗xf7+ ♘xf7 21 ♖d7 which gave White a large advantage in Portisch–Gelfand, Linares 1990) 12 ♗f2 ♘a6 13 ♘f3 ♘b6 14 0-0. Now Black's pieces are working well, and he may choose between Gelfand's suggestion **14 ... ♗f5!?** 15 a3 ♖d8 16 ♕c1 ♘a4 17 ♘xa4 ♕xa4 and **14 ... ♗h6** 15 ♕c1 (15 ♕d2 ♗f5!? △ ... ♖d8) 15 ... ♘a4= 16 ♘xa4 ♕xa4 17 ♖e1 ♗f5 18 ♘h4 ♗e4 19 ♗d1! ♕c6 20 ♗a4! ♕xa4 21 ♖xe4 ♖ae8 22 b3 ♕c6 23 ♖xe8 ♖xe8 24 ♕d2 ♘c7 ½-½ Beliavsky–Gelfand, Munich 1991.

(b2) **11 ♕d2 ♘c6** 12 ♘f3 f5 13 ♗e2 (13 0-0-0 ♕a5 14 ♗d3!? and now Beliavsky's 14 ... ♗xc3 and the 14 ... ♘d4 15 ♗xd4 cd 16 ♘d5 ♕xa2 17 ♕b4 of Mikhalchishin–Stangl, Budapest 1991, both lead to unclear play) 13 ... ♕a5 14 0-0 ♘f6 15 ♘e5 ♖d8 16 ♘xc6 bc 17 ♕c2 ♘g4 18 ♗xg4 fg 19 ♖ad1 ♗f5 20 ♕f2 ♗xc3 21 bc ♕xc3 22 ♗xc5 ♕xc4 23 ♖c1 ♕d5 24 ♖fe1 gave White enough for the pawn in Gofshtein–Smirin, Tel Aviv 1991.

(b3) **11 ♘f3 ♕e8 12 ♕d2 ♘b6 13 ♗e2 ♘a6 14 ♖d1 ♗f5** (*71*):

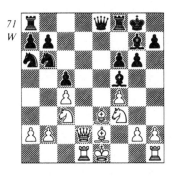

(b31) **15 0-0 ♕e7** (15 ... ♖d8 16 ♕c1 ♕e7 17 a3!, preventing ... ♘b4, left White comfortable in Lautier–Nunn, Belgrade 1991. Then instead of 17 ... ♘c7? 18 ♖fe1 ♖fe8 19 ♖xd8 ♖xd8 20 ♗f1 ♗e6 21 ♘e4 ♘d7 22 ♗f2 ♕f8 23 g3 ♔h8 24 h4!±, Nunn recommends 17 ... ♔h8!±) 16 ♘h4 ♗c2 17 ♖de1 ♖ad8 18 ♕c1 led to trouble for Black in Christiansen–Nunn, Vienna 1991 after **18 ... ♗d3?** 19 f5 since the intended 19 ... ♘xc4 would have failed to 20 ♘d5!; instead the players found that **18 ... f5** 19 ♗f2 ♗xc3 20 bc ♗e4 21 ♘f3 would have given Black reasonable chances.

(b32) **15 ♔f2!?** ♕f7 16 b3 ♖fe8. Now 17 ♖hf1 ♗f8 18 ♘h4 ♗d7 19 ♗f3 ♖ad8 20 ♕c1 ♘b4 21 ♔g1 ♗c6 was fine for Black in Christiansen–J. Polgar, Vienna 1991, but Nunn pointed out that the immediate 17 ♘h4! ♗d7 18 ♘b5 was promising for White.

11   ♕xd8   ♖xd8
12   ♗xc5   ♘c6!

Instead 12 ... ♘a6?! failed to equalise in Razuvaev–Wahls, Bundesliga 1990/91: after 13 ♗a3 ♘g4 14 ♘d5! e6 (14 ... e5!?) 15 ♘e7+, White's knights coordinated well. Razuvaev gave 15 ...

&f7 16 ♘f3 h6 (16 ... ♗f6 17
♘g5+ ♔g7 18 ♘xc8±) 17 ♖c1
♗f6 (17 ... ♗d7 18 ♗d3) 18
♘xc8 ♖axc8 19 b3±; the game
continued 15 ... ♔h8 16 ♘f3 ♗f8
17 ♘g5 ♖e8 18 ♘xc8 ♗xa3 19
ba ♖exc8 20 ♗e2 ♘e3 21 ♔f2
♘xc4 22 ♖ac1 ♘xa3 23 ♘xe6 ♘b4
24 ♖hd1 ♘xa2 25 ♖xc8+ ♖xc8
26 ♖d7 and White won, rather
surprisingly, with a mating attack:
26 ... b5 27 ♖xa7 b4 28 ♘g5 ♖c2
29 ♔e3 ♘c1? 30 ♗g4! ♘c4+
31 ♔e4 h6? 32 ♖h7+ ♔g8 33
♗e6+ ♔f8 34 ♖f7+ 1-0.

However, a very simple and
effective approach was demonstrated in Campos Moreno–Mortensen, European Club Cup 1991:
12 ... ♗f5!? 13 ♘f3 ♘e4 14 ♘xe4
♗xe4 15 ♗a3 ♘c6 16 ♗e2 ♘d4
17 ♘xd4 ♗xd4∓. White, already
fighting for a draw, found a
reasonable way to return the
pawn: 18 ♗f3 ♗xf3 19 gf ♖ac8
20 ♔e2 ♖xc4 21 ♖ac1 ♖xc1 22
♖xc1 ♗b6 23 ♖c4 ♔f7 24 b3
♖d5 and, after a few inaccuracies
by Black, secured half a point.

13 ♘f3
Lobron suggests instead 13
♗e2. If this is indeed a meaningful
improvement, Black may prefer
the move order 9 ... ♘c6 10 ♘f3
f6 11 ef ♘xf6.

13 ... b6!
14 ♗a3
Certainly not 14 ♗e3? ♘g4 △
... ♘b4.

14 ... ♘g4 *(72)*
15 ♘d5

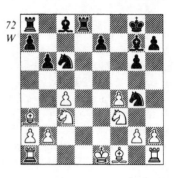

72
W

15 ♖c1 e5!? (Fishbein considers
15 ... ♘e3 16 ♘d5 ♘xf1 17 ♖xf1
♗g4 drawish, whilst Kindermann
suggests 15 ... ♗h6!? 16 g3 e5 17
♘d5 ef 18 gf ♗g7 with compensation) 16 fe ♘cxe5 and now 17
♘d5 ♗b7 18 ♗e2 ♗xd5 19 cd
♖xd5 holds few dangers for either
side. Instead L. Hansen–Fishbein,
Stavanger 1991/2 continued 17
♗e2?! ♘d3+! 18 ♗xd3 ♖xd3 19
♘d5 ♗h6! (Also strong is Kindermann's 19 ... ♗b7!) 20 ♔e2 ♖xd5
21 cd ♗a6+ 22 ♔d1 ♘f2+ 23
♔c2 ♖c8+ 24 ♔b1 ♘xh1 25
♖xh1 ♗d3+ 26 ♔a1 b5 planning
... ♖c2 and ... b4) 20 ♔e2?? (20
♖c3 ♖xc3 21 bc ♗b7 22 h3 ♘e3
23 ♗c1! gives White chances of
survival) 20 ... ♖xd5! 21 cd ♗a6+
22 ♔d1 ♘f2+ 23 ♔c2 ♖c8+ 24
♔b1 ♗xc1 25 ♖e1 ♗d3+ 26
♔a1 ♘g4 27 ♘d4 ♘e3 28 d6
♗d2 29 ♖g1 ♘c4 30 ♘c6 ♖xc6
31 d7 ♗g5 0-1.

15 ... e6
16 h3 ed
17 hg ♗xg4
18 cd ♗xf3

Fishbein's **18 ...** ♘d4 19 ♘xd4 ♗xd4 may be a better try for advantage, since White's king has serious problems.

19 gf ♘d4
20 ♗d3?!

20 ♖c1 b5! 21 ♗d3 ♖xd5 22 ♗e4 ♖e8 23 ♔f2 ♖d7 24 ♖hd1= (Kindermann).

20 ... ♖ac8
21 ♔f2

21 d6?! fails to keep the pawn since Black advances on the queenside with 21 ... b5 and 22 ... a5.

21 ... ♖xd5
22 ♖ac1 ♖dd8!

The situation is now clear: White faces a difficult task to save this ending. There followed 23 ♗c4+?! (23 ♗e4) 23 ... ♔h8 24 ♗f7 (White plays for tactics, but Pandora's box is empty!) 24 ... ♘f5! 25 ♖xc8 ♖xc8 26 ♖e1 (26 ♗xg6? ♖c2+ and 27 ... ♖c1+ wins the bishop) 26 ... ♖c2+ 27 ♖e2 ♗d4+ 28 ♔e1 ♖xe2+ 29 ♔xe2 ♗g7 30 ♗c4 (30 ♗b3 h5 31 ♔f1 allows Black's queenside pawns to advance, whereupon b2 is a problem) 30 ... h5 31 ♔e1 ♘e3 32 ♗b5 ♗c5! 33 ♗xc5? (Hübner pointed out White's only chance: 33 ♔f2! ♘f5+ 34 ♗xc5 bc, but this is ∓) 33 ... bc 34 ♔d2 ♘d5 35 ♔d3 ♘xf4+ 36 ♔c4 (36 ♔e4 g5 37 ♔f5 h4 38 ♔g4 ♔f6) 36 ... h4 37 ♗d7 h3 38 ♗xh3 ♔xh3 39 ♔xc5 ♘g5 40 b4 ♘xf3 41 a4 ♔f6 42 b5 ♔e6 43 a5 ♘e5 0-1.

A. Kuzmin–Shirov
USSR Ch (Moscow) 1991

1 d4 ♘f6 2 c4 g6 3 ♘c3 ♗g7 4 e4 d6 5 f3 0–0 6 ♗e3 c5
7 ♘ge2 ♘c6
8 d5 ♘e5

We now have a type of Benoni which ought to be satisfactory for Black. An alternative form of this arises if White has left the bishop on c1: **6 ♘ge2** c5 7 d5 e6 8 ♘g3. This is not especially dangerous, e.g. 8 ... ed 9 cd a6 (9 ... h5!?) 10 a4 ♘bd7 11 ♗e2 h5!? 12 ♗g5 ♕c7 13 ♕d2 c4 (13 ... ♘h7!?) 14 0–0 ♖b8 15 ♗h6 h4 16 ♘h1 b5 17 ab ab 18 ♘f2 b4 19 ♗xg7 ♔xg7 20 ♘a4 ♘c5 21 ♘xc5 ♕xc5 ½–½ Christiansen–Fedorowicz, San Francisco 1991.

A more popular variance for White on move six is **6 ♗g5 c5 7 d5 e6**:

(a) **8 ♘ge2** ed 9 ♘xd5 ♘c6 10 ♘ec3 h6! 11 ♘xf6+ ♗xf6 12 ♗xf6 ♕xf6 13 ♕d2 ♘d4 14 ♗d3 ♕h4+ gives Black equality.

(b) After **8 ♕d2 ed**, White may play along Benoni lines, or try to leave d6 exposed:

(b1) **9 ♘xd5 ♗e6** 10 ♘e2 ♘c6 11 ♘ec3 ♗xd5 12 ♘xd5 and now Black gains equality with the surprising tactical sequence 12 ... h6! 13 ♘xf6+ ♗xf6 14 ♗xh6 ♗xb2! 15 ♖b1 ♗c3! 16 ♕xc3 ♕h4+ 17 g3 ♕xh6 18 ♕d2 ♕h5, as in Yusupov–Torre, Toluca IZ 1982.

(b2) **9 cd ♗d7!** has caused

Ionescu considerable problems: **10
&d3** &a6 11 &ge2 &b8 12 0–0
(12 a4 &b4 13 &c4 a6 14 a5 b5
15 ab &xb6∞ Ardeleanu) 12 ...
b5 13 &g3 c4 14 &e2 &c5 15
&h1 &e8 16 &d1 h5! 17 &f4
&e5! 18 &h4 &xg5! 19 &xg5
&h7! gave White problems with
his queen and the g3 knight in
Ionescu–Ardeleanu, Romanian
Ch 1986, while **10 a4** &a6 11 &c4
&b4 12 &ge2 a6 13 a5?! (13 0–0)
13 ... &b5! 14 b3 h6 15 &f4 (15
&e3 &xc4 16 bc &d7! 17 f4 b5$\overline{\overline{+}}$
Lobron) 15 ... &h5 16 &e3 f5!$\overline{\overline{+}}$
was Ionescu–Wahls, Novi Sad OL
1990.

>   **9   &g3** *(73)*

9 &c1 e6 10 a4 (10 &e2 ed 11
cd a6 12 a4 &d7 △ ... b5) 10 ...
ed 11 cd h5 12 &e2 &h7 13 0–0 f5
14 &1a2 g5 15 ef &xf5= Dlugy–
Grünberg, New York 1991.

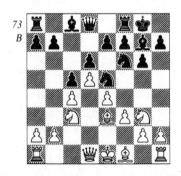

>   **9   ...   e6**

Black can also try **9 ... h5 10
&e2**:

(a) After **10 ... h4** 11 &f1 e6 12
&d2, the knight is comfortably
redeployed but nevertheless 12 ...

ed 13 cd a6 14 a4 &d7 15 0–0
(Psakhis–M. Piket, Amsterdam
1990) 15 ... &h7 is reasonable for
Black. White may consider 15 h3!?.

(b) **10 ... e6** is described by
Shirov as 'mixing up two plans',
but nevertheless after 11 &g5!, he
gives **11 ... ed** as equal: **12 cd** &b6
13 &b3 &c7 with good play (e.g.
14 f4?! c4!), or **12** &xd5 &a5+ 13
&d2 (13 &d2 &xd2+ 14 &xd2
&xd5 17 cd favours Black) 13 ...
&d8 14 &g5 &a5+ etc. Instead,
in Christiansen–Shirov, Biel 1991,
11 ... &b6?! 12 &b3! &c7 13 f4!
gave Black some problems.

>   **10   &e2   ed**
>   **11   cd   a6**

Now White must decide
whether to ignore Black's intended
queenside advance. If allowing 12
... b5 really is good for White,
Black may consider the immediate
11 ... h5!?.

>   **12   a4**

12 0–0 b5 13 &d2 has caused
Kindermann some suffering: **13 ...
&d7** 14 &h6!± &xh6 15 &xh6
b4 16 &d1 &h8 17 &f2 &b5 18
&h3 &g8 19 &d2 &b6 20 f4
left White in control in Van der
Sterren–Kindermann, Prague
1992, while after **13 ... &e8** 14 b3!
&d7 (14 ... b4 leaves c4 wholly
in White's control: 15 &a4 &d7
16 &b2 △ a4) 15 a4, White's
advantage could be kept to a minimum with **15 ... ba!** 16 &xa4 (16
ba!?) 16 ... &b5 (Rogers). Instead
15 ... &b8?! 16 h3! gave Black
serious problems with the e5

knight in Rogers–Kindermann, Prague 1992. After 16 … c4 (16 … b4 17 ♘d1±) 17 ab ab (17 … ♗xb5? 18 f4) 18 b4! ♖c8, White could have maintained a solid advantage with 19 ♖a3!.

12 … h5!?

Also possible is **12 … ♗d7** 13 0–0 (13 f4 ♘eg4 14 ♗d2 h5 15 h3 ♘h6 16 e5 ♘h7 17 0-0 ♖e8 18 ♘ge4 ♘f5∞ Hazai) 13 … b5! 14 h3 (14 ab ab 15 ♖xa8 ♕xa8 16 ♗xb5 ♗xb5 17 ♘xb5 ♕a6 18 ♘a3 ♖b8 19 ♕c2 ♘xd5! 20 ed ♖xb2 gave Black the advantage in Belotti–Piket, Lugano 1989) 14 … ♖b8! 15 b3 ♘e8! 16 ♖c1 ♕h4 as in Gallagher–Nunn, London (Lloyds Bank) 1990; Black could clearly be satisfied.

13 0–0 ♘h7
14 ♕d2 h4

But now **14 … ♗d7?!** gives White the initiative: 15 f4!? ♘g4 16 ♗xg4 ♗xg4 17 e5 ♖e8 18 h3 ♗d7 19 ♘ge4±.

15 ♘h1 f5
16 ♘f2 ♕f6!

Shirov gives no ground in the centre; **16 … fe** 17 ♘fxe4 ♗f5 18 ♖ab1, intending b4, gives White an edge.

17 ef

17 ♗h6?! f4!? 18 ♗xg7 ♔xg7 19 ♘d3 ♘g5∓ only helps Black.

17 … gf *(74)*

Control of e4 is more important than the aesthetic appeal of Black's kingside pawns.

18 f4 ♘g4

Kuzmin considers that **18 …**

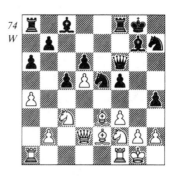

♘f7!? 19 ♘fd1 ♗d7 20 ♖b1 ♖ac8 is unclear.

19 ♘xg4 fg
20 f5

White must not allow 20 … ♗f5, which would give Black a clear positional edge.

20 … ♗xf5
21 ♗xg4 ♕g6
22 ♗xf5 ♖xf5
23 ♖xf5 ♕xf5
24 ♖f1 ♕g6

Kuzmin now gives **25 h3 ♘f6** 26 ♗g5 ♘e4 27 ♘xe4 ♕xe4 28 ♗f6 ♖f8 29 ♗xg7 ♖xf1+ 30 ♔xf1 ♔xg7 31 ♕g5+ with equality.

There followed instead **25 ♖f4?!** ♘f6! 26 h3 (26 ♖xh4 ♘g4) 26 … b5! 27 ♖xh4 b4 whereupon White had to be extremely careful to hold the balance: 28 ♘d1 ♖e8 29 ♘f2 ♕b1+ 30 ♔h2 ♘e4 (30 … ♕f5!?) 31 ♘xe4 ♖xe4 32 ♖xe4 ♕xe4 33 ♗f4 (33 b3? c4∓ ∓) 33 … ♕d4 (33 … ♕xf4+ 34 ♕xf4 ♗e5 35 ♕xe5 is a drawn king and pawn ending. With the text, Black hopes for 34 b3? c4! 35 bc ♕xf4+!) 34

♕xd4 ♗xd4 35 ♗xd6 b3 36 g3
♔f7 37 ♔g2 ♗xb2 38 ♗xc5
♗c3 39 ♗a3 ♔f6 40 ♔f3 ♔e5
41 d6 ♔e6 42 ♔e4 b2 43 ♗xb2
♗xb2 44 h4 ♔xd6 45 ♔f5 ♔e7
46 g4 ♔f7 47 h5 a5 48 g5 ♔e7
49 ♔g6 ♗c1 50 ♔f5 ♔f7 51
g6+ ½–½.

Beliavsky–Ivanchuk
Reykjavik 1991

1 d4 ♘f6 2 c4 g6 3 ♘c3 ♗g7 4 e4
d6 5 f3 0–0 6 ♗e3 c5 7 ♘ge2 ♘c6
8 ♕d2 *(75)*

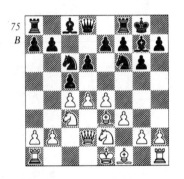

8 ... e6

Black has quite a selection of
moves here. 8 ... a6 and the text,
continuing to offer the pawn, are
perhaps the most consistent, while
8 ... ed and 8 ... b6, leading to
different types of positions, also
have substantial followings. We
should also note the transpos-
itional move 8 ... ♕a5. After 9 d5
♘e5 10 ♘c1 (10 ♘g3 a6) 10 ... e6
11 ♗e2 ed 12 cd ♗d7 13 a4 a6
14 ♖a3 ♕c7 15 0–0 ♖ae8 16 ♘1a2
♗c8 17 a5 h5, Black had an

acceptable Benoni in Psakhis–
Szalanczy, Vienna 1990. 9 0–0–0
a6 transposes to the line 8 ... a6
9 0–0–0 ♕a5, but Hazai prefers
instead 9 ... cd 10 ♘xd4 ♘xd4 11
♗xd4 ♗e6 12 ♔b1 ♖fc8! 13 b3
a6∞.

(a) 8 ... a6 and now:

(a1) 9 ♖d1 may well be best met
by 9 ... cd 10 ♘xd4 ♘xd4 11
♗xd4 ♗e6, when the rook is not
so effective on d1 in this Maroczy
position. Benjamin–Zsu. Polgar,
San Francisco 1991 concluded 12
♗e2 ♕a5 13 0–0 ♖fc8 14 ♘d5
♕xd2 15 ♖xd2 ♘xd5 16 ed
♗xd4+ 17 ♖xd4 ♗d7 18 ♖e1
b5 ½–½. More interesting is 9 ...
♕a5 10 d5 (10 dc dc 11 ♘d5
♕xd2+ 12 ♖xd2 ♘d7=) 10 ...
♘e5 11 ♘c1, when Black can
either try the pawn sacrifice 11
... b5, as in Kupreichik–Smirin,
Sverdlovsk 1987, or Kupreichik's
suggestion 11 ... ♗d7 12 b3 (12
♘b3 ♕b4; 12 f4 ♘eg4 13 ♗g1 b5
14 h3 b4!∓) 12 ... b5! 13 ♗e2∞.

(a2) 9 0–0–0 ♕a5 10 ♔b1 e6
11 dc (Not 11 d5? ed 12 ♘xd5
♘xd5!, but interesting is 11 ♗h6
b5 12 ♗xg7 ♔xg7 13 dc and now
Gheorghiu–M. Piket, Lugano
1989 continued 13 ... b4 14 ♘d5
with complex play; instead the
simple 13 ... dc 14 ♘c1 ♖d8
15 ♕e1 ♖xd1 16 ♕xd1 ♘d4 is
roughly level) 11 ... dc 12 ♘c1 (12
♕d6 ♘d7!) 12 ... ♖d8 13 ♕f2
♖xd1 14 ♘xd1 (A. Schneider–
Hazai, Espoo 1988) 14 ... ♕d8 15
♘c3 b6 (Hazai).

(a3) **9 dc** dc 10 ♕xd8 ♖xd8 11 ♗xc5 ♘d7. The position is now rather similar to those after the immediate acceptance of the gambit pawn with 7 dc. Novikov-Wojtkiewicz, Debrecen 1990 continued 12 ♗e3 ♘de5 13 ♘f4 ♘b4 (Not 13 ... ♘a5?? 14 ♗b6) 14 ♖c1 ♗e6! (14 ... g5 15 ♘fd5 is here a very strong exchange sacrifice due to the weakness of b6) 15 ♗c5 a5! 16 ♗xe7 ♖d7 17 ♗xb4 ab 18 ♘cd5 ♖xa2 19 ♖b1 b3 20 ♗e2 ♘c6 21 ♘d3 ♘a5 22 ♗d1 b5! 23 cb ♗xd5 24 ed ♖xd5 and Black had no problems.

(b) **8 ... b6**. Now, after **9 ♖d1**, **9 ... e6!** transposes to the main game, while Shirov mentions **9 ... e5** 10 dc dc 11 ♘d5 ♘d4 12 ♘ec3±. Play normally continues **9 d5 ♘e5 10 ♘g3** (10 ♘c1 e6 11 ♗e2 ♗a6!= makes good use of the move ... b6) which can lead to Benoni positions, though Black may keep open options of omitting ... e6 in favour of more Benko-like methods. By comparison with the line 8 d5 ♘e5 considered above, Black has the extra move ... b6 (quite useful, but often a slight waste of time), whilst White's queen is here on d2, which encourages Black to fling the h-pawn at the g3 knight, since ♘f1-d2 is impossible.

(b1) **10 ... e6** 11 ♗e2 ed 12 cd a6 13 ♗h6!? (13 a4 h5 14 0-0 h4 15 ♘h1 ♘h7 16 ♘f2 f5 17 f4 ♘f7 18 ♗d3 ♖a7 19 ♖ab1 ♘h6= Gofshtein-Vukić, Hartberg 1991)

13 ... ♗xh6 14 ♕xh6 b5 15 0-0 c4 16 h3 ♖e8 17 ♔h2 ♘ed7 18 b4! blocked Black's counterplay in Fedorowicz-Piket, Wijk aan Zee 1991.

(b2) **10 ... h5 11 ♗e2 h4 12 ♘f1** *(76)*:

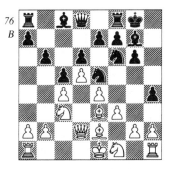

76
B

(b21) **12 ... e6?!** should be met by 13 ♗g5!.

(b22) After **12 ... a6**, on the other hand, **13 ♗g5** achieves little: 13 ... h3 14 g3 b5 15 ♗h6 ♕a5 16 ♗xg7 ♔xg7 17 ♘e3 bc 18 ♘xc4 ♘xc4 19 ♗xc4 was Timoshchenko-Lanka, Riga 1988, when 19 ... ♘d7 would have given Black the better prospects. Instead Shirov gave **13 ♗h6∞** as better.

(c) **8 ... ed 9 ♘xd4 ♘xd4 10 ♗xd4 ♗e6** and now:

(c1) **11 ♖c1 ♕a5** 12 ♘d5? ♕xd2+ 13 ♔xd2 ♘xe4+ 14 fe ♗xd4 15 ♘xe7+ ♔g7 16 ♘d5 ♗xb2 left White with a very poor position in Zaltsman-Gelfand, New York 1989.

(c2) **11 ♘d5 ♗xd5** 12 ed ♕c7 13 ♗e2 a5 14 h4!? (14 0-0) 14 ... ♖fe8 15 0-0-0 b5 16 ♔b1 bc 17

Ic1 ♛b7 18 ♗xc4 was played in Høi–Mortensen, Danish Ch (Århus) 1992. Black should then have tried 18 ... Ieb8; instead 18 ... a4?! 19 h5 ♘xh5? 20 ♗xg7 ♔xg7 21 g4 ♘f6 22 ♛h6+ ♔h8 23 g5 Iab8 24 Ic2 ♘h5 25 ♗d3! gave White a decisive attack.

(c3) **11 ♗e2 ♛a5** *(77)*

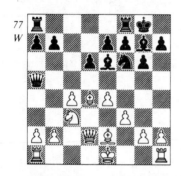

(c31) **12 0–0** Ifc8 13 b3 b5! 14 b4 (14 cb? ♘xe4 15 fe ♗xd4+ 16 ♛xd4 ♛xc3∓) 14 ... ♛xb4 15 Iab1 ♛a5 16 Ixb5 ♛d8= Novikov–Glek, USSR 1984.

(c32) **12 g4** Ifc8 13 g5 ♘d7 (13 ... ♘h5!?) 14 ♗xg7 ♔xg7 15 ♘d5 ♛xd2+ 16 ♔xd2 ♗xd5 17 cd Ic7 18 Ihc1 Iac8 19 Ixc7 Ixc7 20 ♗b5!? gave Black some problems in Høi–Kjeldsen, Lyngby 1991.

(c33) **12 b3** should probably be met by **12 ... a6**, since in Knaak–Kindermann, Hamburg 1991, **12 ... Ifc8** 13 Ib1! prevented ... b5, after which Black could find no constructive plan. There followed 13 ... ♘d7 14 ♗xg7 ♔xg7 15 0–0 ♘f6 16 ♔h1 a6 17 a4! ♛b4

18 ♛b2 ♔g8 19 ♘a2 ♛c5 20 ♛d2 a5 21 ♘c3±.

(c34) **12 Ic1** a6 13 b3 Ifb8 14 0–0 b5 15 c5 ♛b4 16 Ifd1 dc 17 ♗e3 Ia7 (17 ... Ib7!?) 18 ♘d5 (18 ♛d8+? Ixd8 19 Ixd8+ ♗f8 20 ♗h6 fails to 20 ... ♛d4+!) 18 ... ♛xd2 19 ♘xf6+ ♗xf6 20 Ixd2 ♗d4 21 ♗xd4 cd 22 Ixd4 a5 23 Ic5 a4 24 Ixb5 ½–½ Timman–Ivanchuk, Reykjavik 1991.

9 Id1

This is more popular than:

9 dc dc 10 ♗xc5 ♛xd2+ 11 ♔xd2 Id8+ 12 ♔c2 b6! was fine for Black in Miles–Rogers, Mendrisio 1989, which continued **13 ♗e3 ♗a6 14 ♘g3 ♘b4 15 ♔b3 ♘d3 16 ♗e2 Iac8** winning back the pawn with comfortable equality. Gheorghiu notes the variation **13 ♗a3 ♘d7 14 Id1 ♗a6 15 b3 ♘de5** when White has substantial development difficulties.

9 0–0–0 ♘d7 10 ♗h6 ♗xd4!? (Shirov gives 10 ... ♗xh6! 11 ♛xh6 ♛f6 12 ♛e3∞) 11 ♘xd4 cd 12 ♘b5 e5! 13 ♘xd6 ♘c5 14 ♗xf8 ♛xf8 15 ♘xc8 (15 ♘b5 is promising according to Knaak). Now, in Høi–Shirov, Daugavpils 1990, **15 ... Ixc8?!** 16 ♔b1 a5 17 h4! should not have given Black quite enough for the exchange; Shirov recommends **15 ... ♛xc8** △ ... a5–a4.

9 ...   b6! *(78)*
10 ♗g5!?

White has two main alternatives:

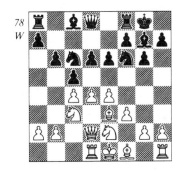

(a) **10 g3** ♗a6 11 b3 ♖e8 12 ♔f2?! (12 ♗g2?! d5!∓; 12 dc dc 13 ♗g2= Shirov) 12 ... d5! led to a quick win for Black in Gheorghiu–Shirov, Moscow 1989: 13 e5 (13 cd ed 14 e5 ♗xe2! 15 ♗xe2 cd 16 ♗xd4 ♘xd4! 17 ♕xd4 ♖xe5∓) 13 ... cd 14 ♗xd4 ♘d7 15 cd ♘cxe5 16 ♘f4 ♗b7! 17 ♗e2 ed 18 ♘fxd5? (18 ♖he1 ♘c5∓) 18 ... ♘f6! 19 ♘f4 ♕e7 20 ♖he1 ♖ad8∓∓ 21 ♕c1 g5! 22 ♗b5 ♖xd4! 23 ♖xd4 ♘fg4+! 24 ♔f1 ♘xh2+ 25 ♔g2 ♘hxf3 26 ♘fd5 ♘xd4 27 ♗xe8 ♕e6 28 ♕e3 ♘c2 0–1.

(b) **10 d5** ♘e5 11 ♘g3 ed 12 cd h5! 13 ♗e2 h4 14 ♘f1 ♘h7 15 f4 ♘g4 16 h3 ♘xe3 17 ♘xe3. Now De Firmian suggested **17 ... g5!**, e.g. 18 0–0 gf! 19 ♖xf4 ♗e5! 20 ♖ff1 ♖e8 intending ... ♘f8–g6, with a good game for Black. Instead **17 ... f5?!** 18 gf gf 19 0–0 a6 20 ♔h2 b5 gave Black a less satisfactory game in Christiansen–Benjamin, US Ch (Jacksonville)

1990.

10 ... h6!?

Beliavsky analyses the long variation **10 ... ♗b7** 11 d5 ♘e5 12 de ♘xc4 13 ♕c1 ♕e7!? 14 ♘f4 ♘e5 15 ♘cd5 ♗xd5 16 ♘xd5 ♕xe6 17 ♘c7 ♕xa2 18 ♘xa8 ♖xa8 19 ♖xd6 ♘e8 20 ♖d2 ♘c7 21 ♗e2 ♘e6 22 ♗e3 ♕b3 when Black has compensation.

Ivanchuk prefers instead to give up a pawn to win some dark squares.

11	♗xh6	♘xe4
12	♘xe4	♕h4+
13	g3	♕xh6
14	♕xh6	♗xh6
15	♘xd6	cd
16	♘xd4	♘xd4
17	♖xd4	♗a6

Black has enough compensation to reach a tenable ending. A variation illustrating Black's counterchances is **18 b4** ♖fd8 19 c5 (19 b5 ♗b7 △ ... ♗f8) 19 ... bc 20 bc ♗e3 21 ♖e4 ♗xc5 22 ♘xf7 ♖db8∓ (Beliavsky), so the game concluded **18 ♖d1** ♗g7 19 b3 ♖fd8 20 ♗g2 (Knaak analysed 20 c5 ♗xf1 21 ♖xf1 bc 22 ♔e2 ♗d4= and 20 ♘e4 f5 21 ♘g5 ♗f6 22 h4∞) 20 ... f5 21 f4 ♖ab8 22 a4 ♗f8 23 ♘b5 ♗xb5 24 ab ♖xd1+ 25 ♔xd1 ♖d8+ 26 ♔e2 ♗b4= 27 ♖d1 ♖xd1 28 ♔xd1 ♔f7 29 ♗c6 ♔e7 30 ♔e2 ♗d6 31 ♔f3 e5 32 fe ♗xe5 33 h3 ♔f6 34 ♗e8 ♗d6 35 g4 g5 36 ♗d7 fg+ 37 ♔xg4 ♗c5 38 ♔h5 ♗b4 39 ♔h6 ♗f8+ ½–½.

9 Classical Main Line: Ideas with a4

1 d4 ♘f6 2 c4 g6 3 ♘c3 ♗g7 4 e4
d6 5 ♘f3 0–0 6 ♗e2 e5

7	0–0	♘c6
8	d5	♘e7 (79)

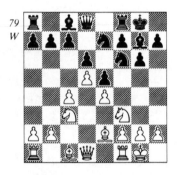

Here we consider some new approaches by White, mostly involving the move a2–a4. This has a number of motives. Firstly, the rook may sometimes be activated via a3, from where it is useful in defending the kingside, in addition to furthering White's queenside ambitions. Consider also the following situation, in which Black has taken pains to secure his queenside, so White switches to the kingside (80):

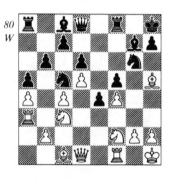

Larsen–Mortensen, Danish Ch (Lyngby) 1991 continued 18 ♘b5! ♗d7 19 ♖h3! with a promising game for White.

White generally envisages the further advance a4–a5 gaining space on the queenside and nailing down a potential weakness on b6. Black can prevent this with ... a7–a5, but must be careful that this does not give White additional targets on the queenside. The following position, from Korchnoi–Hellers, European Club Cup 1987, demonstrates a specific tactical point (81):

White now played 14 ♘b5!. The

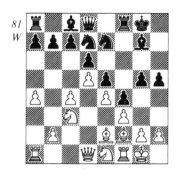

81
W

most natural reply is 14 ... b6, followed by ... a5, or ... a6, driving the knight back. However, Black has no time for this, since 15 a5± begins the dismantling of Black's queenside. In the game, 14 ... ♘f6 15 ♘xa7 ♗d7 16 ♘b5 g4 17 fg hg 18 ♗h4 gave White some advantage.

Kožul–Popović
Novi Sad 1992

1 d4 ♘f6 2 c4 g6 3 ♘c3 ♗g7 4 e4 d6 5 ♘f3 0-0 6 ♗e2 e5 7 0-0 ♘c6 8 d5 ♘e7
9 ♘e1

White has three unusual alternatives which occur from time to time in tournament play:

(a) **9 a4** a5 (9 ... ♘h5?! 10 a5!). The main question is whether these moves disrupt White's queenside advance more seriously than they weaken Black's queenside. 10 ♘e1 (Hellers suggests 10 ♗g5!?) 10 ... ♘d7 11 ♗e3 f5 12 f3 ♘c5! (Blocking the kingside is not recommended: 12 ... f4 13 ♗f2 b6 14 ♘d3 ♘c5 15 b4!± —

Kasparov) 13 ♘d3 b6 14 b4! ♘xd3! (14 ... ab 15 ♘xb4 ♗d7 16 ♘d3 ♘b7 17 ♘b5 ♔h8 18 ♖a3 ♘a5 19 ♘c1 f4 20 ♗d2 g5 21 ♘b3! ♘xb3 22 ♕xb3 ♖g8 23 a5 ♕b8 24 ♖fa1 h5 25 ♗e1!± L. Hansen-Skovlund, Lyngby 1989) 15 ♕xd3 ab 16 ♘b5 ♔h8 17 ♕b3 (17 ♗d2!? c5! 18 dc ♘xc6 19 ♕d5! ♗d7!? 20 ♕xd6 ♘d4! 21 ♘xd4 ed 22 ♕xb4 fe 23 fe d3! 24 ♗xd3 ♗xa1 25 ♖xa1 ♗e6 26 ♕c3+ ♔g8 27 ♗h6 ♕f6∓ is Kasparov's analysis) 17 ... ♘g8 18 ♕xb4. Now **18 ... ♘f6?!** 19 ef gf 20 ♗g5 was unclear in Korchnoi-Kasparov, Barcelona 1989. Instead Kasparov gives **18 ... fe!** 19 fe ♖xf1+ 20 ♖xf1 ♗h6! as promising for Black.

(b) **9 ♔h1 ♔h8** (This has been the most common reply. After the obvious 9 ... ♘h5, Larsen has demonstrated two good methods: 10 g3 f5 11 ef ♘xf5 12 ♘g5 ♘d4 13 ♗d3 ♘f6 14 f3 c6 15 ♘ge4 ♗h3 16 ♖f2± (Larsen-Nunn, Hastings 1987/8) and 10 ♘g1 ♘f4 11 ♗f3 c5 12 a4 h6 13 a5 g5 14 ♖a3 f5 15 ef ♘xf5 16 g3 ♘g6 17 ♘e4± Larsen-C. Hansen, Odense 1988. Instead, the simple 9 ... ♘e8 may be Black's best) 10 a4!? (10 ♘e1 ♘d7 11 ♗e3 is worth considering, since White's king move is then more useful than Black's; 10 ... ♘fg8!?) 10 ... a5 11 ♖a3 b6 (Black fared well with 11 ... ♘fg8 12 ♘e1 f5 13 ♘d3 ♘f6 14 f3 c5 15 dc ♘xc6 16 ef gf 17 ♗g5 ♗e6 in L. Hansen-Kotronias, Bled 1991)

12 ♘e1 ♘d7 13 ♘d3 f5 14 ef gf 15 f4 ♘g6 16 ♗h5 e4 17 ♘f2 ♘c5 18 ♘b5! ♗d7 19 ♖h3 ♔g8 20 ♖g3 ♗xb5 21 cb ♕f6 22 b3 ♖ae8 23 ♘h3 gave White useful kingside pressure in Larsen–Mortensen, Danish Ch (Lyngby) 1991.

(c) 9 ♗g5 is an interesting move, but precise play seems to equalise: 9 ... ♘h5! and now:

(c1) 10 g3 h6 (10 ... f6 11 ♗d2 f5 transposes to an old line considered satisfactory for Black) 11 ♗d2 ♗h3!? (11 ... f5) 12 ♖e1 f5 13 ♘h4 ♘f6 14 ef g5! 15 ♘g6 ♘xg6 16 fg ♗f5 gave Black good play in Bern–W. Watson, Gausdal 1991.

(c2) 10 ♘d2 ♘f4 11 b4 (11 f3 h6 12 ♗h4 c5!=) 11 ... h6 12 ♗h4 g5 (12 ... f5?! 13 f3 ♖f7 14 c5 ♗f8 15 ♖c1 g5 16 ♗f2 ♘eg6 17 ♔h1! Burgess–Coleman,   Hastings Challengers 1989/90) 13 ♗g3 f5.

(c3) 10 ♘e1 ♘f4 11 ♘d3 ♘xe2+ 13 ♕xe2 h6! 14 ♗d2 f5 14 f4 c6!= Burgess–S. Pedersen, Assens 1990.

9   ...   ♘d7

10   ♗e3

10 ♘d3 f5 11 a4!? *(82)*

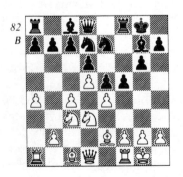

11 ... ♘f6 12 f3 (12 ef is best met by 12 ... ♘xf5, rather than 12 ... gf 13 ♖a3) 12 ... f4 (12 ... ♔h8?! would be inappropriate due to 13 ♗e3) 13 c5 g5 14 b4 ♖f7 15 b5 ♗f8 16 ♗a3 ♘g6 17 a5 h5 18 ♕b3 g4 19 b6 cb 20 cd and now Black should try **20 ... ♘h7!**. Instead Larsen–Heine Nielsen, Valby 1991 continued **20 ... g3** 21 h3 ♘h7 22 ♖fc1 ♕h4 (22 ... ♗xh3 23 gh ♘g5 24 ♔f1!) 23 ♗f1 ♘g5 24 ♘e1 ♗xh3 25 gh ♘xh3+ 26 ♗xh3 ♕xh3 27 ♖a2 ♘h4 28 ♘d1 ♖g7 29 ♖c7! ♖g6 30 ♖cc2 ♖c8 31 ♖d2 g2 (31 ... ba 32 ♕xb7) 32 ♖xg2 ♘xg2 33 ♖xg2 ♖xg2+ 34 ♘xg2 whereupon White took full control.

10 ♗g5!? h6 11 ♗e3 f5 12 f3 is very similar to the text, except that White hopes that the pawn on h6 may be a nuisance for Black, i.e. preventing ... ♗h6 and also ... ♖f6–h6 ideas, while ... h6–h5 prevents a black knight using the h5 square. In Agdestein–I. Soko-lov, Novi Sad OL 1990, Black tried to profit from the extra move: 12 ... g5!? 13 a4 a5 (13 ... f4 14 ♗f2 ♘g6 should be compared with lines below) 14 ♗f2 b6 15 ef (Also possible are 15 ♘d3 and 15 ♘c2 intending b4 — compare with the line 9 a4 above) 15 ... ♘xf5 16 ♗d3 ♘c5 17 ♗b1 ♘d4 18 ♖a3!± ♗d7 19 ♘b5 ♘xb5 20 ab (20 cb!?) 20 ... e4 21 ♗d4 ♗xd4+ 22 ♕xd4 ♕f6 23 ♕xf6 ♖xf6 24 b4! when Black was faced with a difficult defensive task.

10	...	f5
11	f3	f4

One practical advantage of 10 ♗e3 is that since White will proceed at full speed on the queenside, Black is obliged to go in for a race. Moves such as 11 ... ♔h8 (12 ♘d3±) and 11 ... ♘f6 (12 c5±) simply amount to a loss of time, as White will just ignore Black's manoeuvres. A reasonable option is **11 ... ♖f7**, though after 12 a4, Black can hardly do better than transpose with 12 ... f4 13 ♗f2 g5.

12	♗f2	g5
13	a4!?	*(83)*

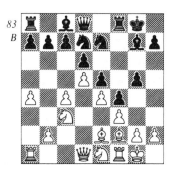

This move has come to the attention of the chess world following its adoption by Korchnoi. He had previously tried **13 ♘b5**, but it seems that 13 ... b6 is an adequate reply, whilst 13 ... a6 14 ♘a7 ♖xa7 15 ♗xa7 b6 16 b4 ♘f6 (16 ... ♗b7? is hopeless) 17 c5 g4 is far from clear. 13 a4, while a very useful move in itself, prepares 14 ♘b5, since in answer to ... b7–b6, White has the powerful

thrust a4–a5. Black's choice of reply is far from simple: Black wishes to leave the knight on d7 until White has lost time preparing c5; 13 ... h5 robs the knight of this square and so blunts Black's attack; 13 ... a5 seriously weakens Black's queenside. Black's standard choice has become kingside regrouping with ... ♘g6 and ... ♖f7, but as we shall see, there is a surprising tactical drawback to this.

13	...	♘g6

Here Black has a choice:

(a) **13 ... h5** 14 ♘b5 (14 a5 ♖f7 15 ♘b5 ♘f6 16 c5 was also convincing in Cooper–Bouaziz, Thessaloniki OL 1984) 14 ... ♘f6 (14 ... b6? 15 a5±) 15 ♘xa7 ♗d7 (15 ... ♖xa7? is nonsense: 16 ♗xa7 g4 17 c5 ♘g6 18 cd cd 19 a5 g3 20 ♗b6 ♕e7 21 ♖c1 ♘h7 22 ♔h1 ♕h4 23 ♗g1 ♘f6 24 ♖c7++ Federau–Heim, Bundesliga 1987) 16 ♘b5 g4 (16 ... ♘g6 17 c5! g4 18 cd cd 19 ♘xd6 g3 20 ♗c5!± ♘e8 21 ♘f5 ♖xf5? 22 ef ♕h4 23 h3 ♗xf5 24 ♗d3 ♗xh3 25 gh ♕xh3 26 ♕e2++ is a line given by Hellers) 17 fg (17 c5 is well met by 17 ... g3! 18 fg hg 19 ♗xg3 ♘g6∞, but White may consider Korchnoi's 17 g3!? △ ♘g2) 17 ... hg 18 ♗h4 ♘xe4 19 ♗xg4 ♘f6 20 ♗xd7 ♕xd7 and now **21 ♘c3!** would leave White better due to his firm control of e4. Instead in Korchnoi–Hellers, European Club Cup 1987, there followed **21 ♖a3** ♘f5 22 ♗f2, when 22 ... ♖ae8 23 ♘c2 c6!? 24 ♘c3 e4 would have left the game very unclear.

(b) **13 ... ♖f7** can perhaps be met by 14 c5. Instead A. Ivanov–Hebden, Hastings 1984 saw 14 a5 ♗f8, when again 15 c5 must be considered, along with 15 ♘b5 ♘f6 16 ♘xa7 when Black is not ready for 16 ... g4, while 16 ... ♗d7 is met by 17 c5!. In the game, 15 b4 ♘g6 16 c5 ♘f6 transposed to note (a) to White's fifteenth move below.

(c) **13 ... a5** compares unfavourably with the lines following 9 a4 above, so can hardly be a good idea. **14 ♘d3** and now:

(c1) **14 ... b6** can be met by **15 b4** h5?! (15 ... ab) 16 ba ♖xa5 17 ♘b5 ♘f6 18 ♗e1 ♖a6 19 a5 g4 20 ab cb 21 ♗b4 ♖xa1 22 ♕xa1 ♘e8 23 ♕a8 g3 24 h3 ♘c7 25 ♕b8++ Korchnoi–Van der Wiel, Brussels (Rapid) 1987 or **15 ♗e1!** c5 (15 ... ♘f6 16 ♘f2 h5 17 h3 intends ♘b5 and b4+) 16 dc ♘b8 (16 ... ♘xc6 17 b4 ab 18 ♘b5) 17 c7 ♕xc7 18 ♕b3 ♔h8 19 ♕a3 ♕d8 20 ♘b5 ♖f6 21 ♖d1 ♘ec6 22 ♗c3 which gave White a wonderful position in Kožul–Popović, Yugoslavia 1991.

(c2) **14 ... ♘g6** 15 c5 ♘f6 16 ♖c1 (16 ♖a3!?) 16 ... ♖f7 17 cd cd. It is difficult to believe that Black can possibly hope to survive here, with the gaping weakness on b6, but White's knight on d3 really obstructs White's exploitation of this. Franco–Reyes, Toledo 1991

continued **18 ♕b3?!** g4 19 ♗b6 ♕e7 20 ♘b5 g3 21 ♖c7 ♗d7 22 ♔h1 ♘h5 (22 ... gh) 23 h3 ♕h4 24 ♖xd7 ♖xd7 25 ♘c7 ♖c8 26 ♘e6 ♘f6 27 ♗xa5 ♕h5 28 ♕d1 ♘f8 when Black could hope for a draw, and in fact obtained one. There is no need to allow ... g4 so readily: **18 ♔h1** looks a better way to start. Naturally White would be delighted if Black played ... h5, since this, as usual, robs the knight of the h5 square and so Black is very slow to create any threats. An obvious move is 18 ... ♗f8, but then 19 ♕b3 g4 20 ♗b6 ♕e7 21 ♘b5 g3 22 ♘c7 is strong.

14   a5

White can also try:

(a) **14 ♘b5** leads to similar play to 15 ♘b5 in the note to White's next move, viz. 14 ... ♘f6 15 ♘xa7 g4! (15 ... ♗d7?! 16 ♘b5 g4 17 fg ♘xe4 18 ♗d3 and White obtains a grip on e4) 16 ♘xc8 g3 17 hg ♘h5 18 gf ef 19 ♘d3 ♕g5! with a dangerous attack (Nunn).

(b) **14 ♘d3** was Korchnoi's surprising choice against Kasparov at Amsterdam 1991. For many years the knight has been believed simply to be in White's way on d3, despite forcing through c5. His new idea was that after 14 ... ♘f6 15 c5 h5, he did not exchange on d6, as Black's standard attack with a ... g3 pawn sacrifice is then very strong. 16 h3 (16 c6 a5!∞) 16 ... ♖f7 17 c6 a5!!, however, ensured that Black's light square bishop was not distracted from its duty of sacrificing on h3 should need be. There followed 18 cb (18 b4 b6! 19 ba ba!) 18 ... ♗xb7 19 b4 ♗c8 20 ba ♗h6! 21 ♘b4? (21 a6! ♗xa6! 22 ♘b4 ♗c8∞ — Kasparov) 21 ... g4 22 ♘c6 ♕f8 23 fg hg 24 hg ♗g5 25 ♗f3 ♕h6 26 ♖e1 ♘h4! 27 ♗xh4 ♗xh4! 28 g5?! ♕xg5 29 ♖e2 ♘g4 30 ♖b1 ♗g3 31 ♕d3 ♕h4 0-1.

14 ...   ♖f7

One of the main subtleties in this variation is that Black tries to avoid playing ... h5, since White's queenside play (e.g. ♘b5) often means that ... g4 is possible without this preparation due to the weakness of e4. Additionally, a pawn on h5 prevents ... ♘h5 ideas; moreover, after the advance of Black's g-pawn and capture on h2, the h-pawn obstructs Black's h-file play. Thus Black seeks to develop, and will only play ... h5 after running out of preparatory moves.

Nevertheless, Ikonnikov-Mamadshoev, Azov 1991 saw **14 ... h5 15 ♔h1 ♖f7** (15 ... ♘f6) **16 ♘b5!?** (16 c5!? — compare the main game) 16 ... a6 (Korchnoi gives 16 ... g4 17 fg± and 16 ... ♘f6 17 ♘xa7 ♗d7 18 c5! ♖xa7 19 c6±) **17 ♘a7 ♘f6 18 ♘xc8 ♕xc8**, and as normal Black's attack has a lot less force without the light-square bishop. There followed **19 ♘d3 g4 20 ♗g1 ♗f8 21 ♖e1 h4** (no other way to open the kingside) **22 ♘f2!** h3 23 fg hg+ 24 ♔xg2 f3+ 25 ♗xf3 ♘xd5 26

cd ♘h4+ 27 ♔h1 ♘xf3 28 ♖e3±.

15   c5!?

(a) Previously played was **15 b4 ♘f6 16 c5 ♗f8 17 cd ♗xd6 18 ♘d3 ♖g7 19 ♘c5 ♘f8 20 ♘b5 g4** and now **21 ♕e1?** ♕e8! 22 fg (White was trying to avoid this move, but now has no choice) 22 ... ♘xg4 gave Black a strong attack in Korchnoi-Nunn, Amsterdam 1990. Better is **21 ♗h4!** *(84)*:

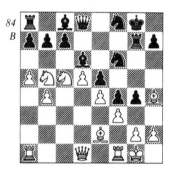

(a1) **21 ... ♘g6 22 ♗xf6 ♕xf6 23 fg±** (Korchnoi).

(a2) **21 ... h5 22 ♗c4** (Korchnoi suggests 22 ♔h1 and 22 fg!? hg 23 g3 with the point that 23 ... f3 24 ♗xf3 is terrible for Black, but 23 ... ♘8h7 24 gf ef 25 ♘xd6 ♕xd6 26 ♕d4 is an unclear mess) 22 ... **♕e7** (22 ... ♔h8) **23 ♔h1** was played in Korchnoi-J. Polgar, Pamplona 1990/1. Judit now blundered with **23 ... a6?** 24 ♘xc7!±±, but simply moving the king is adequate: **23 ... ♔h8 24 ♖c1 a6 25 ♘xd6 cd 26 ♘e6 ♘xe6 27 de ♗xe6 28 ♗xf6 ♕xf6 29 ♕xd6 ♖e8 30 ♗xe6 ♕xe6 31 ♕xe6**

♖xe6= (Wahls) or **23 ... ♔h7** 24
♖c1 a6 25 ♘xd6 cd 26 ♘a4 gf 27
gf ♗h3 28 ♖g1 ♘g6 (28 ... ♘xe4
fails due to the pin on the b1–h7
diagonal) 29 ♗g5 ♖ag8 30 ♕e1
♕f7 31 ♘b6 ♘f8 32 ♕h4 ♗g4!?
when Black has counterplay.

(a3) **21 ... g3** 22 hg ♘g6 (22 ...
fg? 23 ♘xd6 cd 24 f4! ♘g6 25 fe
♘xh4 26 ef ♖f7 27 ♖a3 is very
promising for White) 23 ♗xf6
♕xf6 24 g4 h5 25 ♘xd6 cd 26
♘e6 was considered unclear by
Korchnoi. Wilson–Mason, corres
1991 continued 26 ... ♗xe6 (26
... hg 27 fg ♖h7 28 g5 ♕h8 29
♔f2 ♖h2 30 ♖g1) 27 de hg 28 fg
♕xe6 29 ♖c1 ♔f8 30 ♗c4 ♕d7
31 ♕d5 ♘e7 32 ♕e6 with some
advantage for White due to
Black's problems with his queen's
rook and his king.

(b) **15 ♘b5 ♘f6** 16 ♘xa7 g4! (16
... ♗d7 17 c5!±) 17 fg (17 ♘xc8
g3) 17 ... ♘xe4 18 ♘xc8 ♘xf2 19
♖xf2 e4! (Nunn) ensures plenty of
counterplay. Note the importance
of Black's 19th move: instead capturing the knight would give
White time to control the e4-
square.

Returning to the position after
15 c5!? *(85).*

This astonishing pawn sacrifice
was presumably motivated by
Kožul's previous experiments with
the related idea 13 ♖c1 ♘g6 14 c5
♘xc5 15 b4 ♘a6 16 ♘b5, to which
a convincing answer was provided
in Kožul–Fedorowicz, Wijk aan
Zee 1991: 16 ... ♗d7 17 ♕a4 g4!

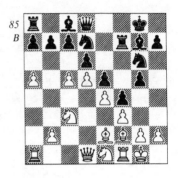

18 fg f3 19 gf ♘f4 20 ♕d1 h5 with
plenty of play for Black. Having
analysed such a possibility, it is
natural that he should seek an
improved version.

15 ...   ♘xc5

Kožul gave detailed analysis of
the alternatives:

(a) **15 ... dc** 16 ♗c4 ♗f8 (16
... ♔h8 18 d6 ♖f8 18 ♘b5!±) 17
d6 ♗xd6 (17 ... cd 18 ♘c2 △
♘a3±) 18 a6±.

(b) **15 ... ♗f8** 16 c6! ♘f6 17 cb
♗xb7 18 a6 ♗c8 19 ♘c2! (19
♘b5 allows 19 ... g4 immediately,
so the other knight becomes active
first) 19 ... h5 (19 ... ♖g7 20 ♘b4
♘e7 21 ♗b5 g4? 22 ♗h4 ♘g6 23
♘c6±±) 20 ♘b4 g4 21 ♘c6 ♕e8
22 ♘b5 g3 23 ♗e1±.

16 ♗xc5   dc
17 ♗c4   ♔h8

No better is **17 ... ♘f8** 18 ♕b3
♔h8 19 ♘d3 b6 (19 ... ♘d7 20
d6 ♖f8 21 ♘b5±) 20 d6 ♖d7 21
dc±.

17 ... ♗f8 should be met by 18
d6, since 18 a6 ♗d6 19 ab ♗xb7
20 ♘d3 a5!? gave Black good play

in Burgess–Beckhuis, Biel 1992.

18 a6!   ba

Kožul also considered **18 ...
♖d7** 19 ab ♗xb7 20 ♘d3 ♗f8 21
♘a4± and **18 ... b6** 19 d6 ♖f8 (19
... ♖d7 20 ♕d5 c6 21 ♕xc6 ♖b8
22 ♘b5±) 20 ♕d5! ♖b8 21 ♘b5
c6 22 ♕xc6 ♗d7 23 ♕d5±.

19 ♘d3   ♗f8
20 ♘a4   ♖b8

White's grip on the queenside is
not shaken by **20 ... ♗d6** 21
♘axc5 ♕e7 22 b4 ♖b8 23 ♗xa6.

21 b3!   ♗d6
22 ♘axc5   ♕e7
23 ♘xa6!   ♖b6
24 ♖a5   g4! *(86)*

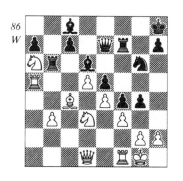

86
W

In these lines, Black always
obtains some sort of attacking
chances. Here, however, with
White having made so much progress on the queenside and in the
centre, it is no surprise that it is
the black king which finds itself in
most danger.

25 fg   ♕g5

26 ♘ac5   ♗xg4
27 ♘e6   ♕h5

27 ... ♗xe6 has the surprising
drawback of opening the fifth
rank: 28 de ♖g7 29 ♖f2 ♘h4 30
♘xf4± ±.

28 ♕a1!   f3
29 ♖xa7   h6

Black's king needs room; alternatively 29 ... ♖b8 30 ♖a8 ♖xa8
31 ♕xa8+ ♘f8 32 ♕e8 leaves
Black tied up.

30 ♖a8+   ♔h7
31 ♕a4   ♗xe6

Kožul gives **31 ... ♖e7** as necessary.

32 de   ♕g5
33 ♖f2   ♖g7
34 ♖xf3   ♘f4

The alternatives are **34 ... ♘h4**
35 ♖g3 ♗c5+ 36 ♔f1 ♕f6+ 37
♔e2± and **34 ... ♗c5+!?** 35
♘xc5! (35 ♔f1?? ♕xg2+!!) 35 ...
♘h4 36 ♖g3 ♕c1+ 37 ♗f1
♕xc5+ 38 ♔h1 whereupon
White's own attack takes over.

35 ♘e1!   ♗c5+

Typical lines after **35 ... ♗b4**
36 e7! are **36 ... ♗xe1** 37 ♖h8+
♔xh8 38 e8(♕)+ ♔h7 39 g3± ±
and **36 ... ♘h3+** 37 ♔h1! ♗xe1
38 ♖h8+ ♔xh8 39 e8(♕)+ ♔h7
40 ♕a2± ±.

After the text White's moves
were easier to find: **36 ♔f1 ♘xg2**
37 ♕e8! ♘e3+ 38 ♔e2 ♘xc4 39
♕h8+ ♔g6 40 ♖g3 ♖xb3 41
♖xg5+ hg 42 ♘d3 1–0.

10 ♘d3 and ♗d2: New Approaches

1 d4 ♘f6 2 c4 g6 3 ♘c3 ♗g7 4 e4
d6 5 ♘f3 0–0 6 ♗e2 e5 7 0–0
♘c6 8 d5 ♘e7

9	♘e1	♘d7
10	♘d3	f5
11	♗d2	*(87)*

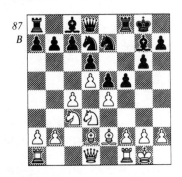

87
B

Until fairly recently, play would
generally continue 11 ... ♘f6 12
f3 f4 13 c5 g5 14 cd cd 15 ♖c1 (or
sometimes 15 ♘f2) 15 ... ♘g6 16
♘b5 ♖f7 17 ♕c2 and a race would
ensue. These variations became
very heavily analysed, with Black
generally finding enough counterplay against the white king to
balance White's c-file invasion.

In the late 1980s White began
to have remarkable success with a
new approach: 13 g4 *(88)*.

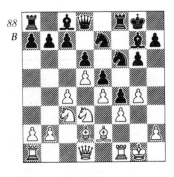

88
B

Presumably, it had always been
assumed that 13 ... fg would open
lines for Black's attack, but closer
examination revealed that the
extra space and lines around the
king actually help White to defend
(♗e3, ♔g2, ♖h1) so Black has
difficulty even obtaining a single
real threat. A further point is that
the knight on f6 obstructs Black's
most natural forms of counterplay: ... ♗f6 activating the bad
bishop; or ... g5, ... h5 and ...
♖f6–h6 with quick play on the h-
file. Since 13 ... h5 14 g5 ♘h7 15

h4 ♘xg5 appears not to work, Black generally plays 13 ... g5 and aims for h-file play with ... ♔f7 and ... ♖h8 or ... ♖f7, ... ♗f8 and ... ♖h7, followed by swinging the other heavy pieces over. White will reply bringing the bishop to f2, ready to exchange it for a knight on h4, and the rook to h1. White is happy to exchange the major pieces on the h-file, since then all that will be left in the position is White's queenside initiative. The following position, from Shirov–Hebden, London (Lloyds Bank) 1991, is a good example of what White is aiming for *(89)*:

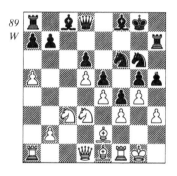

White now played 20 ♔g2 hg 21 hg ♗e7 (21 ... ♘h4+ is met by 22 ♗xh4; Black hopes to gain a tempo) 22 ♗f2 ♘h4+ 23 ♗xh4 gh (23 ... ♖xh4 will do no harm, with White always able to play ♖h1 when necessary) 24 ♘f2 h3+ 25 ♔h1. White's king is very safe indeed and his queenside play decided the game in his favour. Note that Shirov did not hurry to

play ♖h1 — a case perhaps where 'the threat is stronger than the execution'.

So how is Black to respond? Our illustrative game, Gelfand–Kasparov, shows an idea with a ... ♘h5 piece sacrifice; clearly this cannot be a general method, but is worth bearing in mind if White has spent time on the queenside rather than kingside prophylaxis. Black should also be alert to possibilities of sacrificing on g4. In the following position *(90)*, from Haugli–Badea, Haifa 1989, this was combined with h-file invasion:

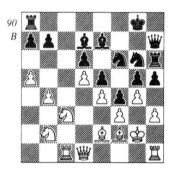

25 ... ♖f8! now threatened 26 ... hg 27 hg ♘xg4 28 fg f3+ 29 ♗xf3 ♘f4+ when 30 ♔g3 ♖h3+ mates, and 30 ♔g1 ♖xh1+ 31 ♗xh1 ♘h3+ is also catastrophic. So White prevented the mate, with **26 ♕f1**, whereupon Black continued 26 ... ♔g7, preparing to treble on the h-file. White, rather tied up, played 27 ♗b5 ♗c8 28 ♗d3 ♖h8 (Threatening 29 ... hg 30 hg ♖h2+) 29 ♕g1 hg 30 hg ♖h3! 31 ♗e2 ♘xg4! 32 fg f3+ 33 ♗xf3

♗xg4! 34 ♗xg4 ♘f4+ 35 ♔f1
♖xh1 0–1. For another example
of Black trebling on the h-file, see
the note to Black's seventeenth
move in Gelfand–Kasparov.
Observe that there is little point
in Black opening the h-file until
he has a definite idea in mind; this
denies White use of the h3-square
and the possibility of initiating
exchanges.

As a result both of dislike of the
long theoretical variations following 13 c5 and the problems caused
by 13 g4, Black started looking for
other ways to play, avoiding 12
... f4. There have emerged two
principal methods, which can
clearly transpose: 11 ... ♔h8 and
11 ... ♘f6 12 f3 ♔h8. The motiv-
ation behind ... ♔h8 is similar to
that behind the line 9 ♘d2 a5 10
♖b1 ♘d7 11 a3 f5 12 b4 ♔h8:
the manoeuvre ... ♘g8 is prepared, the king steps off the
a2–g8 diagonal, but most of all
the tension is retained on the kingside, keeping open possibilities of
... fe, ... f4 or ... ♗h6. Attacking
White's centre with ... c6 is very
often an idea. For instance, if
White tries to proceed as if nothing
has happened, with (11 ... ♘f6 12
f3 ♔h8) 13 c5, then Black has the
strong reply 13 ... c6!.

One very important idea is illustrated by the following position,
from Murugan–Bologan, Gausdal
International 1991 *(91)*:

Now 14 ... f4 could well be met
by 15 g4, when Black has similar

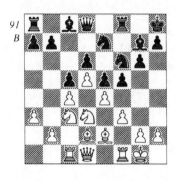

problems to those discussed
above. Instead Bologan played **14
... h5!?**, preparing 15 ... f4 followed
by ... g5, etc. Not wishing to face
such an attack, White replied 15
ef ♘xf5 (15 ... gf 16 f4 e4 17 ♘f2
♘g4 18 ♘xg4 hg is a standard
alternative — Black will attack on
the half-open h-file, and White on
the b-file) 16 ♘f2 ♘d4 17 ♗d3
♗f5 when Black had reasonable
piece play.

An idea specific to the line 11
... ♔h8 *(92)* is that leaving the
knight on d7 causes White some
problems in organising a queenside advance.

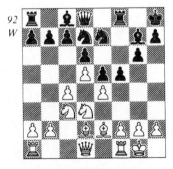

After 12 b4 ♘g8, the move b4 may

turn out to be a loss of tempo, whilst in Khalifman–Shirov, Lvov Z 1990, 12 ♖c1 c5! 13 b4?! cb 14 ♘xb4 ♘c5! left Black already a little better.

Sometimes, Black can develop an initiative on the queenside with ... c6 and ... b5 *(93)*:

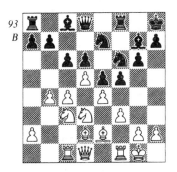

Frias–Sznapik, Thessaloniki OL 1984 continued 14 ... b5 15 dc bc 16 ♘f2 ♘xc6 17 ♗xc4 ♘d4! 18 ♘d5 ♗b7 19 ♗e3 ♘xd5 20 ♗xd5 ♗xd5 21 ed ♕b6 with reasonable prospects for Black. In the illustrative game Bareev–A. Kuzmin, we see White playing a4 to prevent such a ... b5 idea, whereupon Black plays directly on the kingside and, surprisingly enough, is able to make good use of the c7 square.

A further important scenario occurs if White captures on c6 after Black plays ... c6 or ... c5. Then Black's piece play and pressure on e4 stand him in good stead, e.g. Lautier–Wahls, Biel 1990 *(94)*:

14 ... ♘xc6! 15 ♗e3 ♗e6 16

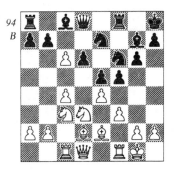

♕a4 ♘d4 17 ♖fe1 a6 18 c5 ♖c8 19 ♕a3 ♗c4 20 cd ♗xd3 21 ♗xd3 ♖c6 22 ef gf 23 ♘e2 ♖xd6 24 ♘xd4 ed 25 ♗f4 ♖d5. Black's position looks ugly, but the d-pawn is quite strong; White must watch out for ... ♘d5–e3. In the game White actually lost a piece after 26 ♗c7 ♕a8 27 ♗c4 ♖d7 28 ♗e6 d3! 29 ♖ed1 d2! 30 ♖c2 ♖e8! 31 ♕b3 ♖de7.

Gelfand–Kasparov
Reggio Emilia 1991/2

1 d4 ♘f6 2 c4 g6 3 ♘c3 ♗g7 4 e4 d6 5 ♘f3 0–0 6 ♗e2 e5 7 0–0 ♘c6 8 d5 ♘e7 9 ♘e1 ♘d7 10 ♘d3 f5

11	♗d2	♘f6
12	f3	f4
13	g4	g5

If permitted, White will follow up with h4, whereupon Black will find it very difficult to open lines on the kingside. The text has become Black's standard choice; two other moves fail to give adequate counterchances:

(a) **13 ... h5?! 14 g5! ⟐h7 15 h4**
⟐xg5 (15 ... c6?! 16 ⟐e1! ⟐f7
17 ⟐f2 ⟐h3 18 ⟐e1 ⟐xg5? 19
⟐h2!±± Lautier–Nunn, Groningen 1988/9) **16 hg ⟐f5** (16 ...
⟐xd5 17 ⟐f2 ⟐xc3 18 ⟐xc3 ⟐h3
19 ⟐b3 ⟐xg5+ 20 ⟐h2 ⟐e7 21
c5+± Khenkin–Konikov, USSR
1989) **17 ⟐f2** (17 ef allows a perpetual check) **17 ... ⟐xg5+ 18
⟐g2 ⟐g3 19 ⟐f2 ⟐f6** (19 ... ⟐f7
20 ⟐d3! ⟐f8 21 ⟐e2! h4 22
⟐h2! ⟐h7 23 ⟐g1! ⟐e7 24 ⟐c3
⟐h5 25 ⟐g4 h3 26 ⟐e2! ⟐h4 27
⟐e1 1–0 Khalifman–M. Schlosser, Groningen 1989/90) **20 ⟐f1!**
(20 ⟐h2 ⟐g5 gives White nothing
better than repeating with 21 ⟐g2,
but 20 ⟐d3 g5 21 ⟐e1 g4 22 fg
hg 23 ⟐xg3 fg 24 ⟐h1 worked
well in Steingrimsson–Dannevig,
Gausdal International 1991) **20 ...
g5 21 ⟐h2** *(95)* with the following
possibilities:

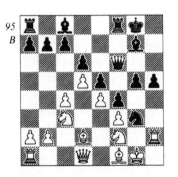

95
B

(a1) **21 ... ⟐g6** 22 ⟐h3 g4 23
fg hg 24 ⟐xg4 f3 25 ⟐xf3 ⟐xe4+
26 ⟐g2 1–0 Lukacs–Spiriev,
Budapest 1991.

(a2) **21 ... ⟐xf1** 22 ⟐xf1! ⟐g6

23 ⟐e2 (Djurhuus–Scholseth,
Gjøvik 1991 saw the weaker 23
⟐g2 ⟐f6 24 ⟐e2 g4 25 ⟐d3 g3
26 ⟐e2 h4 27 ⟐g1 ⟐d8∞) 23 ...
g4 24 ⟐h1! g3 (24 ... gf+ 25 ⟐d3
⟐g4 26 ⟐g1±±) 25 ⟐g1 ⟐f6 26
⟐xh5 gf 27 ⟐h8+ ⟐f7 28 ⟐xg7+
wins (Lautier).

(a3) **21 ... g4** 22 fg hg (22 ...
⟐xf1 23 ⟐xf1) 23 ⟐xg4! ⟐g6 24
⟐h3 f3 25 ⟐e1! ⟐h5 26 ⟐h4 was
analysed by Lautier as insufficient
for Black: 26 ... ⟐f6 27 ⟐xh5!;
26 ... ⟐f4 27 ⟐f2! ⟐xh3+ 28
⟐xh3 ⟐xg4 29 ⟐h7+ ⟐f7 30
⟐g1; 26 ... ⟐f6 27 ⟐f2!! ⟐xg4
28 ⟐g1 ⟐xe4+ 29 ⟐xe4 ⟐xe4 30
⟐xg4 ⟐e2+ 31 ⟐g3 f2 32 ⟐e6+
and White wins.

(b) **13 ... fg?!** **14 hg** has little
to recommend it. White intends
⟐e3, ⟐g2 and ⟐h1, while Black
has no visible counterplay:

(b1) **14 ... h5** 15 ⟐e3 ⟐h7 16 c5
g5 17 ⟐c1 ⟐g6 18 cd cd 19 ⟐b5
⟐f7 20 ⟐xa7 ⟐h3 21 ⟐f2 ⟐f4
22 ⟐b5 ⟐xe2+ 23 ⟐xe2 ⟐c8 24
⟐xc8 ⟐xc8 25 ⟐c2 ⟐f8 26 ⟐c3
⟐d7 27 ⟐e2 ⟐f6 28 g4± Rago-
zin–S. Ivanov, Leningrad 1989.

(b2) **14 ... ⟐h8** 15 ⟐e3 ⟐eg8
16 ⟐d2 ⟐d7 17 ⟐g2 ⟐f7 18
⟐h1 c6 19 dc± Malaniuk–Bokan,
Sverdlovsk 1989.

(b3) **14 ... h6** 15 ⟐g2 (15 f4 ef
16 ⟐xf4 (16 gf c6!∞) 16 ... g5 17
⟐e3 ⟐g6∞ — Shirov) 15 ... g5
16 ⟐c1 ⟐g6 17 c5 ⟐f7 18 cd cd
19 ⟐f2 ⟐f8 20 ⟐h1 ⟐h7 21 a4
⟐e8 22 ⟐b5± Tunik–Kaminski,
Kecskemet 1989.

(b4) **14 ... c6** 15 ♗e3 h6 (15 ...
♔h8 16 ♔g2 a5 17 ♘f2 ♘h5 18
♖h1 cd 19 cd ♘g8 20 ♕d2 a4 21
♖h2 a3 22 b4 ♖f7 23 ♖ah1± P.
Schlosser–Pähtz, Altensteig 1990)
16 ♔g2 g5 17 ♘f2 cd 18 cd ♘g6
19 ♖h1 ♖f7 20 a4 ♗f8 21 a5 ♖h7
22 ♘b5± Lutz–Fedorowicz, Porz
1988.

14 b4

More normal is **14 ♗e1 h5 15
h3**:

(a) **15 ... ♔f7** 16 ♔g2 ♖h8 17
♖h1 (17 ♗f2) 17 ... hg (17 ...
♖h6!?) 18 hg ♖xh1 19 ♔xh1 ♘g6
20 ♔g2 ♕h8 should be met by **21
♗f2** (21 ... ♗d7 22 c5?! ♘h5!?).
Instead, in Martinez–J. Romero,
Las Tunas 1990, **21 c5?** gave
Black the possibility 21 ... ♘h5!
22 gh (22 ♗f2 ♘g3 23 ♗xg3 fg
24 ♕h1 ♕h4) 22 ... ♕xh5 23 ♘f2
(23 ♗f1 ♗d7!) 23 ... ♗h3+! 24
♔g1 (24 ♘xh3 ♖h8) 24 ... ♖h8
25 ♗f1 ♗d7 with a very strong
attack (Romero).

(b) **15 ... ♘g6** *(96)* gives White
a wide choice of plans:

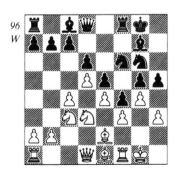

(b1) **16 ♗f2** c5 should be met

by **17 dc** bc 18 ♘b4 ♗b7 19 c5
a5 20 ♕b3+ ♔h8 21 ♘d3 △ cd
(Knaak), since **17 ♖b1** (17 b4 b6
18 bc bc 19 ♕a4 hg 20 hg ♘xg4 21
fg f3 22 ♗d1 ♘f4∓ Miladinović–
Todorović, Belgrade GMA 1988)
17 ... ♖f7 18 b4 b6 19 ♔g2 ♗f8
20 ♖h1 ♖h7 21 ♕b3 ♗d7 gave
White nothing in Kir. Georgiev–
Spraggett, Terrassa 1990.

(b2) **16 ♔g2 ♔f7** (16 ... ♖f7
17 ♖h1 ♗f8 18 ♗f2 ♘h4+ 19
♗xh4 gh 20 b4 ♘h7 21 ♘f2 ♘g5
22 a4 ♖h7 23 a5 ♕f6 24 ♕d3 ♗e7
25 ♖ag1 hg 26 ♘xg4 ♗xg4 27 fg
f3+ gave Black activity for the
pawn in L. Hansen–Berg Hansen,
Lyngby 1989) 17 ♗f2 ♖h8 (17 ...
♘h4+ 18 ♗xh4 gh 19 b4 ♖g8
20 c5 ♗f8 21 ♔h2 ♗e7 22 cd
♗xd6!? 23 ♘a4 b6 24 ♘ab2 △
♘c4± is analysis by Lautier) 18
♖h1 ♘h4+ 19 ♔g1 (19 ♗xh4)
19 ... ♖h6 20 c5 hg 21 hg ♗d7
22 ♖c1 ♕h8 23 ♗xh4 ♖xh4 24
♔g2 ♕h6 25 ♖xh4 ♕xh4 26 ♕e1
♕h6 27 ♕h1 ♕g6 28 ♔g1 ♖h8
gave Black enough h-file play to
balance White's queenside pressure in Sokolin–Monin, Leningrad
1990.

(b3) **16 c5 ♖f7 17 cd** (17 ♔g2
♗f8 18 b4 ♖h7 19 ♖h1 ♗d7 20
♕b3 hg 21 hg ♖xh1 22 ♔xh1
♔g7 23 ♗f2 ♗e7 24 ♔g2 ♕c8
½–½ Lazarev–Hazai, Hungary
1991) **17 ... cd**. White has two
ideas:

(b31) **18 ♖c1 ♗f8** 19 ♕b3 (19
♗f2 ♖h7 20 ♕b3 hg 21 hg ♘h4
22 ♗xh4 ♖xh4 23 ♘f2 a6! 24 a4

♖h7!? 25 ♔g2 ♗d7 26 ♘b1 b5!
27 ab ab 28 ♘a3 ♕b6 29 ♘xb5!
♗xb5! 30 ♕xb5 ♕xb5 31 ♗xb5
♖b8 reached an ending in Khalifman–V. Spasov, Manila IZ 1990,
which Black should have held, but
subsequently missed his chance to
manoeuvre his knight to d4, and
was squashed) 19 ... ♖h7 20
♔g2!? a6! (20 ... hg 21 hg ♘h4+
22 ♗xh4 ♖xh4 23 ♘f2±) 21 a4
♗d7 22 ♗f2 ♖c8 23 ♖h1! ♕e8?!
(23 ... ♖g7 would be better since
24 ♕b6?! can be met by 24 ...
♘h4+) 24 ♕b6! ♖g7 25 b3 intending ♘b1–d2–c4 gave White an
edge in Lobron–Renet, Novi Sad
OL 1990.

(b32) **18 a4** ♗f8 19 a5 (19 ♔g2
♗e7 should presumably be met
by 20 a5, since in Bareev–Belotti,
Aosta 1989, 20 ♖c1?! ♕f8! 21 a5
♗d8 22 b4 ♗d7 was fine for
Black) 19 ... ♖h7 20 ♔g2 hg 21
hg ♗e7 22 ♗f2 ♘h4+ 23 ♗xh4
gh 24 ♘f2 h3+ 25 ♔h1 a6 26 b4
b5 27 ab ♕xb6 28 b5± Shirov–
Hebden, London (Lloyds Bank)
1991.

| 14 | ... | **h5** |
| **15** | **h3** | **♔f7** *(97)* |

Kasparov brings his rook to the
h-file as quickly as possible. In
Gavriushin–Temirbaev, USSR
1990, Black's counterplay came
too slowly: 15 ... ♘g6 16 c5 ♖f7
17 a4 ♗f8 18 a5 ♖h7 19 a6 ba
20 c6 hg 21 hg ♕e7 22 ♖f2 ♖b8
23 ♗e1 ♖h6 24 ♖h2±.

| 16 | **♗e1** | **♖h8** |
| 17 | **♔g2** | **♘g6** |

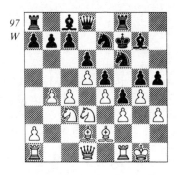

Gelfand proposes an immediate
h-file build-up: **17 ... ♖h6!?** 18
♗f2 ♕h8 19 ♖h1 ♗d7 20 ♕b3
♕h7 21 ♖ag1 ♖h8 22 ♕d1 hg 23
hg ♖h2+ 24 ♖xh2 ♕xh2+ 25
♔f1∞.

| **18** | **c5** |

This allows Black a very
surprising resource. Ftačnik
recommends instead **18 ♖h1**,
while Gelfand and Khuzman give
the line **18 ♗f2** a5 19 a3 hg 20
hg ♘h4+ 21 ♗xh4 ♖xh4 22 ♖h1
♕h8=. The possibility of opening
the a-file ensures that Black is not
starved of counterplay, while b5 is
met by ... b6, ruining White's
queenside chances.

| 18 | ... | **hg** |
| **19** | **hg** | **♘h5!** *(98)* |

19 ... ♘h4+ 20 ♗xh4 ♖xh4 21
♖h1 gives Black no substantial
counterplay against White's eventual queenside invasion — the
extra tempo over the previous note
makes all the difference.

| 20 | **♖h1** |

Acceptance is highly dangerous:
20 gh ♖xh5!? (20 ... ♗h3+ 21

98
W

♔g1! ♖xh5 22 ♖f2 ♕h8 23
♗f1∞) 21 ♖h1 (21 ♘f2 ♘h4+!
22 ♔g2 ♕h8 leaves White
defenceless) 21 ... ♖xh1 22 ♔xh1
♕h8+ 23 ♔g2 ♕h5 24 ♗f1 g4∓
(Gelfand).

| 20 | ... | ♘g3 |
| 21 | ♗xg3 | fg |

**21 ... ♖xh1 22 ♕xh1 fg 23
♔xg3 (23 ♕h3 ♕f6!?) 23 ... ♘f4
24 ♕h2 ♗d7 25 ♕f2 ♕h8 26 ♕h2
♕xh2+ 27 ♔xh2 a5! 28 cd cd 29
ba∓ (Gelfand).**

| 22 | ♕d2 | ♖h4 |

Gelfand suggests that **22 ...
♕f6!?** 23 ♔xg3 ♗d7 gives Black
better chances of keeping the
initiative. After the text, Black
merely has enough compensation.

23	♔xg3	♗d7
24	♖xh4	gh+
25	♔h2	♗f6
26	b5	

26 ♕h6 ♗g7 kicks the queen
back.

| 26 | ... | ♗g5 |
| 27 | ♕e1 | ♗e3 |

Gelfand prefers **27 ... ♔g7 28
c6 ♗c8 29 a4 a6.**

28	c6	♗c8
29	♘d1	♗d4
30	cb	♗xb7
31	♖c1	a6!
32	♕d2	ab
33	♕h6	

Now White has secured
counterplay, e.g. **33 ... ♖xa2?** 34
♖xc7+ ♕xc7 35 ♕h7+ ♔f6 36
♕xc7 ♖xe2+ 37 ♔h1 ♖d2 38
g5+! wins.

The game concluded **33 ... ♘f8
34 ♖c2 (24 ♘e3 ♗xe3 35 ♕xe3
♖xa2 36 ♖b1 ♕a8 37 ♘b4 ♕a7=)
34 ... ♗b6 35 ♘e3 ♕f6 36 ♕h5+
♕g6 37 ♘f5 ♕xh5 38 gh ♖c8 (38
... ♘d7!?) 39 ♘xh4 ♘h7 40 f4 ef
41 ♘xf4 ♘g5 42 ♗xb5 ♘xe4 43
a4 ½-½.**

Hjartarson–Shirov
Reykjavik 1992

**1 d4 ♘f6 2 c4 g6 3 ♘c3 ♗g7 4 e4
d6 5 ♘f3 0-0 6 ♗e2 e5 7 0-0
♘c6 8 d5 ♘e7 9 ♘e1 ♘d7 10 ♘d3
f5**

| 11 | ♗d2 | |

The older move order **11 f3** has
the point that 11 ... ♔h8 12 ♗e3!
robs the king move of its point,
and that Skembris' idea 11 ... ♘f6
12 c5!? gives Black nothing better
than 12 ... f4, when 13 ♗d2 is the
traditional main line. Black's best
is **11 ... f4**, when **12 g4 ♗f6!** 13
♗d2 h5 14 h3 ♔f7 15 ♗e1 ♖h8
16 ♔g2 ♘g8 17 ♖c1 ♗h4 18 ♖h1
♔g7 gave Black easy equality in
Dreev–Gelfand, Kramatorsk
1989, while after **12 ♗d2, 12 ...**

♔**h8** transposes to Hjartarson–
Shirov, but there is no reason why
Black shouldn't just get on with
it: **12 ... h5** 13 ♖c1 g5 14 b4 ♘f6
etc. Moreover, **12 ... g5** 13 g4 h5
14 g3 is an improved version for
Black of the line 11 ♗d2 ♘f6 12
f3 f4 13 g4 g5 since Black has the
option of ... ♖f6–h6.

11   ...   ♔h8

11... ♖f7?! was brutally treated
in Khalifman–Watson, London
(WFW) 1991: 12 f3 f4 13 ♖c1
(White is waiting for ... g5 before
playing g4, since this clogs up
Black's dark-square play) 13 ... h5
(Logical, but too slow) 14 c5! ♘xc5
(Otherwise White has gained too
much time) 15 ♘xc5 dc 16 ♗c4
(A nightmare scenario following
... ♖f7) 16 ... ♔f8 17 ♗e1! b6
18 b4! cb 19 ♘b5 c5 20 d6 ♘c6
21 ♕d5 ♕d7 22 ♗h4! 1–0. The
threat is 23 ♗e7+.

12   f3

White has two major alternatives:

(a) **12 ♖c1 c5!** seems very adequate for Black. Knaak suggests
the aggressive **13 f4**, while **13 b4?!**
cb 14 ♘xb4 ♘c5 15 ♗f3 ♗d7 16
♗e3 b6 17 ♘d3 ♘g8 18 ♘xc5 bc
19 ♖b1 ♗h6 20 ♗xh6 ♘xh6∓
½–½ was Khalifman–Shirov, Lvov
Z 1990. On **13 dc**, Shirov has
shown both recaptures to be playable:

(a1) **13 ... bc** 14 c5 d5 15 ed cd
16 ♗g5 ♗b7 (16 ... ♗f6 17
♗xf6 ♖xf6 18 f4!) 17 ♘b5 ♗c6
18 ♘b4 ♘f6 19 ♘d6 (19 f4!?) 19

... ♕d7= Dreev–Shirov, World
Junior (Tunja) 1989.

(a2) **13 ... ♘xc6** 14 f3 (14 b4
♘f6! 15 f3 ♘xb4!∞ — Shirov) 14
... ♘c5 15 ♗e3 ♘e6 16 ♕d2 b6
17 ♖fd1 ♗b7 18 ♘e1 ♘cd4 19
♘c2 ♕h4 20 ♗f2 ♕h5 21 ef ♖xf5
Akopian–Shirov, World Junior
(Santiago) 1990.

(b) **12 b4** can be met by **12 ...
♘f6** 13 f3 transposing to the next
game. Alternatively, **12 ... ♘g8** 13
♖c1 (13 f3 ♗h6) **13 ... ♘df6** 14
f3 (14 ef gf 15 f4 e4 16 ♘f2 a5 17
a3 ab 18 ab c6 19 ♗e3 ♖a3 gave
Black reasonable prospects in Kir.
Georgiev–Ghinda, Stara Zagora
Z 1990) **14 ... ♗h6** *(99)* is playable. Then:

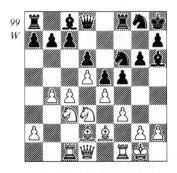

(b1) **15 ef!?** gf 16 f4 argues that
Black's bishop is misplaced on h6.
In Lutz–Pähtz, Dortmund 1991,
16 ... ♘e4?! 17 ♗e1 ♘gf6 18 fe!
de 19 ♘xe4 ♘xe4 20 ♘xe5 won a
pawn for insufficient compensation, since Black can hardly
contemplate grabbing the
exchange. Maybe **15 ... ♗xf5** 16
♘f2 ♘h5 is worth investigating.

(b2) **15 c5** ♗xd2 16 ♕xd2 f4 17 ♘f2 g5?! (17 ... h5∞ prevents White's next move) 18 g4! h5 19 h3 ♖f7 20 ♖c2 ♖h7 21 a4 hg (21 ... ♕f8!?) 22 hg ♕f8 23 ♔g2 ♘e7 24 ♖h1 ♖xh1 25 ♔xh1 a6 26 ♔g1 ♘g6 27 ♘d3 ♗d7 28 ♗d1!± Malaniuk–Gelfand, USSR Ch (Leningrad) 1989.

(b3) **15 ♗xh6** ♘xh6 16 ♕d2 ♘f7 (16 ... f4?! 17 g4± Milos–Fiorito, Buenos Aires 1990) 17 c5 ♗d7∞ 18 a4 f4 19 a5 g5 20 ♘f2 h5 21 h3 ♘h6 22 cd cd 23 ♘b5 ♗xb5 24 ♗xb5 g4∓ Chabanon–V. Spasov, Sofia 1990.

12 ... **f4** *(100)*

12 ... ♘f6 is considered in the next two games. The text gives 11 ... ♔h8 independent significance.

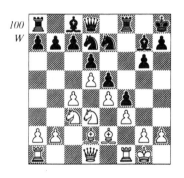

100
W

13 ♖c1

13 g4 was tried in Shirov–Lanka, Moscow 1991. There followed 13 ... ♗f6!? 14 ♗e1 h5 15 h3 ♘g8 16 b4 ♗h4 17 c5 ♖f7 18 ♔g2 ♖h7 19 cd cd 20 ♗xh4 ♕xh4 21 ♕e1 ♕f6 22 ♕f2 ♘f8 23 a4 g5 24 ♖fc1 ♗d7 and White was successful with a king march to the queenside. Nevertheless, Black's logical plan can hardly be condemned on this basis.

With the text, White plans to meet **13 ... g5** with 14 g4. Shirov's next move cuts out this option.

13	...	h5
14	b4	g5
15	c5	♘f6
16	♘b5	♘e8
17	♕c2	♗d7
18	♘f2	*(101)*

White could prefer **18 a4**, as Black now has an interesting way to delay White on the queenside.

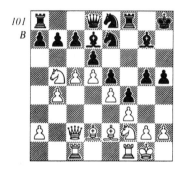

101
B

18	...	a6
19	♘a3	b5!
20	cb	cb
21	♘c4?	♖c8
22	♕d1?!	b5
23	♘a5	♖xc1
24	♕xc1	♕b6!

Black, threatening 25 ... g4, is now clearly better.

There followed: **25 ♔h1** ♘f6 26 ♘d3 ♖c8 27 ♕d1 g4 28 ♗e1 ♘g6 29 ♗f2 ♕c7 30 ♘c6 h4 (Shirov is not, of course, interested in winning a pawn when there is bigger

game) 31 fg ♘xe4 32 ♗e1 ♘g5 33
♘a5 ♕c2 34 ♘c6 ♕xa2 35 ♘c1
♕a3 36 ♘b3 h3 37 gh ♖xc6 38 h4
(38 dc ♗xc6+ 29 ♔g1 ♘xh3#)
38 ... ♕b2 39 ♗d3 e4 40 ♖f2
♕e5 0–1.

Bareev–A. Kuzmin
Moscow Ch 1989

**1 d4 ♘f6 2 c4 g6 3 ♘c3 ♗g7 4 e4
d6 5 ♘f3 0–0 6 ♗e2 e5 7 0–0
♘c6 8 d5 ♘e7 9 ♘e1 ♘d7 10 ♘d3
f5 11 ♗d2 ♔h8 12 f3**

12 ... ♘f6

13 b4 *(102)*

Again White has a wide choice:

(a) **13 c5** is met by 13 ... c6!?∞,
e.g. 14 cd ♕xd6 15 ♗e3 b6 or 15
... ♘d7!?.

(b) **13 g4** c6 14 ♔h1 (14 a4!?)
14 ... b5!? 15 b3 (15 g5 ♘h5 16 cb
cb 17 ed∞) 15 ... ♖b8 16 a3 a5 17
♘f2 b4 18 ab ab 19 ♘a2 fe 20
fe cd 21 cd (Polugaevsky–Gufeld,
Sochi 1981) 21 ... ♘fxd5 22 ed
♘xd5 23 ♘e4 ♗b7 24 ♖xf8+
♕xf8 25 ♗f3 ♖a8 (Gufeld) is
good for Black.

(c) **13 a4!?** a5 14 g4 (14 c5 c6;
14 ♕c2 c5 15 dc ♘xc6 16 ♗e3
♘d4 17 ♕d1 ♗e6 gave Black a
defensible position in L. Hansen–
Berg, Græsted 1990) 14 ... c5 (14
... c6!?) 15 ♖f2 (15 ♔g2 f4 16 h4
h5 17 g5 ♘e8 18 ♖h1 ½–½ was
Khalifman–Gelfand, Reggio
Emilia 1991/2; the entire board is
blocked and there are no feasible
break-throughs) 15 ... b6 (An idea
worth noting: the rook is trans-

ferred along the second rank) 16
h4 ♖a7 17 ♖h2 (Kožul–Gufeld,
Tbilisi 1988) 17 ... ♘eg8!? 18 h5
gh!? 19 gf ♗h6∞ (Gufeld).

(d) For **13 ♖c1** see the next
game.

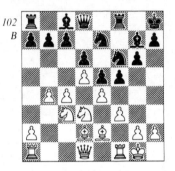

102
B

13 ... c6

Black can also try:

(a) **13 ... ♘eg8** 14 c5 ♗h6!?
transposes after **15 ♖c1** (Malaniuk–Gelfand) or **15 ♗xh6** ♘xh6
16 ♕d2 ♘f7 17 ♖ac1 to lines
considered in the note (b) to
White's twelfth move in the previous game.

(b) **13 ... h6** was successful in
Hjartarson–Shchekachev, Philadelphia 1991: 14 ♖c1 g5 15 ♘f2
♘g6 16 ef ♗xf5 17 g3 a5 18 a3
ab 19 ab c6 20 ♕b3 ♘e7 21 dc bc
with a very promising position for
Black.

(c) **13 ... h5** 14 ef gf (14 ... ♘xf5
15 ♘f2 c6! 16 ♗d3 cd 17 ♘xd5
♘xd5 18 cd ♗d7 gave Black a
good game in Lutz–Shirov, World
Junior (Santiago) 1990) 15 f4 e4
16 ♘f2 ♘g4 17 ♗xg4 (17 ♘xg4!?
hg∞; 17 ♘h3? c6!∓ Gouret-

Lanka, Torcy 1990) 17 ... hg 18
♖c1 (Bologan considers 18 g3!?
♘g8 19 h3 gh 20 ♕h5+ ♘h6 21
♘xh3 ♗d7 22 ♘g5 ♕e8! equal)
18 ... c6!? 19 ♗e3 a5! 20 b5
c5= Barkhagen–Bologan, World
Junior (Mamaia) 1991.

14 a4

White prevents 14 ... b5, so
Black now plays vigorously on the
kingside, in the hope that the last
two moves are helpful.

For 14 ♖c1 b5, see the note to
Black's 13th move in the next
game.

	14	...	f4
	15	g4	h5
	16	g5	

16 h3 ♘h7 17 ♗e1 ♗f6∞ (Kuzmin).

	16	...	♘h7
	17	h4	♘xg5
	18	hg	♘xd5!
	19	♖f2	

Capturing the knight allows a
perpetual check.

| | 19 | ... | ♘c7! (103) |

19 ... ♘e3?! 20 ♗xe3 fe 21 ♖g2
♗e6 22 ♕c1 ♗xc4 (22 ... d5? 23
cd cd 24 ♘c5±± Rashkovsky–
Tsarëv, Kiev 1989) 23 ♕xe3 ♗g8
△ ... ♕e7 is analysed by Rashkovsky, but his assessment (equality)
is rather hard to believe.

	20	♖g2	♗h3
	21	♖h2	♕xg5+
	22	♔h1	♗e6
	23	♗e1	♕f6
	24	♗h4	

Better is 24 b5.

| | 24 | ... | g5 |

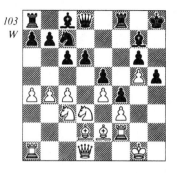

103
W

| | 25 | ♗f2 | ♕g6 |
| | 26 | b5 | c5! |

White must open as many lines
as possible on the queenside, or
Black will have plenty of time
to organise an eventual kingside
advance.

	27	b6!	ab
	28	♖b1	♖a6
	29	♘e1	♗d7

White has obtained some activity and is able to put many tactical
obstacles in the way of Black's
kingside push. There followed 30
♖b2 ♗h6 31 ♘g2 ♖g8 32 ♖d2
♘e8 33 ♘b5 ♗f8 34 ♗e1 ♖g7
35 ♖d3 ♔g8 36 ♗c3 ♗c8 37
♖d5 ♖a8 (37 ... g4 38 ♘xf4! gives
White counterplay) 38 ♗f1 ♗e7
39 ♗e2 ♖h7? (39 ... ♔f8 and 40
... ♖g8 would finally prepare ...
g4∓. Now White seizes a chance
for counterplay) 40 ♘h4! gh 41
♖g2 ♗g4 42 fg ♖g7 43 g5 ♕xe4!
44 ♗f3 ♕f5 45 ♕d3 (45 ♘xd6
♗xd6 46 ♖xd6 ♘xd6 47 ♕xd6
e4! 48 ♗xg7 ef ∓) 45 ... ♕xd3 46
♖xd3 ♖xa4 47 ♗xh5 ♔f8 48
♗xe8 ♔xe8 49 ♘xd6+ ♗xd6 50

♖xd6 ♖xc4 51 ♗xe5 f3! 52 ♗xg7
fg+ 53 ♔xg2 ♖g4+ 54 ♔f3
♖xg5 55 ♗f6 ♖g1 56 ♗xh4 ♖b1
57 ♔g4 ♖b4+ 58 ♔h5 ♖d4
$\frac{1}{2}$–$\frac{1}{2}$.

Gelfand–Kasparov
Linares 1990

1 d4 ♘f6 2 c4 g6 3 ♘c3 ♗g7 4 e4
d6 5 ♘f3 0–0 6 ♗e2 e5 7 0–0
♘c6 8 d5 ♘e7 9 ♘e1 ♘d7 10 ♘d3
f5

11	♗d2	♘f6
12	f3	♔h8

12 ... h5 appears less accurate
than 12 ... ♔h8 13 b4 h5 (as in
the note to Black's 13th in the
previous game) since White's
queenside is more secure here, so
opening the long diagonal has less
drawbacks for White. Shirov–
Nunn, Bundesliga 1991/2, continued 13 ef! gf (13 ... ♘xf5
14 ♘f2±; 13 ... ♗xf5 14 g4!?)
14 f4 e4 15 ♘f2 ♘g4 (15 ... h4 16
♘h3±) 16 ♘xg4!? fg? (16 ... hg 17
♗e3±) 17 ♘xe4 ♗xb2 18 ♖b1
♗d4+ 19 ♔h1± ♘f5 (on 19
... ♗f5 Shirov gives 20 ♗d3 b6
21 ♕c2) 20 ♗d3 b6 21 ♖e1! ♗d7
22 ♘g5 ♖f6 23 ♗b4!!±± a5
24 ♗a3 ♗c3 25 ♖e2 h4 26 ♖e6!
♘h6 27 ♗h7+ ♔g7 28 ♕d3!
♗xe6 29 ♕xc3!! ♗g8 30 ♗b2!
1–0.

13 ♖c1 c5 (104)
This is far from Black's only
choice here:
(a) 13 ... ♘eg8 14 c5 (14 g4 fg
15 fg h6 16 h4 ♘xg4 17 ♗xg4

♕xh4= Ftačnik) 14 ... ♗h6
nearly equalises according to
Ftačnik.

(b) 13 ... c6 14 b4 (14 dc — see
next note) 14 ... b5 is an important
alternative. White's inferior
options are 15 cb?! cd 16 ed ♘exd5,
15 c5?! cd 16 cd ♕xd6 17 ♘xb5
♕b6+ 18 ♘f2 de∓ and 15 ♕b3?!
bc 16 ♕xc4 cd 17 ed ♕b6+ 18
♔h1 ♗b7∓ (Ftačnik). More critical:
(b1) 15 ♗e3 bc 16 ♘b2 cd 17
ed ♗b7 18 ♗xc4 a5 19 b5 ♖c8
20 ♕b3 f4 21 ♗f2 ♘f5 22 ♘ba4
♘d4 with lively, balanced play in
Michelet–Troffiguer, corres 1985.
(b2) 15 dc bc 16 ♘f2 (16 ♘b2
♘xc6 17 ♘xc4 ♘d4∞ Ftačnik–P.
Littlewood, Hastings 1982/3) 16
... ♘xc6 17 ♗xc4 ♘d4! (17 ...
♘xb4 18 ♘b5 ♘c6 19 ♗g5±)
18 ♘d5 ♗b7 19 ♗e3 ♘xd5 20
♗xd5 ♗xd5 21 ed ♕b6 22 ♗xd4
ed 23 ♘d3 (Frias–Sznapik, Thessaloniki 1984) 23 ... a5!? 24 ♖c6
♕b5 25 a4! ♕xd5 26 b5 with
enough compensation (Frias).

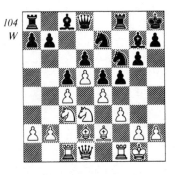

104
W

14 g4

White could also try:

(a) **14 dc** ♘xc6 (14 ... bc?! 15 ♗e3 ♕e8 16 ♕a4 ♗e6 17 ♖fd1± Hübner–Nunn, Bundesliga 1984/5) 15 ♗e3 ♗e6 16 ♕a4 (16 b3 ♘d4 17 ♘f2 ♘h5 18 ♖e1 ♘f4 19 ♗f1 ♗g8 20 ♘e2 ♘fxe2+ 21 ♗xe2 fe 22 ♘xe4 d5= Schlacht-Schubert, Bundesliga 1985/6) 16 ... ♘d4 17 ♖fe1 a6 18 c5 ♖c8 19 ♕a3 ♗c4 20 cd ♗xd3 21 ♗xd3 ♖c6 led to a sharp struggle in Lautier–Wahls, Biel 1990.

(b) **14 ♖b1** can be met by **14 ... h5** 15 ef gf (15 ... ♘xf5) 16 f4 e4 17 ♘f2 ♘g4 18 ♘xg4 hg 19 ♗e3 ♘g8 20 ♕d2 ♖f6 21 g3 ♖h6 22 b4 b6 23 ♔g2 ♘f6 24 ♖b3 ♗d7 25 bc bc 26 ♖fb1 ♔h7 27 ♔g1 ♔g6 28 ♗f1 ♕h8 29 ♖b7 ♗c8 30 ♖7b3 ♗d7= Berg Hansen-Mortensen, Danish Ch (Århus) 1992; Belov's **14 ... ♘eg8** 15 b4 b6 16 bc bc 17 ♕a4 a6! 18 ♕c6 ♖a7 19 ♖b8 ♖c7∞; or **14 ... a5** 15 a3 ♘eg8 16 b4 ab 17 ab b6 18 ♕c1 (Neverov–Belov, Voskresensk 1990) 18 ... ♘h5 19 g3 ♘hf6 20 ♘f2 ♘e8 △ ... f4∞ (Belov).

(c) **14 a3** gives Black a similar choice: **14...a5** 15 ♖b1 transposes to Neverov–Belov; **14 ... ♘eg8** 15 b4 bc 16 bc bc 17 ♖b1 h5 18 ♕a4 (Titov–Kudriashov, Azov 1991) 18 ... a6; or **14 ... h5** 15 ef ♘xf5 (15 ... gf) 16 ♘f2 ♘d4 17 ♗d3 ♗f5 18 ♘ce4 ♘xe4 19 ♘xe4 ♗f6 20 b4 b6 21 ♖b1 ♕e7 22 ♗e3 ♗xe4 23 ♗xe4 ♗g5 with no great problems for Black in Murugan-Bologan, Gausdal Inter-national 1991.

14 ... a6!

This, together with the next move, is Kasparov's idea. Other moves fail to equalise: **14 ... h6** 15 h4 fg 16 fg g5?! 17 h5± (Ftačnik) restricts Black's knights; **14 ... ♗d7** 15 ♘f2 ♘eg8 16 ♔h1 f4 17 b4!?± Ftačnik–Geller, Sochi 1977; **14 ... ♘eg8** 15 ♔g2! ♘e8 (15 ... f4 16 h4 ♘xg4!? 17 fg ♕xh4 18 ♗e1 ♕g5 19 ♘f2 h5 (19 ... ♘h6 20 ♘h3 ♕f6 21 g5!) 20 ♘h3 ♕f6 21 gh g5 22 ♘f2± Ftačnik) 16 g5 f4 (16 ... ♖f7 17 h4 ♗f8 18 ef ♗xf5 19 f4 and 16 ... ♕d7 17 ♘f2 do not help Black) 17 h4 ♖f7 18 ♖h1 ♗f8 19 ♕g1 ♘g7 20 ♗d1! with ideas of ♗a4 gave White a distinct edge in Ftačnik–Nunn, Vienna 1986.

15 ♘f2

To prevent 15 ... b5. Of course, **15 a4** a5 ruins White's queenside chances.

15 ... h6!

Black intends 16 ... fg 17 fg g5 followed by ... ♘g6–f4.

16	h4	fg
17	fg	♘eg8
18	♔g2	♘h7
19	♖h1	♗f6
20	g5	*(105)*

Black's surprising manoeuvre exploits White's awkwardness in defending the h-pawn due to the knight on f2: **20 ♔g3?** ♗xh4+ 21 ♖xh4 ♖xf2. Thus the text, a fully reasonable pawn sacrifice.

| 20 | ... | hg |
| 21 | h5 | ♕e8 |

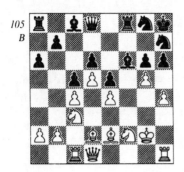

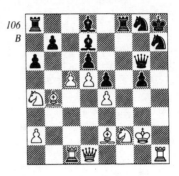

21 ... ♘e7 22 ♗g4 is good for White, who plans ♕e2 and play on the h-file.

22   b4!?

22 ♕a4 is best met by 22 ... b5! 23 cb ♗d7∞. Gelfand suggests **22 ♗e3**, whilst Kasparov considers **22 hg** ♕xg6 23 ♗h5 ♕g7 24 ♗g4 to be unclear.

22   ...   cb
23   ♘a4   ♗d8
24   ♗xb4

24 c5 leads to complications after, e.g. 24 ... ♖xf2+!? 25 ♔xf2 ♘gf6 26 cd ♘xe4+ 27 ♔g2 ♗d7 (Gelfand).

24   ...   ♗d7
25   hg

Kasparov queries this, preferring **25** ♘b2 ♖xf2+ 26 ♔xf2 ♘gf6, but Gelfand felt that Black would have the initiative after 27 ♕d3 ♗b6+! 28 ♔e1 gh 29 ♗xd6 ♗d4 and 30 ... ♕g6.

25   ...   ♕xg6
26   c5 *(106)*
26   ...   g4?!

Kasparov analysed **26 ...** ♘f6 as a better try: 27 c6 (27 ♘c3 g4

28 c6 g3∓) 27 ... ♘xe4 28 cd (28 ♘xe4 ♕xe4+ 29 ♗f3 ♕xb4 30 cd g4∓∓) 28 ... ♖xf2+ 29 ♔g1 ♕f5 30 ♗e1 (30 ♖c3 ♖g2+ 31 ♔xg2 ♕f2+ 32 ♔h3 g4+ leads to mate) 30 ... ♕f4! 31 ♕d3 (31 ♖h3 g4∓∓) 31 ... ♕xc1 32 ♖xh7+ ♔g8∓∓ and White is defenceless. After the text, Black still has good chances, but White's resources seem adequate.

27   c6   g3
28   ♘d3   bc
29   dc   ♖c8!
30   ♗f3?!

30 ♗xd6! ♕xd6 (30 ... ♕xe4+ 31 ♗f3 ♖xf3 32 ♕xf3 ♗xc6 33 ♗xe5+ ♗f6 34 ♗xf6+ ♘xf6 35 ♖xc6 draws) 31 cd ♖xc1 32 ♘xc1! ♕g6 (not 32 ... ♖f2+ 33 ♔xg3 ♕f6 34 ♗f3!) 33 ♗f3 ♘h6 is given by Gelfand as unclear.

30   ...   ♖xf3!

30 ... ♗xc6 31 ♘xe5! leads to equality.

31   ♕xf3   ♗g4
32   ♕xg3   ♕xe4+
33   ♔g1   ♘f6

White would also have considerable difficulties to overcome after **33 ...** ♗**g5** or **33 ...** ♗**f3**.

34	♗xd6!	♕d4+
35	♘f2	♕xd6
36	♘xg4	♕d4+
37	♘f2	♕xa4
38	♕xe5	♖c7

After **38 ...** ♖**xc6**, Kasparov demonstrated White's saving resource: 39 ♖xh7+! ♔xh7 40 ♕h2+!! ♘h5! 41 ♕xh5+ ♔g7=.

After the text this great fight began to fizzle out with some exchanges: 39 ♖h2 ♖g7+ 40 ♖g2 ♗c7 41 ♕f5 ♕xa2 42 ♕c8+ ♕g8 43 ♕xg8+ ♔xg8 44 ♖xg7+ ♔xg7 45 ♘d3 ½-½.

11 Classical Main Line with 9 ♘d2 a5

1 d4 ♘f6 2 c4 g6 3 ♘c3 ♗g7 4 e4 d6 5 ♘f3 0–0 6 ♗e2 e5 7 0–0 ♘c6 8 d5 ♘e7
9   ♘d2 *(107)*

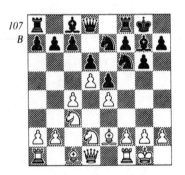

107
B

Since the mid 1980s 9 ♘d2 has been a tremendously popular way to meet the Classical Main Line. The knight looks a little clumsy on d2, but White envisages b4, c5 and ♘c4, putting great pressure on the black queenside.

This chapter concentrates on the reply 9 ... a5, and in particular the line 10 ♖b1 ♘d7 11 a3 f5 12 b4 ♔h8 which has become by far Black's most popular choice. To see why, the alternatives should

be considered.

Alternatives to 9 ... a5

9 ... c5 is the traditional move. Capturing *en passant* is not especially harmful provided Black is familiar with the subtleties, so normally there follows 10 ♖b1 ♘e8 11 b4 b6. White's knight will then never obtain its dream-posting on c4, but nevertheless White can hope for good queen-side chances. Black's position is reasonably solid, but winning chances are limited. A sample line is 12 bc bc 13 ♘b3 f5 (13 ... ♔h8 14 ♕c2!? f5 15 f4! Baikov–Krasenkov, Moscow Ch 1988) 14 ♗g5!? *(108)*.

This is Eingorn's idea, which has both tactical and positional points, viz. **14 ... h6** 15 ♗xe7 ♕xe7 16 ♘a5 and **14 ... ♘f6?!** 15 ♘xc5! dc 16 d6 both allow White a substantial edge, while **14 ... ♗f6** 15 ♗d2! (Eingorn–Hebden, Moscow 1986) leaves the bishop seriously misplaced on f6. The

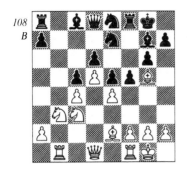

108
B

main line is **14 ... ♔h8** 15 ef gf 16 f4!? (16 ♘xc5 dc 17 d6 ♘xd6 18 ♘d5 ♖e8 appears to force a drawish ending) 16 ... h6 17 ♗h4 ef 18 ♕d2 (Chernin–A. Kuzmin, Naberezhnye Chelny 1988) which leaves Black having to defend very carefully for a draw. **9 ... a5** 10 ♖b1 c5 11 a3 ♘e8 12 b4 ab 13 ab b6 14 bc bc 15 ♘b3 f5 leads to a similar position, but without the a-pawns. The consequence of this is that 16 ♗g5 is not so powerful since ♘a5 ideas are not on; on the other hand 16 ♗d2 followed by ♖a1 gives White a queenside initiative since the knights invade quickly.

A more wild idea for Black is to ignore White's queenside play, and stake everything on the king-side attack. Sample lines are **9 ... ♘e8** 10 b4 f5 11 c5 ♔h8 (The idea is to avoid transposition to the next line, with 11 ... ♘f6 12 f3) 12 a4 (12 f3?! f4 justifies Black's idea) 12 ... ♘g8 13 ♗a3 f4 (What else? Note how valuable White's control of e4 is here) 14 a5 h5 15

b5 b6 16 cd cd 17 ♘c4 ♖b8 18 ab ab 19 ♘a2 ♘h6 20 ♘b4 ♖b7 21 ♘c6 ♕f6 22 ♗b4 and Black's queenside collapsed without a single real threat being created on the kingside (Blees–Danailov, Vienna 1990) and **9 ... ♘d7** 10 b4 f5 11 c5! (Typically, White is prepared to sacrifice this pawn to open lines and gain c4 for the knight) 11 ... ♘f6 12 f3 f4 13 ♘c4 g5 14 a4 (14 ♗a3!?) 14 ... ♘g6 15 ♗a3 ♖f7 16 b5 ♗f8 *(109)*

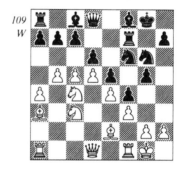

109
W

Now with 17 b6! White detonates Black's queenside. Shirov and especially Akopian are the only grandmasters who have shown any interest in playing Black here. **17 ... dc** 18 bc ♖xc7 19 ♘b5 ♖g7 20 d6± was Ftačnik–Pribyl, Czech Ch 1984; while **17 ... ab** 18 cb cb 19 ♖b1± also leaves White walking in; Akopian's idea is **17 ... cb** 18 cd (18 ♘xd6?! ♖g7! Epishin–Akopian, Minsk 1990) 18 ... ♘e8 when White can try **19 ♖c1 ♗d7** 20 ♕b3 h5 21 h3 ♖f6 22 a5 ♘xd6 23 ♘xd6 ♗xd6 24 ♗xd6 ♖xd6 25 ♕a3 ♕f6?! 26 a6 which led to success in Epishin–Akopian, Daugavpils 1989, or **19 ♘b5!?** ♗d7 20 ♗b2 ♕f6 21 ♖a2 ♘xd6 22 ♘bxd6 ♗xd6 23 ♘xd6 ♕xd6 24 ♗a3 ♕f6 25 ♕b3 ♖c8 26 ♖c2 ♖xc2 27 ♕xc2 h5 28 ♗b5 g4 29 ♗xd7 ♖xd7 30 ♕c8+ ♕d8 31 ♕xd8+ ♖xd8 32 ♖c1 which left Black with a difficult, though certainly not hopeless, ending in Ftačnik–Akopian, Groningen 1991/2.

A further approach which has enjoyed some popularity is **9 ... c6**, intending to meet 10 b4 with 10 ... a5! 11 ba ♕xa5 12 ♕c2 and then 12 ... c5 blocking lines on the queenside before playing as normal on the kingside, or Murey's 12 ... ♗d7!? intending play on the c-file. However, the problem for Black is **10 ♖b1!**. Then **10 ... b5** 11 dc b4 12 ♘d5 ♘xc6 13 ♘xf6+ ♗xf6 14 ♘f3 ♗g4 15 ♘e1! ♗e6 16 ♘c2 ♖c8 17 b3 gave White an enduring positional edge in Sher–Gallagher, Hastings 1989/90, so Black started trying **10 ... a5** 11 a3 b5 (11 ... ♕c7!? 12 b4 ab 13 ab cd 14 ed ♗f5 15 ♖b3!? Krasenkov–Marković, Vienna 1990) 12 dc b4 13 ab ab *(110)* with the point that if White continues with 14 ♘d5, Black has more queenside play than in Sher–Gallagher. Unfortunately, the lack of a-pawns gives White a strong possibility:

14 ♘b5! ♘xc6 15 ♘b3! ♗e6! 16 ♕d3! ♘e8 17 ♗e3 f5 18 f3 and in Epishin–Nunn, Vienna 1991,

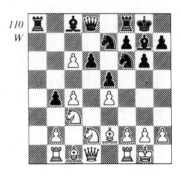

Black found no solution to the problem of the weak d-pawn; there followed 18 ... fe 19 fe ♖xf1+ 20 ♖xf1 ♕d7 21 h3 ♗f8 22 ♗g4! ♗xg4 23 hg ♕e6 24 ♘d2 ♖c8 25 ♕d5 ♘d8 26 b3 ♗e7 27 ♗b6 ♘f6 28 ♖xf6! ♗xf6 29 ♘xd6 ♖b8 30 ♗c7 ♕xd5 31 ed ♖a8 32 ♘6e4 when White's pawns were unstoppable.

The Ideas Behind 9 ... a5

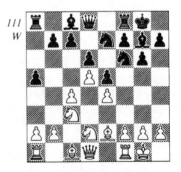

The system with 9 ... a5 aims to avoid some of the problems outlined above. Black frustrates White's ambitions of a quick b4 and c5, keeping the knight on

the less than ideal square d2, but avoiding the passive positions characteristic of the 9 ... c5 variation, and the structural weaknesses to which 9 ... c6 leads. Black also wishes to attack on the kingside, but with more subtlety than 9 ... ♘d7 or 9 ... ♘e8. The idea is not new, but for a long time was considered dubious, since Black would play too inflexibly (e.g. clarifying the kingside situation too early, or losing time with ... ♗h6) whereupon 9 ... a5 would turn out just to have weakened Black's queenside and opened lines for White, e.g. 10 ♖b1 ♘d7 11 a3 f5 12 b4 ab 13 ab ♘f6?! 14 c5 ♗h6 15 f3 ♘h5 (15 ... dc 16 ♘c4!) 16 ♘c4 ♗xc1 17 ♖xc1 ♘f4 18 g3 ♘xe2+ 19 ♕xe2 fe 20 fe ♗h3 21 ♖xf8+ ♕xf8 22 ♕f2 gave Black a truly miserable position in Dorfman–Balashov, USSR Ch (Lvov) 1984.

Black's new approach is to meet 10 ♖b1 ♘d7 11 a3 f5 12 b4 with 12 ... ♔h8!. The knight remains on d7 to hold up White's c5-advance, while the manoeuvre ... ♘g8(–f6–h5) is prepared, activating Black's worst placed piece. Above all, Black maintains the tension on the kingside. White must always be ready to meet the following black plans: advancing ... f5–f4 and a standard pawn storm; ... ♗h6 to activate or exchange this bishop; exchanging on e4 followed by piece play; the knight invasion ... ♘f6–h5–f4.

The following position *(112)*, from Karpov–Kasparov, Skellefteå 1989, illustrates the knight manoeuvre:

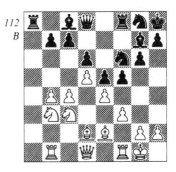

Black now played 16 ... ♘h5!. Not wishing to have a knight land on f4, Karpov replied 17 g3, which was met with 17 ... ♘hf6!. The knight's work on h5 is done, so it returns to put pressure on e4. Meanwhile, Black has provoked a weakness as a target for the ... f4 advance, and gained the possibility of a future ... ♗h3; White already has quite serious problems. Nowadays this is an entirely standard idea for Black, but was quite a surprise at the time.

If Black pushes ... f5–f4, then White must play for c4–c5 as quickly as possible. Clearly ♘b3 prepares this, but puts the knight on a bad square. Much more to the point is a pawn sacrifice, viz. *(113)*:

Vladimirov–Temirbaev, Alma Ata 1989 continued 15 c5! bc (15 ... dc 16 ba ♖xa5 17 ♘c4±) 16 bc ♘xc5 17 a4 g5?! (17 ... c6 18 dc

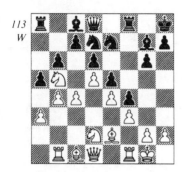

113
W

♘xc6 19 ♘c4±) 18 ♗a3 ♘a6 19 ♕c2 when White had superb queenside play. Not only does the pawn sacrifice activate all White's pieces, but by seizing the initiative so firmly, White ensures that the tempi Black has spent preparing a kingside attack are more or less wasted.

An important idea for Black is the advance ... c7–c6 to break up White's centre. Sometimes this is a reply to a premature c5 and ♘b5 (i.e. Black exchanges pawns on c5, then plays ... c6), but normally occurs after White has exchanged pawns on f5 and played f2–f4: *(114)*

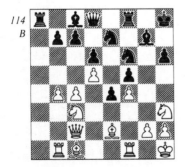

114
B

Observing that White's pieces are not terribly active, and in particular cannot control many squares on the d-file, Black, in Van der Sterren–Fishbein, Kerteminde 1991, played 20 ... c6! 21 dc (else d5 just becomes a weakness) 21 ... bc 22 ♖d1 d5 23 cd cd 24 ♘b5 ♗a6 25 ♘d4 ♗xe2 26 ♕xe2 ♕b6. Black has freed his position and has good chances.

In some instances, ... ♗g7–h6 is a good positional idea. However, this is not necessarily Black's bad bishop if White retains the option of exchanging on f5, followed by f2/f3–f4, and may represent a loss of time; consider Ivanchuk–Gelfand, Linares 1992 *(115)*:

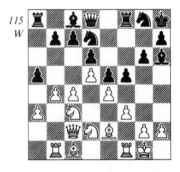

115
W

White now played highly energetically: 15 ♘b5 ab 16 ab ♘df6 17 c5 fe (17 ... ♗d7!?) 18 ♘xe4! ♘xd5? 19 cd c6 20 ♕c5 ♗d7? 21 ♗xh6 ♘xh6 22 ♘c7 and Black was soon swept aside, partly because his dark squares were defenceless.

In these variations, Black is

faced with the question of when to exchange pawns on b4. If Black exchanges too early, White may benefit from contesting the a-file, or placing the bishop on a3; additionally, Black loses the, albeit rarely useful, possibility of blocking the queenside with ... a4. Black will normally exchange the pawns when capturing on a5 is a good idea for White (e.g. when Black cannot recapture, or White can use the b-file), when the black rook wishes to use the a-file, or just when there is no point delaying it further.

The following theoretical and practical material will hopefully illuminate these and many other points.

Shirov–Fishbein
Kerteminde 1991

1 d4 ♘f6 2 c4 g6 3 ♘c3 ♗g7 4 e4 d6 5 ♘f3 0-0 6 ♗e2 e5 7 0-0 ♘c6 8 d5 ♘e7 9 ♘d2 a5

10　♖b1

10 a3 is sometimes met by 10 ... ♗d7, but there is no reason to avoid 10 ... ♘d7 on account of 11 ♖a2, since then 11 ... f5 12 b4 ♘f6 13 f3 c6!? 14 ba (14 ♔h1) 14 ... fe! 15 ♘dxe4 (15 fe ♕xa5 16 ♘b3 ♕xc3 17 ♗d2 ♘xe4) 15 ... ♘f5 16 a6 (16 c5 ♖xa5) 16 ... ♖xa6 17 c5 ♖a5 18 ♗c4 (18 dc bc 19 cd ♗e6 20 ♖b2 ♘d5∞ — Nikolić) 18 ... b5! was fine for Black in P. Nikolić–Nunn, Reykjavik 1988.

In Karpov–Kasparov, Seville

Wch (17) 1987, White sacrificed a tempo to force Black into a line with ... a5 and ... c5: **10 b3 c5! 11 a3 ♘e8 12 ♖b1 f5 13 b4 ab 14 ab b6**, but as would be expected, this is harmless — Black's position is fairly solid, even without the extra tempo.

10	**...**	**♘d7**
11	**a3**	**f5**
12	**b4**	**♔h8** *(116)*

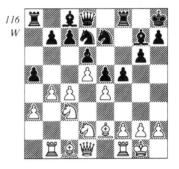

116
W

The main line is now 13 f3 ♘g8 14 ♕c2, which we consider in the third and fourth games of this chapter. The subject of the next game is the line 13 f3 f4.

Very often 13 ♕c2 is merely a transposition (after 13 ... ♘g8 14 f3); the current game deals with alternatives for Black and White.

13　♕c2

13 ♘b3 is rather ineffective: 13 ... ab 14 ab ♘f6 15 ef (15 f3?! f4 16 c5 g5 transposes to the note 'a' to White's 14th in Hernandez–Frolov below) 15 ... ♗xf5! 16 ♗d3 ♕d7 17 f3 ♘h5 18 ♗e4?! (18 ♘e4= Belov) 18 ... ♘g8 19 ♗e3 ♗h6! 20 ♕d2 ♗xe3+ 21

♕xe3 ♘gf6 22 ♕a1 ♘f4 left Black better in Kulikov–Belov, USSR 1988.

13 ba!? was successful in Azmaiparashvili–Hellers, Reyk-javik 1990, but has not been tried since, perhaps because after 13 ... ♘c5 14 a4 ♖xa5 15 ♗a3, Black could well have tried **15 ... ♘xe4!?** with equality according to *ECO*.

13 ... ♘g8

The older move is **13 ... b6** and now:

(a) **14 ♘b3** ab 15 ab fe 16 ♘xe4 ♘f6 17 ♗d3 ♘xe4 18 ♗xe4 gives Black few real problems; in Gavri-kov–Kasparov, USSR Ch (Moscow) 1988, **18 ... ♘f5** 19 ♕d3 ♕h4 20 g3 ♕f6 21 f3 ♗d7 22 ♗d2 ♘d4 23 ♘xd4 ed 24 ♖a1 ♗h3 gave adequate play, as did **18 ... ♘g8** 19 ♗d2 ♕h4 20 f3 ♘f6 21 ♖a1 ♗d7 22 b5 ♗h6 in Ruzhiale–A. Kuzmin, Blagovesh-chensk 1988.

(b) **14 ♗b2** ♘f6 (14 ... ♘g8 transposes to note (b) to White's fourteenth move) 15 ♗d3 ab 16 ab c5 17 bc bc 18 f3 h5 Sakaev–Daugela, Pinsk 1989.

(c) **14 ♔h1!?** ♘f6 15 f3 f4 16 c5 ab 17 ab g5 18 ♘b5 ♘e8 19 ♗b2 h5 20 ♖a1 ♖b8 21 ♘a7 ♗d7 22 cd cd 23 ♘c6 ♘xc6 24 dc ♗c8 25 ♖a7± Ruban–Tuzan, Sochi 1990.

(d) **14 f3 f4** is usual, and now:

(d1) **15 ♘b5 g5 16 c5 bc** (16 ... dc can be met by 17 ba ♖xa5 18 ♘c4 ♖a8 19 ♖d1±, or 17 bc ♘xc5 18 ♘c4! ♗a6 19 ♖d1 ♗xb5 20 ♖xb5 ♘b7 21 d6! ♘xd6 22 ♖xe5!

♘g6 23 ♖ed5 ♕e7 24 ♘xd6 cd, as in Østenstad–A. Kuzmin, Biel 1990, when 25 ♕c6! would have yielded a small advantage) **17 bc dc** *(117)* (17 ... ♘xc5 18 ♘b3 c6 19 dc ♘xc6 20 ♘xc5 dc 21 ♕xc5 ♗d7 22 ♗b2!± was Sakaev–Tkachev, Pinsk 1989) and now:

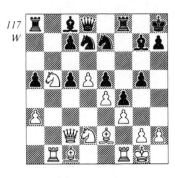

(d11) **18 ♘c3?!** ♘f6 19 ♘c4 g4 20 ♘xe5 g3 21 h3 ♘e8 22 ♘g4 (22 ♘d3 ♘g6 △ ... ♕h4) 22 ... h5 23 ♘b5 ♘d6 24 ♘e3 fe 25 ♕xc5 ♘g6 gave Black a winning attack in Sakaev–Frolov, Sochi 1990: 26 ♗xe3 ♕h4 27 ♘xc7 ♗xh3 28 ♖fc1 ♘xe4! 29 ♕b6 ♗xg2 30 ♔xg2 ♕h2+ 31 ♔f1 ♘f4 0–1.

(d12) **18 ♘b3?!** c6 is promising for Black.

(d13) **18 a4** c6 19 d6 cb 20 de ♕xe7 21 ab, when White has compensation, is given by A. Kuz-min.

(d14) **18 ♖d1** ♖f6 19 ♘c4 c6 20 ♘c3 ♖h6 21 d6± Danielian–Minasian, USSR Junior Ch 1991.

(d15) **18 ♘c4!?** c6 19 d6! cb 20 de ♕xe7 21 ♖xb5 a4 22 ♖a5! ♖xa5 23 ♘xa5 ♘b6 24 ♗d2 ♗e6

25 ♖b1 ♕c7 26 ♖b5 ♖c8 27 ♕b2 with good compensation in Boguszlavsky–V. Gurevich, Berlin 1991.

(d2) **15 ♘b3** ab 16 ab g5 17 c5 (17 g4 fg 18 hg ♘g6 19 ♘d1 ♖g8 20 ♖f2 ♘df8 21 ♖h2 ♕f6 gave Black a reasonable position in Lerner–H. Grünberg, Moscow [GMA] 1989) 17 ... ♘f6 18 ♘b5 g4! (The queenside must be abandoned to its fate) 19 cd cd 20 ♕c7 gf 21 gf (Smirin analysed 21 ♕xd8 f2+! 22 ♖xf2 ♖xd8 when the weakness of e4 and the potentially exposed rook on b1 give Black counterplay) 21 ... ♕e8!. Now bad would be **22 ♕xd6?** ♗h3 23 ♖f2 ♕g6+ 24 ♔h1 ♘xe4!, while in Gavrikov–Smirin, Klaipeda 1988, **22 ♔h1?!** ♘h5!, with ... ♘g3+ ideas, gave Black a very strong attack. Critical is **22 ♘xd6** ♕g6+ 23 ♔h1 ♘exd5 24 ed ♕xb1 25 ♖g1 ♘h5 and now Smirin gave **26 ♘f7+** ♔g8 27 ♘h6+ ♔h8 28 ♘f7+ with a perpetual, but after **26 ♘d2!?** Shevelev–Bezman, Leningrad 1989 terminated abruptly: 26 ... ♕xb4? 27 ♕e7±± ♔g8 28 ♘xc8 ♕d4 29 ♘d6 ♖f6 30 ♘2e4 1-0. Instead *ECO* recommends **26 ... ♕a2!∞** (e.g. 27 ♗c4 ♕a7 or 27 ♘f7+ ♔g8 28 ♗c4 ♕a7 29 d6 b5).

There are also three other methods for Black:

(a) **13 ... ab** 14 ab ♘f6 15 f3 g5! (15 ... f4 16 c5 g5 17 ♘c4!? is promising for White) 16 c5 ♘g6! is Kasparov's latest attempt to rip open lines towards the white king. 17 ♘c4 (17 ef ♘f4!) 17 ... ♘f4 18 cd! cd 19 ♗e3 g4 produced great complications in Vaganian–Kasparov, Manila OL 1992: 20 ♗b6! ♕e7 21 ef ♘xe2+ 22 ♘xe2 gf 23 ♖xf3 ♘xd5 (23 ... ♗d7!?) 24 ♕d2! e4! 25 ♖ff1 ♖xf5! 26 ♖xf5 ♘xb6!! and a draw resulted in the end.

(b) **13 ... ♗h6** 14 ♘b3 (14 c5!? is also critical; with the a-pawns already exchanged, Lputian–A. Kuzmin, USSR Ch (Moscow) 1991 continued 15 ... ♘f6 16 f3 fe 17 fe ♗e3+ 18 ♔h1 ♘g4 19 ♗xg4 ♗xg4 20 ♗b2 ♗xd2 21 ♕xd2 ♘g8 22 ♖xf8 ♕xf8 23 ♘b5 ♕e7, whereupon 24 ♘xc7! ♕xc7 25 cd ♕xd6 26 ♕g5 won a pawn) 14 ... ♗xc1 was tried in Komarov–Gelfand, Kramatorsk 1989, but both 15 ♖bxc1 and 15 ♕xc1 △ 15 ... ♘f6 16 f4! (Gelfand) would then have been promising for White.

(c) **13 ... fe** 14 ♘cxe4 ♘f5 15 ♘f3!? gives White some advantage. With the a-pawns (rather unnecessarily) already exchanged, Hertneck–J. Polgar, Munich 1991, continued 16 ... h6?! 17 ♗d2 ♘f6 18 ♗d3 ♘h5, when 19 ♘g3! △ 19 ... ♘f4 20 ♘xf5 ♗xf5 21 ♗xf5 ♖xf5 22 ♕e4! would have left White with a clear positional advantage. Instead 15 ... ♘f6 (Li Wenliang–Smirin, Beijing 1991) can be met by 16 ♗g5!?± △ 16 ... h6 17 ♗xf6 or 16 ♗d3 ♘h5 17 c5 ♘f4 18 ♗c4± (Li).

14 ef

White reasons that in the type of position arising after this exchange, the knight will be misplaced on g8. Black argues that the time to re-position the knight is well spent, since in return White has given ground in the centre.

14 ♗b2 is a reasonable alternative:

(a) **14 ... ♘gf6** allows White some advantage with either **15 ♖be1** f4?! 16 c5!? dc 17 bc ♘xc5 18 ♘b5 (Salov–Short, Skellefteå 1989) or **15 ♖bd1** ♘e8 16 ef gf 17 ♔h1 ♕h4 18 g3 ♕h3 19 ♘f3 ♕h6 20 ♗c1 (Pinter–Sznapik, Haifa 1989).

(b) **14 ... b6** 15 ♖be1 ♗h6 16 ef gf 17 g3 f4 18 ♗f3 ♘df6 19 ♗g2 ♘g4! 20 ♘f3 ♗f5 21 ♕d1 ab 22 ab fg 23 hg ♕e8 24 ♘h4 ♕h5 25 f4 ♗g7 26 ♗h3 ♗f6 27 fe ♗xh4 28 gh ♕xh4 29 ♕f3 ♘xe5 30 ♖xe5 ♗xh3 31 ♘e4! led to interesting complications and an eventual draw in Dokhoian–Griego, Philadelphia 1990.

(c) **14 ... ♘df6** 15 ♖bd1 (15 ♖be1!?; 15 ♖bc1 ♗h6!; 15 c5 fe 16 ♘dxe4 ♘xe4 17 ♘xe4 ♘f6=) 15 ... ♗d7 16 ef (16 c5? ab 17 ab fe 18 ♘dxe4 ♘xe4∓ 19 ♘xe4? ♗a4∓∓ illustrates a point of Black's previous move) 16 ... gf. Now Illescas–Khalifman, Manila IZ 1990 continued **17 f4?!** ef! 18 ♖xf4 ab 19 ab ♘e7! when Black had good kingside play. Instead Khalifman gives **17 c5!** ♕e7 18 cd cd 19 ♘c4±.

14 ♘b5 is perhaps not so troublesome. Khalifman recommends simply **14 ... fe** 15 ♘xe4 ♘gf6=, while in Lipman–Gezalian, Moscow 1989, **14 ... ab** 15 ab ♘df6 16 ef?! c6!? 17 dc bc 18 ♘c3 gf gave Black good prospects. Khalifman–Torre, Manila IZ 1990 proceeded **14 ... ♘df6** 15 f3 (15 ♗d3 ab 16 ab ♘h5 17 ♘f3 ♘gf6 18 ♗g5 ♘f4 left Black with no problems at all in Vaganian–Marin, Manila IZ 1990) 15 ... ♗d7 (15 ... ♘h5 16 c5! ♘f4 17 ♘c4 gives White some advantage, but Black should try 15 ... ab 16 ab ♗d7) 16 ba!? ♖xa5 17 c5! fe 18 fe ♘g4 19 ♘f3 ♗xb5 20 ♖xb5 ♖xb5 21 ♗xb5 ♗h6 22 ♕c3 ♗xc1, when 23 ♖xc1 (Khalifman) would have given White powerful play on the c-file.

14 ... gf
15 f4 ♘e7

Three other plans have been adopted:

(a) **15 ... ♘h6** 16 ♘f3 e4 17 ♘e1 ab 18 ab ♘f6 19 h3 c6 20 ♗e3 cd 21 cd (Knaak suggests 21 ♘xd5!?) 21 ... ♗d7 22 ♕d2 ♖c8 23 ♘c2 ♘h5 24 ♗xh5 ♖xc3 25 ♗e2 ♕c7= Danielian–Anapolsky, Jurmala 1991.

(b) **15 ... ab** 16 ab e4 17 ♘b3 ♖f6!? (17 ... ♘df6 18 ♗e3 ♕e7 19 ♘d4 ♘h6 20 h3 ♗d7 21 c5 ♖g8 22 c6 bc 23 dc ♗e8 24 b5 ♖b8 25 ♖a1 ♕f7 26 ♖a7 gave White strong pressure in Lputian–Loginov, Azov 1991) 18 ♘d4 (18 g4!?) 18 ... ♘f8 19 ♗e3 ♖g6 20 g3 ♘f6 21 ♖a1 ♖b8 22 ♔h1 h5 23 ♖g1 ♗d7 24 c5 dc 25 bc c6 26 dc bc 27 ♖a6 ♕c8 28 ♖b6 h4 29 ♕b3 ♖a8 30 ♔g2 ♕e8 31 ♖b1 ♖h6 led to an impressive Black win in Browne–Fedorowicz, San Francisco 1991: 32 ♖b8 ♖xb8 33 ♕xb8 ♕g6 34 ♖b7 hg 35 hg ♕h7 36 ♗g1 ♖h1 37 ♕d6 ♕h3+ 38 ♔f2 e3+ 39 ♔xe3 ♖xg1 40 ♘f3 ♖c1 41 ♘a2 ♖c2 42 ♖b8 ♗e8 43 ♘b4 ♖b2 44 ♘xc6 ♖xe2+ 45 ♔xe2 ♕g2+ 46 ♔e1 ♕xg3+ 47 ♔d2 ♕xf3 48 ♘d4 ♕h1 49 ♔e2 ♗h5+ 50 ♔d3 ♕d1+ 51 ♔c4 ♗f7+ 52 ♔b5 ♘e8 0–1.

(c) **15 ... ef 16 ♘f3 ♘e5** (16 ... ♘e7 17 ♗xf4 ♘g6 18 ♗g5 ♘f6 19 ♖be1 ab 20 ab h6 21 ♘h4 ♘e5 22 ♗f4 ♘h5 23 ♗xe5 ♕xh4 24 ♗xg7+ ♘xg7 25 ♕d2± Arlandi–J. Polgar, Portorož/Nova Gorica 1991) **17 ♗xf4** *(118)* and now:

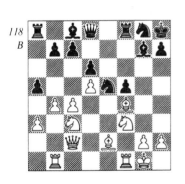

(c1) **17 ... ♘xf3+** 18 ♗xf3 ab 19 ab ♘h6 20 ♔h1 ♘g4 21 c5 ♘e5 22 ♘b5± Lputian–Torre, Manila IZ 1990.

(c2) **17 ... ♘g6** 18 ♗g5 ♗f6 19 ♗xf6+ ♕xf6 20 ♖bd1± Ambart-

sumian–Nalbandian, Erevan 1991.

(c3) **17 ... ab 18 ab ♗d7!?**, introduced by Bagaturov, has been the starting point for a number of games:

(c31) **19 ♘b5!?** ♘e7 20 ♕d2 (Sulipa–Tondivar, Groningen 1991/2) 20 ... ♘xf3+ 21 ♖xf3 ♘g6 22 ♗h6± (Sulipa).

(c32) **19 c5!?** ♕f6! 20 ♘xe5 (20 ♗b5 c6∞) 20 ... de 21 ♗e3 (21 ♗d2 ♖ae8 22 ♗h5 ♖d8 23 ♔h1 ♕h4 24 ♗f3 ♘f6 25 ♗e1 ♕h6 26 ♖d1 ♖de8 27 ♗d2 ½–½. Dokhoian–Heissler, Bundesliga 1991/2) 21 ... ♕g6! (21 ... e4 22 ♖b3 ♕e5 23 ♗f4! is good for White) 22 ♘b5!? (22 b5?! f4!∞ Ambartsumian–Edelman, Los Angeles 1991) 22 ... ♗xb5 23 ♗xb5 c6 24 ♗d3 e4 25 ♗c4± (Lputian).

(c33) **19 ♘xe5** de 20 ♗e3 ♖a6! 21 c5 ♖g6 22 ♗h5 ♖g5! 23 ♗xg5 ♕xg5 24 ♗e2 e4! with good compensation was Bagaturov's rather astonishing idea.

(c34) **19 ♖bd1** is best met by 19 ... ♘xf3+ 20 ♗xf3 (20 ♖xf3 ♘f6! 21 ♗g5 ♕e8 22 ♖df1 ♘g4!) 20 ... ♖a3 21 ♘e2 (21 ♖d3 ♕f6 22 ♘e2 ♖fa8!∞) 21 ... ♗a4 22 ♕c1 ♖a1 23 ♕xa1 ♗xa1 24 ♖xa1 ♗d7 25 ♗e3!? ♘e7! 26 ♗d4+ ♔g8 27 ♗h5!? ♘g6 28 ♖a3 f4! 29 ♗xg6 hg 30 ♘xf4 ♕h4∞, as analysed by Ambartsumian and Lputian. Instead, the game Ambartsumian–Bagaturov, USSR 1991 continued 19 ... ♕f6?! 20 ♘d4±.

16 ♘f3

Rather harmless was 16 fe ♘xe5
17 ♘f3 (17 ♘b3 ab 18 ab ♗d7)
17 ... ♘xf3+ 18 ♗xf3 ♘g6= 19
♘e2 ab 20 ab ♕e7 21 ♘f4 ♗d7 22
♔h1 ♘xf4 ½–½ in Berg–Fishbein,
Kerteminde 1991.

16 ... e4

16 ... ♘g6 17 ♘g5 ♘f6 18 fe de
19 ♔h1 ab 20 ab ♘f4 21 ♗xf4 ef
22 ♗f3 gave Black a difficult,
though not hopeless game in G.
Georgadze–Neverov, Podolsk
1989.

17 ♘g5 ♘f6 *(119)*

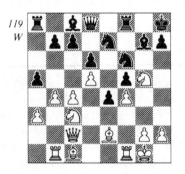

119
W

18 ♗b2

The alternatives are no better:
(a) **18 ♔h1** ab 19 ab h6 20 ♘h3
c6 dissolved White's centre, giving
Black fully adequate play in Van
der Sterren–Fishbein, Kerteminde
1991. Play continued 21 dc bc 22
♖d1 d5 23 cd cd 24 ♘b5 ♗a6 25
♘d4 ♗xe2 26 ♕xe2 ♕b6 27 ♘f2
♘d7 (27 ... ♖a4!?) 28 ♗e3 ♕g6
29 ♖a1? (29 b5) 29 ... ♖xa1 30
♖xa1 ♘c6 21 ♕d2 (31 ♕d1) 31 ...
♘b6 32 ♖a6 ♘c4 33 ♖xc6 ♕xc6
34 ♘xc6 ♘xd2 35 ♗xd2 where-

upon 35 ... d4 would have left
White's pieces unable to cope with
the active rook and the two passed
pawns.

(b) With the a-pawns already
exchanged, M. Gurevich–Wahls,
Tåstrup 1992 continued **19 ♖d1**
c6 20 ♗e3 h6 21 ♘e6 ♗xe6 22
de ♘c8! 23 g4 ♕e8! 24 gf ♘e7 25
♘xe4 ♘xf5 26 ♗f2 ♘xe4 27 ♕xe4
♕g6+ 28 ♕g2 ♕xe6 29 ♕f3 ♖a2
30 ♗f1 ♘d4! 31 ♗xd4 ♗xd4+
32 ♖xd4 (32 ♔h1 ♖f2) 32 ...
♕g6+ when Black won an
exchange for no substantial compensation.

18 ... ab
19 ab c6

The standard freeing move for
Black.

20 dc bc
21 ♖fd1 ♕c7!

The indirect pressure on f4 is
very useful.

22 ♕d2 h6
23 ♘h3 ♖d8

Shirov pointed out that Black
could obtain equal play with **23
... ♕b6+** 24 ♔h1 ♕xb4 25 ♘xe4
♕xd2 26 ♘xd2. Fishbein's actual
choice leads to a more complicated game.

24 b5 ♗e6
25 ♕e3! c5
26 ♕g3! ♖g8?!

This natural move has the tactical drawback of boxing in the
black king. Fishbein indicates **26
... ♗f7** and **26 ... ♔h7** as preferable.

27 ♖d2 d5?

After this, Black has serious problems. **27 ... ♘d7** invites **28 ♘g5!**, but Black should try **27 ... ♖ad8**, still with a reasonable position.

28	cd	♘exd5
29	♘xd5	♘xd5
30	♕h4!	♗xb2
31	♕xh6+	♕h7
32	♕xh7+	♔xh7
33	♖dxb2	♔h6

Now **34 ♖c1!** would have been strong: **34 ... ♖a3 35 ♘g5! ♘xf4 36 ♘xe6 ♘xe6 37 ♗c4++** or **34 ... ♘b6 35 ♘g5 ♗d5 36 ♖xc5 ♘a4 37 ♖xd5 ♘xb2 38 ♖xf5++**. Instead in the game, a series of time trouble mistakes gave Black a decisive endgame advantage, which was converted accurately to a full point:

34 b6? ♘b4! 35 ♖c1?! ♖a5! 36 ♖d2?! ♗d5 37 ♖cd1? e3!∓∓ 38 ♖xd5 ♘xd5 39 ♖xd5 ♖a1+ 40 ♖d1 ♖xd1+ 41 ♗xd1 ♖d8! 42 ♔f1 (42 ♗e2 c4!) 42 ... ♖xd1+ 43 ♔e2 ♖d2+ 44 ♔xe3 ♖xg2 45 ♘f2 ♖g6 46 ♘d3 ♖xb6 47 ♘xc5 ♖b2 48 ♘e6 ♖xh2 49 ♘d4 ♖h3+ 50 ♔f2 ♔g6 51 ♔e2 ♖a3 52 ♘c2 ♖a2! 53 ♔d3 ♖a4! 54 ♔e3 ♖c4! 55 ♘d4 ♖c3+ 56 ♔e2 ♖c5 57 ♘f3 ♔h5 58 ♘e5 ♖c3 59 ♔f2 ♔h4 60 ♔g2 ♖b3 0-1.

Hernandez–Frolov
Havana 1991

1 d4 ♘f6 2 c4 g6 3 ♘c3 ♗g7 4 e4 d6 5 ♘f3 0-0 6 ♗e2 e5 7 0-0 ♘c6 8 d5 ♘e7 9 ♘d2 a5 10 ♖b1

♘d7 11 a3 f5 12 b4 ♔h8 13 f3 f4 *(120)*

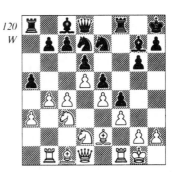

14 c5

Again White has a choice of several alternatives:

(a) **14 ♘b3?!** is rather too slow. After **14 ... ab 15 ab g5 16 c5 ♘f6!**, White has suffered badly in practice:

(a1) **17 g4 h5 18 h3 ♘g6 19 ♗d2 ♘h4 20 ♖a1?! ♖xa1 21 ♕xa1? hg 22 hg ♘xg4! 23 fg f3 24 ♗c4 ♕d7! 25 ♔f2 ♕xg4 26 ♖g1 ♕h3 0-1** Gofman–Belov, USSR 1988.

(a2) **17 ♗d2 ♘g6 18 c6 b6 19 ♗e1 ♖g8 20 ♘d2 h5 21 ♘b5 g4 22 ♖a1 ♖xa1 23 ♕xa1 g3 24 ♕a8 (24 ♕a7 ♘e8; 24 hg fg 25 ♗xg3 ♗h6 26 ♘c4 ♘f4∓∓) 24 ... ♘h7∓∓ 25 hg fg 26 f4 ef! 27 ♕b8 ♘e5 28 ♖xf4 ♕g5 29 ♖f3 ♘xf3+ 30 ♗xf3 ♕e3+ 31 ♔f1 ♗a6 0-1** Dreev–Shirov, Borzhomi 1988.

(b) **14 ♘a4** (decentralising) is best met by **14 ... ab 15 ab c6!?**, attacking the centre:

(b1) **16 ♗b2 ♘f6 17 dc ♘xc6 18 c5 dc 19 ♘xc5** should perhaps be met by Ftačnik's **19 ... ♘xb4!?**

20 ♘c4 ♕e7 21 ♕d6 ♕xd6 22 ♘xd6 b6!?∞. Instead **19 … ♘d4** 20 ♘c4 ♘h5 (20 … ♖a2!?) 21 ♖f2! b6 22 ♘d3 ♘g3 23 ♗f1 ♘xf1 24 ♖xf1 ♖a2 25 b5!± gave Black problems on the long diagonal in Polugaevsky–Hellers, Biel 1989.

(b2) **16 c5** cd (16 … dc!?) 17 cd ♘c6 18 ed ♘d4 gave Black plenty of play in Salov–Nunn, Rotterdam 1989. Nunn then gave **19 ♘c5** ♘xc5! 20 bc ♕a5 21 ♘e4 ♗f5 22 ♗d2 ♕a3 as equal, since 23 ♗b4? ♕e3+ 24 ♖f2 ♗xe4 25 fe ♖a2 wins for Black. The game in fact continued **19 ♘c3?!** ♘b6 20 ♘de4 ♗f5 21 ♗d3 ♖c8 22 ♗b2 (22 ♘c5 ♖f7∓) 22 … ♗xe4 23 ♗xe4? (23 fe ♕xd6∓) 23 … ♘c4 24 ♕d3 ♕xd6∓.

(c) **14 ♘b5** may well be White's best — an active move, preparing the c5 thrust. Practice has seen:

(c1) In W. Schmidt–Sznapik, Krynica 1988, **14 … g5** 15 c5 dc 16 bc ♘xc5 17 a4 c6 18 ♗a3 ♘a6 (18 … cb 19 ♗xc5 b4 20 ♘c4) 19 dc bc 20 ♘d6 ♘b4 21 ♘2c4 ♗e6 allowed White the strong possibility 22 ♘xa5! ♕xa5 23 ♗xb4 ♕xa4 24 ♕xa4 ♖xa4 25 ♘b7±.

(c2) Vladimirov–Temirbaev, Alma Ata 1989, varied with **14 … b6** 15 c5 bc (15 … dc 16 ba ♖xa5 17 ♘c4+) 16 bc ♘xc5 17 a4 g5?! (17 … c6 18 dc ♘xc6 19 ♘c4 ♘d4 20 ♘cxd6 leaves White only marginally better, according to Vladimirov) 18 ♗a3 ♘a6 19 ♕c2 ♖f7 20 ♖fc1 ♘g6 21 ♕c6 ♗d7 22 ♕b7 ♗e8 23 ♘a7! and White's

queenside invasion turned out successful: 23 … ♘b4 (23 … c5 24 dc ♖xa7 25 ♗xa6++) 24 ♗xb4 ab (24 … c5 25 ♗xa5 ♖xb7 26 ♗xd8 ♖bxa7 27 ♗b6 ♖xa4 28 ♘c4 ♗f8 29 ♗c7+) 25 ♖xb4! c5 26 dc ♖xa7 27 ♕b8+.

(d) **14 ♕c2** waiting for a committal reply, is worth considering. **14 … g5** 15 ♘b5 b6 is considered under the move order 13 ♕c2 b6 14 f3 f4 15 ♘b5 g5, while for **14 … ab** 15 ab ♘f6 see 13 ♕c2 ab 14 ab ♘f6 15 f3 f4. Both these lines are promising for White.

14	**…**	**dc**

A new plan, introduced in this game. Previously Black had inserted the exchange of a-pawns: **14 … ab 15 ab** and now:

(a) **15 … ♘f6?!** 16 ♘c4 ♘e8 17 ♗a3 g5 18 b5 b6 19 cb cb 20 ♘a4 ♖b8 21 ♗b4 h5 22 ♘axb6!?± Lputian–Timoshchenko, Belgrade (GMA) 1988.

(b) **15 … dc** 16 bc ♘xc5 17 ♘c4 b6 18 ♗a3 ♗a6 19 ♗xc5 (19 ♘b5 ♘c8 20 ♗xc5 bc 21 ♘a5 ♘d6 22 ♘c6 ♕d7 23 ♕c2 g5 24 ♕xc5 g4 25 ♕f2 gf 26 gf ♗xb5 27 ♗xb5 ♗f6 28 ♔h1 ♕h3 29 ♖g1 ♕h5 30 ♗d3 ♘f7 31 ♖g4 ♖g8= Kantsler–Loginov, Azov 1991) 19 … bc 20 ♕c2 c6 (20 … ♗xc4 21 ♗xc4 c6 22 ♖fd1 cd 23 ♗xd5 ♖b8 (Shirov–Safin, Dimitovgrad 1988) would have favoured White after 24 ♘b5!±) 21 ♘b6 ♗xe2 22 ♘xe2 ♖b8 23 d6 (Van der Sterren–Gelfand, Amsterdam 1989) 23 … ♕xd6 24 ♖bd1 ♘d5 25 ♘xd5 (25

♘c4 ♘b4!) 25 ... cd 26 ♖xd5 yields equality.

15	bc	♘xc5
16	a4	♘e6!? *(121)*

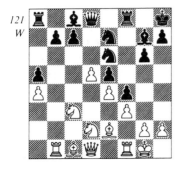

17 ♗a3

In Lerner–Frolov, USSR Ch (Moscow) 1991, White refused to allow the knight to reach d4, but his suspect idea turned out badly: 17 de ♕d4+ 18 ♔h1 ♕xc3 19 ♘c4 ♕d4 20 ♗a3 ♖e8 21 ♕c2 ♘c6 22 ♖b5 ♕a7 23 ♕b2 ♖xe6 (White's compensation is nebulous, to say the least) 24 ♖d1 ♖e8 25 ♗f1 b6 26 ♕c3 ♗a6 27 ♖bd5 ♘d4 28 ♖d7 b5 29 ♘xa5 ba 30 ♗c5 ♕b8 31 ♖xg7 ♔xg7 32 ♗xd4 c5! 33 ♗xc5 ♗xf1 34 ♖xf1 ♕b5 35 ♖c1 and 0–1.

17	...	♘d4
18	♗c4	g5
19	♘e2	c6!
20	d6	♘g6
21	♘xd4	ed
22	♘b3	♘e5

An alternative is **22 ... g4!?**; Frolov gives 23 d7 ♗xd7 24 ♘xd4 c5 25 ♗xc5 ♖c8 26 ♗b6 ♖xc4 27 ♗xd8 ♗xd4+ 28 ♔h1 ♖xd8

as the critical line.

23	♗e2	g4
24	d7	

After **24 ♘xd4 g3** 25 d7 ♕h4 26 h3 ♗xd7 27 ♗xf8 ♖xf8 28 ♘f5 ♗xf5 29 ef ♘f7! Black's rather blunt threats force White to act with caution.

24	...	♗xd7
25	♗xf8	♕xf8
26	♘xd4	♖d8!
27	♕c1	

27 ♕c2 gf followed by ... ♘g4 would give Black good chances. After the text, some forcing play leads to the return of the sacrificed exchange and an agreement to end hostilities: 27 ... ♘d3! 28 ♕c4 (28 ♗xd3? ♗xd4+ 29 ♔h1 g3 leads to mate) 28 ... ♗c8 29 ♘f5 (29 ♘c6? lets Black's attack flare up anew: 29 ... bc 30 ♗xd3 ♕d6! 31 ♗e2 ♗d4+ 32 ♔h1 g3∓∓. The text prevents ... ♗xh3 ideas, so Black has no choice but to chop wood) 29 ... ♗xf5 30 ef ♗d4+ 31 ♔h1 ♘f2+ 32 ♖xf2 ♗xf2 33 ♕xf4 ♕e7! 34 ♗f1 gf 35 ♕xf3 ♗d4 ½–½.

Ftačnik–Wang Zili
Sydney 1991

1 d4 ♘f6 2 c4 g6 3 ♘c3 ♗g7 4 e4 d6 5 ♘f3 0–0 6 ♗e2 e5 7 0–0 ♘c6 8 d5 ♘e7 9 ♘d2 a5 10 ♖b1 ♘d7 11 a3 f5 12 b4 ♔h8

13	♕c2	♘g8
14	f3	♘gf6 *(122)*

It is too early to move the knight from d7, as this gives White too free a hand on the queenside: **14 ... ab** 15 ab ♘df6?! 16 c5 ♘h5 17 ♘c4! (No need for 17 g3 here) 17 ... ♘f4 **18 ♗e3 ♛g5** 19 ♗d3 ♗d7 20 ♔h1 ♛e7 21 b5 dc 22 b6 c6 23 ♗xf4 ef 24 e5 pushes Black off the board (Epishin–Kindermann, Vienna 1991). This certainly seems convincing, but Kasparov played the same line against Khalifman (Paris Immopar 1991), who played weakly: **18 cd** cd 19 ♘b5 ♖a6 20 ♖b3? fe 21 fe ♗d7! 22 ♘c3 ♖a1∓. What he intended after 18 ♗e3 remains a mystery.

14 ... b6 is perhaps playable: 15 ♘b5 ♗h6 16 ♘b3 a4 17 ♗xh6 ♘xh6 18 ♘d2 f4 19 ♖bc1 g5 20 g4 fg 21 hg ♗a6 22 ♔g2 ♖f6 23 ♖h1 ♖g6 24 ♘f1 ♘f6 25 g4 ♘hg8 26 ♘e3 ♗xb5 27 cb ♖a7; Black's position is passive, but he survived in Dautov–Timoshchenko, Podolsk 1990.

14 ... ♗h6 is unpopular, but has achieved reasonable results:

(a) **15 ♘b3** ab 16 ab ♘df6 17 ♘a5 (17 c5 fe 18 fe ♘g4!?; 17 ♗xh6 ♘xh6 18 ♖a1 ♖xa1 19 ♖xa1 fe 20 ♘xe4 ♘xe4 21 fe ♛h4 22 g3 ♛e7 23 ♗f1 ½–½ L. Hansen–Berg, Gausdal (Arnold Cup) 1990; 17 ef?! ♗xf5 18 ♗d3 ♘h5 19 g3 ♗xc1 20 ♖bxc1 ♛g5 was more than fine for Black in Schüssler–Zapata, Palma (GMA) 1989) 17 ... ♘h5 18 g3 ♘hf6! 19 ♖f2 ♛e7 (19 ... ♔g7; 19 ... f4 20 ♗d2 fg 21 hg ♘h5 22 ♔g2∞ Epishin) 20 ♗d2 ♔g7 21 ♖c1 ♗xd2 22

♛xd2 ♘h6 23 ♗d3! fe 24 fe ♗h3 25 ♗f1 (25 ♘xb7?! ♘fg4 allows Black dangerous play on the f-file) 25 ... b6! 26 ♗xh3 (26 ♘c6 ♛d7) 26 ... ba 27 ba ♖xa5 28 ♗e6 (28 ♖cf1 ♖a3! threatens ... ♖xc3) 28 ... ♖aa8 29 ♖cf1 ♘fg4 30 ♖xf8 ♖xf8 31 ♖xf8 ♛xf8 32 h3 ♘f6 33 g4 ♘f7 34 ♗xf7 ♛xf7 35 ♛f2 ♛e7 36 ♛a7 ½–½ Epishin–A. Kuzmin, USSR Ch (Moscow) 1991.

(b) **15 ef** ab! (Exchanging pawns now allows Black to preserve his dark-square bishop from exchange — desirable now that the long diagonal is less obstructed) 16 ab gf 17 ♘b3 ♗g7 18 ♗d3 ♘df6 19 ♗g5 ♘e7 20 ♖a1 ♖xa1 21 ♖xa1 c6! gave Black good play in Polugaevsky–Wahls, Biel 1990.

(c) **15 c5** ab 16 ab dc 17 bc ♘xc5 18 ♘b5 b6 19 ♗b2 ♗g7 20 ♘c4 ♛e7 21 d6 cd 22 ♘xb6 ♖b8 23 ♘d5 ♛d7 24 ♘xd6 ♛xd6 25 ♗a3 ♖xb1 26 ♖xb1 ♗e6! 27 ♖b6 ♛d7 28 ♗xc5 ♖a8 29 ♛d1 ♛c8 30 ♖b5 ♛d7 31 ♖b1 fe ½–½ Illescas–B. Ivanović, Manila IZ 1990.

(d) **15 ♘b5** seems the critical test of Black's plan, on the current evidence: **15 ... ab** (15 ... b6 — see 14 ... b6) **16 ab ♘df6 17 c5** and now Black must choose carefully:

(d1) **17 ... fe** 18 ♘xe4! (18 fe ♘g4 19 ♗xg4 ♗xg4 20 ♘f3 ♗xf3 21 gf ♖f7∞ Ivanchuk) 18 ... ♘xd5? (18 ... ♗xc1 19 ♖fxc1 ♘xe4 20 fe ♗d7± Ivanchuk) 19 cd c6?! 20 ♛c5?! (20 ♗xh6 ♘xh6 21 ♛c5) 20 ... ♗d7? (20 ... ♗xc1) 21

♗xh6 ♘xh6 22 ♘c7 b6 23
♕c1+± ♘f4 24 ♕b2 ♘xe2+ 25
♕xe2 ♖c8 26 ♕b2 ♘f7 27 f4 ♘xd6
28 ♕xe5+ ♔g8 29 ♘e6! ♗xe6
30 ♕xe6+ ♘f7 31 ♖bd1 ♕c7 32
♖d7 ♕b8 33 f5 1-0 Ivanchuk–
Gelfand, Linares 1992.

(d2) Ivanchuk considers that
after **17 ... ♗e3+ 18 ♔h1 ♗d7
19 cd** (19 ♖b3 f4) 19 ... cd (19 ...
♗xb5!?) **20 ♘xd6 ♗a4 21 ♕d3
♗xd2 22 ♘xb7 ♕b6 23 ♗xd2
♕xb7 24 ♗c3** (△ b5) White has
good compensation.

(d3) **17 ... ♗d7!?** may well be
best. Then **18 cd** cd 19 ♘xd6? fails
to 19 ... ♗a4 20 ♕c5 b6, while
18 c6 bc 19 dc ♗e6 △ ... ♕b8
gives counterplay. Ivanchuk
recommends **18 ♘b3!?**.

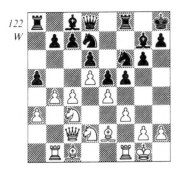

15   ♘b5

In the game Ivanchuk–Kasparov, Linares 1992, White introduced a new plan, investing a
tempo to encourage Black to close
the position: **15 ♗d3!?** f4. Now
the irritating ... ♘h5–f4
manoeuvre is impossible, but following White's standard version

of the c5 pawn sacrifice, a black
knight on c5 will attack the d3
bishop. So there followed **16 ♘b5
b6 17 c5** (M. Gurevich has sought
to improve White's game with 17
♗b2!?) **17 ... dc** (After 17 ... bc,
Seirawan gives 18 ♘b3! ♘e8! 19
♘xa5 g5∞, while 18 ba ♖xa5 19
♘c4 ♖a8 20 a4 is also possible)
**18 ba ♖xa5 19 ♘c4 ♖a8 20 a4
♘e8 21 a5** *(123)*:

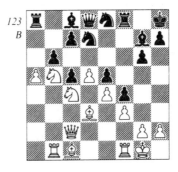

(a) Kasparov found a way to
ensure that White could only
regain the pawns by exchanging
off most of the pieces liable to
harm Black: **21 ... ♗a6 22 ♗d2
♗xb5 23 ♖xb5 ♘d6 24 ♖b2** (24
♘xd6?! cd 25 ab ♘xb6 26 ♗a5
♖xa5! 27 ♖xa5 ♘xd5∓) **24 ...
♕e7!?** (24 ... ♖f6) 25 ♘xd6 (25 ab
♘xb6 26 ♘xb6 cb 27 ♖xb6? fails
to 27 ... c4 followed by ... ♕a7)
**25 ... ♕xd6 26 ♗b5 ba! 27 ♗c6
♖ab8 28 ♖a2 ♖f7 29 ♖xa5 ♗f8**
(Black's kingside counterplay is
finally becoming organised.
Kasparov felt that the position is
dangerous for White, if Black can
avoid the exchange on d7 with

a well-timed ... ♘b6) 30 ♗c1
(Seirawan suggests 30 ♖b1 as a
quicker way to obtain play on the
long diagonal, as White intends
♗c3 and ♕b2) 30 ... g5 31 ♗b2?
♕f6? (31 ... ♘b6!) 32 ♗xd7 ♖xd7
33 ♖fa1 ♗d6 34 ♗a3 g4 35
♗xc5 ♖g8 36 ♖a8 ♖g7 37 ♔h1
♕g6 38 ♗xd6 cd 39 ♖c8 gf 40
♖xg8+ ♖xg8 41 gf ½–½.

(b) The World Champion later
indicated a promising alternative:
21 ... ba!? 22 ♗d2 a4 23 ♖a1 (23
♘a5 ♗a6 24 ♕xa4 ♘d6) 23 ...
c6! 24 dc ♘b8∓.

Ftačnik mentions a further idea
with ♗d3: **15 ef** gf 16 ♗d3 ab 17
ab ♘b6.

15 ...   ♘h5

It is more normal for Black to
insert the exchange of a-pawns at
this point (White could now try
16 ba!?) as Black seems to gain
nothing from delaying this further.
15 ... b6?! 16 ef! gf 17 f4 ab 18
ab gave White the advantge in
Lerner–Smirin, USSR Ch (Leningrad) 1989, since ... b7–b6 has
only weakened the c6-square.

**16   g3   ♘df6
17   c5**

With the a-pawns already
exchanged, Lobron–Gelfand,
Dortmund 1990 continued **18 ♖b3**
fe 19 ♘xe4 (19 fe ♗h3 20 ♖e1
♗d7) 19 ... ♗h3 20 ♖d1! ♘xe4
21 fe ♕d7 and now Gelfand gave
22 c5!? ♘f6 23 c6 bc 24 ♕c8
(24 ... ♕f7 25 ♗c4) 25 ♘c3 as
slightly favouring White. Instead
after **22 ♖f3** ♘f6 23 ♘c3 ♖f7

24 ♖e1 h5 25 ♘d1 ♗g4 26 ♖ff1
♖af8 Black had at least equalised
comfortably.

17   ...   fe

For 17 ... ab 18 ab ♗d7 and
the plan of sacrificing on g3, see
the next game, Karpov–Kasparov.

**18   fe   ab
19   ab**

Ftačnik felt there was little to
be gained from 19 cd cd 20 ♕c7
ba 21 ♕xd6 a2 22 ♖a1∞, so the
game reverts to normal channels.

**19   ...   ♗h3
20   ♖f2**

20 ♖e1 may turn out to be a
better try for advantage. 20 ...
♗h6 would well be a decent reply
(compare 18 ... ♗d7 19 ♖b3 fe
20 fe ♗h3 21 ♖e1 ♗h6), whilst
20 ... ♕d7 21 ♖b3 gives White
ideas with c6 (as in the main game).
After **20 ... ♘g4 21 ♖f3**, Van Wely
suggests that 21 ... ♗h6 may be
OK: 22 ♖b3 (22 ♗xh6 ♘xh6 23
♕d2 ♘f7 △ ... ♘f6∞) 22 ... ♖a1!?
intending exchanges on c1, followed by ... h6 and ... ♘hf6 with
pressure on e4; but practice has
seen **21 ... h6** *(124)* (planning ...
♖f7):

(a) **22 ♖b3!?** ♖f7 (Van Wely's
recommendation is 22 ... ♘hf6
intending ♘e8, ... ♖f7 and ...
♕d7. If White meets this with c6,
then the queen will find its way to
the g1–a7 diagonal via c8 and b8)
23 ♗f1 ♗xf1 24 ♖xf1 ♗f8 25
c6! (White is alert and prevents 25
... dc 26 bc c6) 25 ... bc 26 dc ♕e8
(26 ... d5 27 ♔g2 de 28 ♕xe4

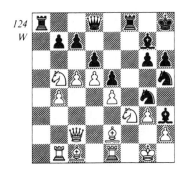

124
W

♖a2+ 29 ♖b2 ♖xb2+ 30 ♗xb2
♘hf6 31 ♕e2 ♘d5 32 ♘xe5!±
Khuzman) 27 ♕c4! ♖a2 28 ♖a3!
♖xa3 29 ♘xa3 d5! 30 ♕xd5!
♗xb4 (Khuzman–J. Ivanov, Wijk
aan Zee 1992) 31 ♘c2 ♘gf6 32
♕c4 ♗f8 33 ♗b2±± (Khuz-
man).

(b) **22 cd** cd 23 ♕c7 ♕xc7 24
♘xc7 ♖a2 25 ♖b2 ♖a3 (Gelfand
gives 25 ... ♖xb2 26 ♗xb2 ♖c8
27 ♖c1 ♘hf6 28 ♗d3! h5 29
♘e6!±) 26 ♘h4 ♔h7 27 ♘b5!
(Black has problems with the d6-
pawn and with his kingside pieces,
which are rather bogged down) 27
... ♖a6 28 ♖c2 ♖f7?! (28 ... ♖f2?
29 ♗xg4 ♖xc2 30 ♗xh3 ♖a1 31
♗d2 ♖aa2 32 ♗e3±± is no
good, but Van Wely argues that
there was no desperate need to
keep the rook out of c7, so 28 ...
♗f6!? was correct) 29 ♘f3 ♗f6
and now **30 ♗f1!** ♗xf1 31 ♖xf1
♖b6 32 ♘c3 ♖c7!? 33 h3 ♘xg3 34
♖e1 ♖xb4 35 hg ♖bc4 36 ♗d2
(Gelfand) gives White a decisive
material advantage. Instead **30
♘d2?** ♗d8 31 ♘c4 ♖f2 32 ♘e3

♗b6? (32 ... ♖xh2! 33 ♗xg4
♖xc2 34 ♗xh3 ♗b6∓∓) 33
♖c7+! ♗xc7 34 ♗xg4 ♗b6 35
♗xh3 ♖c2 36 ♔h1 ♖xc1 was
agreed drawn in Gelfand–Van
Wely, Wijk aan Zee 1992, since
after 37 ♖xc1 ♗xe3 White can do
no better than take the perpetual,
which Black dare not avoid.

20 ... ♕d7

Of the alternatives, the last two
are worth attention:

(a) **20 ... ♖c8?!** (passive) 21 ♖b3!
♕d7 22 ♖c3 ♘g4 23 ♖xf8+ ♖xf8
24 ♘f3± Browne–Root, Santa
Monica 1990.

(b) **20 ... ♗h6** 21 ♘c4 ♘xe4?
does not work: 22 ♕xe4 ♖xf2
23 ♔xf2 ♗f5 24 ♕f3 ♗xb1 25
♗xh6±.

(c) **20 ... dc!?** is a suggestion of
Polugaevsky's.

(d) **20 ... ♘g4** 21 ♖xf8+ ♗xf8
22 ♘f3 and now in Polugaevsky–
J. Polgar, Aruba (2) 1991, **22 ...
h6?!** 23 ♘h4! ♕f6?! (23 ... ♔h7
24 c6! bc 25 dc ♕b8 26 ♗xg4
♗xg4 27 ♘c3!±) 24 ♗f3! gave
Black serious problems. Instead
both players recommended **22 ...
♗e7!** 23 ♗f1! (23 c6? bc 24 ♕xc6
♖a2! 25 ♕c4 ♖xe2! 26 ♕xe2 c6!∓)
23 ... ♗xf1 24 ♔xf1 dc 25 bc c6!
26 d6 cb 27 de ♕xe7 28 ♖xb5,
considering the chances roughly
level.

21 c6! *(125)*
21 ... bc
22 ♕xc6

In Epishin–Van Wely, Wijk aan
Zee 1992, White chose instead **22**

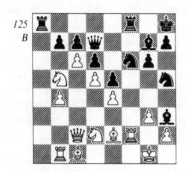

dc ♕e7 23 ♘c3, when Black could try **23 ... ♖ad8** 24 ♘f1 d5∞ (Ftačnik), **23 ... ♗e6** △ ... d5 or **23 ... ♗h6!?** 24 ♘c4 ♗xc1 25 ♖xc1 ♘g7 when the knight heads for d4 (Van Wely). Instead Black speculated with **23 ... d5?!** 24 ed e4 and was rewarded with a devastating attack: **25 ♘c4?** ♘g4 26 ♗xg4 ♖xf2 27 ♕xf2 ♗xg4 28 ♕e3? (28 ♕e1! ♖f8∓) 28 ... ♖f8 29 ♗d2 ♕f7 30 h4?! (30 ♘xe4 ♕xd5) 30 ... ♗f3 31 ♗e1 ♕f5 32 ♖b2 ♘xg3!?∓∓. However, Van Wely analysed as good for White **25 ♘dxe4!** ♘xe4 26 ♕xe4 ♕xe4 27 ♘xe4 ♗f5 (27 ... ♗d4 28 ♗b2) 28 ♗d3 ♘f6 (28 ... ♖ae8 29 ♗b2!±±; 28 ... ♖fe8 29 ♘c5±) 29 ♘c5 ♗xd3 30 ♘xd3 ♘xd5 — Black has only slight drawing chances.

22	...	♗h6
23	♘c4!	♗xc1
24	♖xc1	♘xe4

Black must allow the exchange of queens: **24 ... ♕g7** 25 ♕xc7 ♖f7 26 ♕xd6 ♘xe4 27 ♖xf7 ♕xf7 28 ♕xe5+.

25	♖xf8+	♖xf8
26	♕xd7	♗xd7
27	♘xc7	♖b8 *(126)*

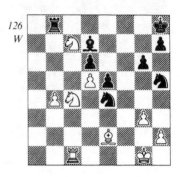

28   b5?!

The first diversion from previous play! Instead **28 ♘a6?!** ♖c8 29 ♖e1 ♘hf6 30 ♘b6 ♖c3 31 ♘xd7 ♘xd7 32 b5 was good for Black in Epishin–Nijboer, Groningen 1990/1, although White went on to win. A better alternative is **28 ♗d3!** ♘hf6 29 b5 ♘c5 (after 29 ... ♗xb5 30 ♖b1 ♘c3 31 ♖b3 Black loses a piece) 30 ♗f1 ♘fe4 31 b6!± — Ftačnik.

28	...	♗xb5
29	♘xb5	

29 ♗xh5 gh 30 ♖b1 ♘c3 31 ♖b3 ♖c8 32 ♘xd6 leads to a draw.

29	...	♖xb5
30	♘xd6	

Others giving nothing: **30 ♘d2?** ♖c5; **30 ♗xh5?** gh 31 ♖e1 ♘g5∓; **30 ♘xe5** ♖xd5 31 ♖c8+ ♔g7 32 ♖c7+ ♔f8! 33 ♘d7+ ♔e8∓∓.

Ftačnik's actual choice forces an ending with no real losing chances. The game finished: **30 ... ♘xd6** 31

♗xb5 ♘xb5 32 ♖e1 ♘f6 33 ♖xe5 ♔g8 34 h3 ♔f7 ½–½.

Karpov–Kasparov
Tilburg 1991

1 d4 ♘f6 2 c4 g6 3 ♘c3 ♗g7 4 e4 d6 5 ♘f3 0–0 6 ♗e2 e5 7 0–0 ♘c6 8 d5 ♘e7 9 ♘d2 a5 10 ♖b1 ♘d7 11 a3 f5 12 b4 ♔h8
18 f3 ♘g8 *(127)*

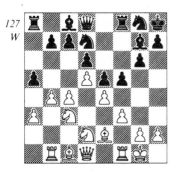

14 ♕c2

With this move we return to the paths of the previous game, but White does have some independent options:

(a) **14 ♘b3?!** has been regarded as much too slow since Karpov–Kasparov, Skellefteå 1989: 14 ... ab 15 ab ♘df6 16 ♗d2 (16 c5 ♘h5 17 g3 ♘hf6 and now 18 ♗d2 fe 19 fe ♗h3 20 ♖f2 ♘h6! gives Black excellent play, whilst 18 g4 ♘e8 19 ♗d2 ♘h6 20 h3 ♘f7 21 ♔g2 ♗f6 22 cd cd 23 ♘a5 h5 led to a straightforward kingside attack in Amura–Dolmatov, Buenos Aires 1991) 16 ... ♘h5 17 g3 ♘hf6 18 ♖f2 (Kasparov notes 18 ♗d3 fe 19 ♘xe4 ♘xe4 20

♗xe4 ♘f6=) 18 ... ♘h6 19 ♖a1 ♖xa1 20 ♕xa1. Black has many possibilities to attack, whereas White is yet to make any real progress. Kasparov gave as Black's most incisive 20 ... f4 21 g4 ♘fxg4 22 fg ♘xg4 23 ♗xg4 ♗xg4∓.

(b) **14 ♘a4** has often been suggested, but has received few practical tests. After 14 ... ab 15 ab ♘df6 (15 ... ♘gf6 16 c5 ♘h5 17 g3 ♘df6 18 ♘c3 (Danielian–Temirbaev, Voroshilovgrad 1989) ought not be a problem for Black) 16 c5 ♘h5 17 g3 ♘hf6 18 b5 fe 19 fe ♗h3 20 ♖f3 ♗h6 21 ♖b4 ♘g4, Black had active play in Flear–Bibby, British Ch (Eastbourne) 1990; the game concluded 22 ♘f1 ♘8f6 23 ♗xh6 ♘xh6 24 ♕c1 ♘fg4 25 b6 cb 26 cd ♖xf3 27 ♗xf3 ♗xf1 28 ♕xf1 ♕g5 29 ♗xg4 ♘xg4 30 d7 ♕e3+ 31 ♔h1 ♘f2+ 32 ♔g2 ♖f8 0–1.

(c) **14 ef** gf 15 ♕c2 ♘e7 16 f4 transposes to Shirov–Fishbein with a whole extra tempo for Black, though it is not clear how best to use it. Lputian–Smirin, Podolsk 1990, continued 16 ... ab 17 ab ♘g6 18 fe ♘dxe5 19 ♘f3, when 19 ... ♕e7 was best.

(d) **14 c5!?** is an energetic pawn sacrifice, which should certainly be accepted: 14 ... ab (14 ... dc 15 bc ♘xc5 16 a4 allows White more than adequate compensation) 15 ab dc (15 ... ♘gf6?! 16 ♘c4 ♘e8 17 c6 ♘df6 18 cb ♗xb7 19 ♘a5 ♗c8 20 ♘c6 ♕d7 21 b5 ♕f7 22 b6 cb 23 ♘a4± Lanka–Shirov, Riga rapid 1988) 16 bc ♘xc5 17 ♘b3 (After 17 ♘c4 fe, Black's pressure on e4 gives counterplay: 18 ♗a3 ef 19 ♗xf3 ♖xa3!? 20 ♘xa3 ♗f5 21 ♖c1 e4 and 18 fe ♖xf1+ 19 ♕xf1 ♕e7 were analysed by Ftačnik) 17 … ♘d7 (17 … ♘xb3 18 ♕xb3 allows White too free a hand on the queenside) 18 ♗e3 c6 (18 … ♗h6 19 ♗f2; 18 … fe 19 ♘xe4 ♘gf6 20 ♘g5 ♘b6 21 ♗c5) 19 ♕d2 fe (19 … ♘gf6 20 ♖fd1 cd 21 ed) 20 dc (20 fe!?) 20 … bc 21 ♘xe4 was Ftačnik–H. Grünberg, Stara Zagora Z 1990. Now Ftačnik suggested **21 … ♘df6!?** 22 ♕xd8 ♖xd8 23 ♘g5 ♘h6 24 ♗b6 ♖e8 25 ♘a5 when White has compensation, whilst the game continued **21 …** ♘gf6 22 ♘g5 when **22 …** ♕e8 23 ♕d6 ♘d5 24 ♕xc6 ♘xe3 25 ♕xa8 ♘xf1 would have equalised. Instead after **22 …** ♕e7?! 23 ♘a5 ♘d5 24 ♘xc6 ♕a3 25 ♗f2 ♘c3 26 ♗c4! Black still had many pitfalls to negotiate.

14	…	♘gf6
15	♘b5	ab
16	ab	♘h5
17	g3	

Wahls suggests that White may refuse to weaken his kingside, by playing 17 ♖d1 ♘f4 18 ♗f1.

17	…	♘df6
18	c5 *(128)*	

For deviations from this sequence, and now the consequences of 18 … fe, see the previous game.

18	…	♗d7

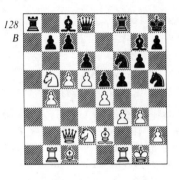

Knaak proposes the immediate knight sacrifice: **18 …** ♘xg3!? 19 hg ♘h5 20 ♖f2 (20 f4? ♘xg3; 20 ♔f2? ♘xg3 21 ♖g1 ♕h4 22 ♖xg3 f4∓∓) 20 … ♘xg3 21 ♘f1∞. This is a logical idea, since ♖b3 looks more useful than … ♗d7 in these lines.

19	♖b3	

White prepares to bring the rook to the c-file. White cannot grab the d-pawn (**19 cd** cd 20 ♘xd6) because of 20 … fe 21 fe ♗h3∓.

19	…	♘xg3

19 … fe 20 fe ♗h3 was played in Gelfand–Kasparov, Paris (Immopar) 1991. It is hard to believe that this can be an improvement over 18 … fe 19 fe ♗h3, but Black obtained interesting play: 21 ♖e1 ♗h6 22 ♘f3 (22 ♖c3 transposes to the two Epishin–J. Polgar games below) 22 … ♗xc1 23 ♖xc1 ♘g4 24 ♕d2 ♕e7 25 ♖bc3 h6 26 ♗f1 ♗xf1 27 ♖xf1 g5 28 cd cd 29 ♘c7 ♘gf6!? 30 ♘xg5!? hg 31 ♘xa8 ♘xe4 32 ♖xf8+ ♕xf8 33 ♕e2 ♘hf6 34 ♖a3

♕c8 and the practical problems proved too much for Gelfand.

19 ... ♗h6 has been played in two games Epishin–J. Polgar. Despite Black's positive score in these games, White's prospects appear better. After **20 ♖c3 fe 21 fe ♗h3** (21 ... dc 22 bc fails: 22 ... ♗xb5 23 ♗xb5 c6 24 ♗c4 cd 25 cd ♘xd5 26 ♖d3±± or 22 ... c6 23 dc ♗xc6 24 ♘d6±) **22 ♖e1!** (22 ♖f2 ♕d7!∞), 22 ... ♘g4 23 ♘f3 looks good for White, so Judit has tried two other moves:

(a) at Brno 1991, **22 ... dc** 23 bc c6 24 dc ♗xd2 25 ♗xd2 bc 26 ♘d6 ♘g4 27 ♖f3! ♕e7 28 ♖b1! ♖xf3 29 ♗xf3 ♖f8 30 ♗xg4 ♗xg4 31 ♗h6 ♘g7 32 ♖b7 left White with an enormous advantage, though by a miracle (and Epishin's habitual time trouble) the game was drawn.

(b) a few weeks later in Vienna 1991, **22 ... ♕d7** 23 ♘f3! ♗xc1 24 ♖xc1 ♘f4 25 ♘g5! ♘xe2+ 26 ♕xe2 ♗g4 27 ♕c4 ♘e8 28 ♖f1 ♖xf1+ 29 ♕xf1 ♔g8 30 h3 h6 31 c6 bc 32 dc ♕e7 33 hg hg also gave White a big edge, but rather than **34 ♕c4+ ♕f7** 35 ♕xf7+ ♔xf7 36 ♖c4 with a very promising ending, Epishin contrived to lose his queen: **34 ♖f3?** d5! 35 ed?! (35 ♘c3!) 35 ... ♕xb4 36 d6 ♘xd6 37 ♘xd6 cd 38 ♖f6 ♕b3 39 ♔h2 ♔g7 40 ♖xd6?? ♖h8+ 0-1.

After 20 ♖c3, the startling **20 ... ♗f4!?** was tried in Kamsky–Kasparov, Dortmund 1992. How-ever, 21 cd ♘xg3 22 hg ♘h5 23 gf ♘xf4 24 ♗c4+ was perhaps more a punishment of the over-zealous follow-up, than the novelty itself.

The text is a fascinating and unclear piece sacrifice. Should it turn out to be insufficient, Black must either demonstrate a play-able alternative, or vary on move 18 or earlier.

20 hg ♘h5
21 f4! *(129)*

White must not be greedy: **21 ♔f2?** (or **21 ♔g2?**) 21 ... ♘xg3! 22 ♔xg3 f4+ 23 ♔f2 ♕h4+ 24 ♔g1 ♗h3∓∓ (Wahls). Also after **21 ♖f2?** ♘xg3 22 ♘f1 ♘xe2+ 23 ♕xe2 fe White has serious problems.

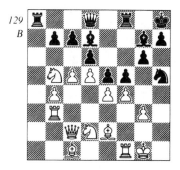

129
B

21 ... ef

Black's best chance seems to be **21 ... ♗xb5 22 ♗xb5 ef** and now:

(a) **23 ♗b2** ♘xg3 (23 ... ♕g5!? 24 ef ♘xg3 25 ♘f3 ♕h5∞) 24 ♗xg7+ ♔xg7 25 ♕c3+ ♔g8 26 ♖xf4 ♘h5 27 ♖f2 fe 28 ♖xf8+ ♕xf8 29 ♘xe4 (Khalifman gives instead 29 ♗d7! ♘f4 30 ♕e3±) 29 ... ♕f5 30 ♕f3 ♕xd5 31 ♖d3 ♕e5 32 ♖d1 (32 ♗c4+!?) 32 ...

d5 33 ♘f2 c6 34 ♗f1 ♖f8 gave
Black three good pawns and continuing play against the white king
in Beliavsky–Khalifman, Reggio
Emilia 1991/2.

(b) **23 gf** ♘xf4 24 ♘f3 fe 25
♕xe4 ♕c8 26 ♘h2 (26 ♗xf4? fails
to 26 ... ♕g4+ 27 ♔h1 ♖xf4 28
♕e6 ♕h5+ 29 ♘h2 ♖h4 etc.) 26
... ♘h3+ 27 ♔g2 ♖a2+ 28 ♗b2
(28 ♗e2? ♖e8∓∓) 28 ... ♖xf1 29
♗xf1 ♖xb2+ 30 ♖xb2 ♗xb2 31
♕e3! dc 32 bc ♕f5 33 ♕e8+ ½–½
Khalifman–Kindermann, Munich
(rapid) 1991.

(c) **23 ef!?** ♘xg3 (23 ... ♖xf5 24
♘e4±) 24 ♖xf4 ♘xf5 (24 ... ♘h5
25 ♖g4 ♖xf5 26 ♘e4±) 25 ♘f3 dc
26 bc ♖a1? 27 ♖d3! ♕e7 (27 ...
♗h6 28 ♔g2 ♗xf4 29 ♗b2+)
28 ♔h2 ♖fa8 29 ♗b2 ♖1a2 30
♖b3 ♘e3? (Epishin recommends
30 ... h6!, but considers this ±) 31
♕e2 ♕xc5 (31 ... ♘xd5 32 ♖e4
♕f8 33 ♘e5±±) 32 ♖e3±± c6?!
33 ♖exe3 ♗xb2 34 ♖xb2 35
♕xb2+ ♔g8 36 dc bc 37 ♖e5
1–0 Epishin–Piket, Wijk aan Zee
1992.

Black should try **26 ... ♕xd5!?**
27 ♖d3 ♖a2! (27 ... ♕e6 28 ♗d7±
Epishin) 28 ♖xd5 (28 ♕c4? ♕xc4
29 ♖xc4 ♖a1∓) 28 ... ♖xc2 29
♗d2 c6 30 ♗a4 cd 31 ♗xc2 ♖c8
32 ♗xf5 gf 33 ♗b4 ♗f8 ½–½
Rublevsky–Pugachëv, Russia
1992.

| 22 | c6! | bc |
| 23 | dc | ♘xg3 |

23 ... ♗e6? would be best met
by 24 ♗xh5 followed by ♗b2±

(Speelman).

| 24 | ♖xg3 | fg |
| 25 | cd | g2! *(130)* |

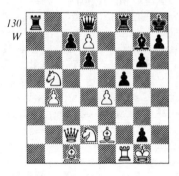

130
W

| 26 | ♖f3?! |

Kasparov recommends **26 ♖f2!**
♕xd7 (26 ... ♕h4 27 ♖xg2 fe 28
♘f1) 27 ef± as the basis for his
condemnation of the sacrifice.

| 26 | ... | ♕xd7? |

Kasparov considers **26 ... ♕h4**
27 ♔xg2 ♕g4+ 28 ♔f1 fe 29
♕xe4 ♕xd7 to be unclear. After
the text, he recommends **27 ef!±**,
since 27 ... c6? is met by 28 ♗b2!
when Black faces disaster on the
long diagonal.

27	♗b2?	fe
28	♖xf8+	♖xf8
29	♗xg7+

29 ♘xe4! looks a better try.
Speelman then gave **29 ... d5** 30
♘f2 d4 31 ♕c5 △ 31 ... ♖f5
32 ♕xc7!, while Van der Wiel's
suggestion **29 ... c5** 30 ♘bxd6 cb
31 ♗c4 leaves Black with major
problems still to solve.

29	...	♕xg7
30	♕xe4	♕f6
31	♘f3	♕f4!

32	♕e7	♖f7
33	♕e6?!	

Repeating with 33 ♕e8+ ♖f8 34 ♕e7 is the most prudent, as Black could now play 33 ... g5! followed by ... g4 with good chances.

33	...	♖f6?!
34	♕e8+	♖f8
35	♕e7	♖f7
36	♕e6?!	♖f6?!
37	♕b3	g5?!

Afterwards Kasparov pointed out the improvement 37 ... c6! 38 ♘bd4 g5, e.g. **39 ♕c3?** g4 40 ♘e6 ♕h6 41 ♘h2 g3∓∓; **39 ♘e6** ♕e4 △ 40 ♘fd4? ♕h3∓∓; **39 b5** cb 40 ♕c3 b4!∓ (and not 40 ... g4? 41 ♘e6 ♕h6 42 ♕c8+). Probably best is **39 ♘xc6** ♕c1+ 40 ♔xg2

♕xc6 41 b5 with roughly level chances (Speelman).

38	♘xc7	g4
39	♘d5	♕c1+
40	♕d1	♕xd1+
41	♗xd1	♖f5
42	♘e3	♖f4
43	♘e1	♖xb4
44	♗xg4!	

With White's last pawn eliminated, Black is now relatively safe. Note, however, that giving up the rook for the bishop would give Black a lost two knights versus pawn(s) ending, so White can try to give mate with the three minor pieces. Black had to defend very carefully until move 114 to obtain half a point.

12 Classical Fianchetto: Romanishin Variation

1 d4 ♘f6 2 c4 g6 3 ♘f3 ♗g7 4 g3
0–0 5 ♗g2 d6 6 0–0 ♘bd7
    7   ♕c2   e5
    8   ♖d1 *(131)*

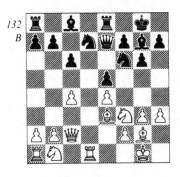

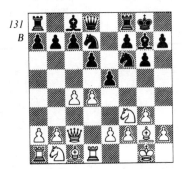

In this variation, pioneered by Romanishin, White's knight stays on b1 for the time being, keeping open possibilities of a ♘d2–c4–d6 manoeuvre. Meanwhile b2, c4 and d4 are more securely defended than in the main lines with the rook on e1 and the queen on d1. Thus one would expect Black's methods of obtaining counterplay to be quite different from in those.

Firstly, we should consider what White is aiming for *(132)*:

White is threatening 13 c5, whereupon the d6-square would be an ideal post for a white knight, so Black has little choice: 12 ... ♘c5 13 ♘c3 ♘fd7 (Probably dubious, as it fails to prepare very effective kingside counterplay) 14 b4 ♘e6 15 ♖ab1 ♕f8 16 c5 (Now White intends ♘f3–d2–c4) 16 ... f5 17 ♘e2 fe?! (17 ... f4 had to be tried) 18 ♘d2 ♘f6 19 ♘xe4 ♘xe4 20 ♗xe4 was positionally overwhelming in Sideif Zade–Imanaliev, Azov 1991.

While the position in the above diagram is certainly playable for Black, it may be considered more pleasant for White, so generally Black delays ... ♖e8 until the exchange on e5 is no longer effective (or indeed feasible). The following position, from Mirallès–Todorčevic, Budel Z 1987, illustrates an important theme in the type of position that typically arises *(133)*:

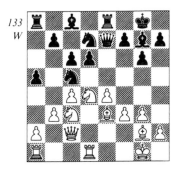

133
W

To prevent ... f5 ideas, White now played 15 ♗f2, which was met by 15 ... h5!?. This is not just a random thrust, but has the point that if White replies h4, then the e5-square will be very secure for a black knight, since White can only drive it away (with f4) to the even better square g4. Thus White must constantly reckon with the possibility of the further thrust ... h5-h4. Play continued 16 ♘ce2 ♘f8 17 ♖ab1 ♘cd7 18 ♕d2 a4 19 ♘c3 ab 20 ab ♘h7 21 ♘de2 ♗f8. Black's position has only one (easily defended) weakness and contains much latent dynamism, as the sequel demonstrates: 22 f4 h4 23 g4 h3! 24 ♗f3 (24 ♗xh3 ♘df6) 24 ... g5! 25 e5 de 26 f5 e4 27

♗xe4 ♘e5 28 ♗d4 ♗g7. Black has plenty of dark square control and a serious initiative.

In the first game we consider the move 8 ... ed, with which Van Wely has experimented successfully, and an attempt by Black, on move four, to avoid the Romanishin Variation entirely. The main lines, 8 ... ♖e8 and 8 ... ♕e7 are considered in subsequent games.

J. Piket–Van Wely
Dutch Ch (Eindhoven) 1991

**1 d4 ♘f6 2 c4 g6 3 ♘f3 ♗g7
4 g3   0–0**

It is worth mentioning an attempt to take advantage of White leaving his knight on b1, viz. **4 ... c5!?**. Then:

(a) **5 d5** d6 (5 ... b5 is a line of the Benko Gambit) 6 ♗g2 a6!? 7 a4 (7 0-0 b5) 7 ... e5 8 de ♗xe6 9 ♘g5 ♗xc4 10 ♘bd2 ♗e6 11 ♗xb7 ♖a7 (The point of Black's play — the insertion of ... a6 and a4 has given this rook a square) 12 ♗g2 0-0 13 ♘xe6 fe 14 0-0 ♘bd7 led to a complicated struggle in P. Nikolić–Epishin, Wijk aan Zee 1992.

(b) **5 ♗g2**. The position after **5 ... d6** was reached in Ionov–Shirov, USSR Ch (Moscow) 1991; there followed 6 0-0 cd 7 ♘xd4 h5!? 8 h3 ♘c6 9 ♘xc6 bc 10 ♘c3 (10 ♗xc6+ ♗d7 11 ♗g2 ♖c8) 10 ... 0-0 11 ♗e3 ♗e6 12 ♕d3 ♕c8∞. More normal is **5 ... ♕a5+** *(134)*:

134
W

(b1) **6 ₩d2?!** ♘c5 7 d6 ♘e4 8 ₩xa5 ♘xa5 9 ♘a3 ♘d6 10 ♘d2 ♖b8 11 e3 a6 12 ♖b1 b5 13 ♗f1 e6 left Black better in a five-minute game Karpov–Kasparov, Brussels 1987.

(b2) **6 ♘c3** ♘e4 7 ₩d3!? (7 0–0?! ♘xc3 8 bc ₩xc3 9 ♗g5 ₩a5! 10 d5 d6 11 ♖b1 ₩xa2!∓ Yusupov–I. Sokolov, Belgrade 1991; 7 ♗d2 ♘xd2 8 ₩xd2 can be met by 8 ... 0–0!? 9 e3 d6 10 h3 (Kir. Georgiev–I. Sokolov, Yugoslavia 1991) 10 ... ♘d7!?= or Yusupov's 8 ... cd 9 ♘xd4 ♘c6 10 e3 ₩c5!?) 7 ... cd 8 ♘xd4 ♘c5 9 ₩d1 ♘c6 10 e3 (10 ♗e3 ♘e6 11 ♘xe6 ♗xc3+ 12 bc de∞) 10 ... ♘e6 11 0–0 ♘cxd4!? (11 ... 0–0?! 12 ♘xe6 de 13 ♗d2± Dizdar–Vaganian, Sarajevo 1987) 12 ed ♗xd4 13 ♘d5 ₩d8 14 ₩e2 ♗g7∞ (Dautov).

(b3) **6 ♗d2** ₩b6 7 ♘c3!? (7 ♗c3 ♘e4 8 0–0 ♘c6 9 e3 0–0=; 7 dc ₩xc5 8 ₩b3 can be met by 8 ... ♘e4!? or 8 ... ♘c6 9 ♘c3 0–0 10 ♖c1 d6= Smejkal–Nunn, Bundesliga 1987/8) 7 ... cd 8 ♘a4

₩c7 (8 ... ₩d6!?; 8 ... ₩c6? 9 0–0 ♘e4?! 10 ♘g5 f5 11 ♘xe4 fe 12 e3!± Dautov–Shirov, Brno 1991) 9 ♘xd4 0–0 10 ♖c1 ♘c6 11 ♘b5 ₩d8 (11 ... ₩e5!?) 12 0–0 d6 and Black's position is 'perhaps slightly worse but certainly playable' (Shirov).

5	♗g2	d6
6	0–0	♘bd7
7	₩c2	e5
8	♖d1	

This is the starting point of the variation popularised by Oleg Romanishin. The first point to note is that White is threatening to win the e5-pawn, so **8 ... c6?**, as in Romanishin–Adianto, Indonesia 1983, will not do. Van Wely's choice here is very similar, in appearance at least, to the Gallagher Variation, considered in the next chapter.

8	...	ed
9	♘xd4	♖e8
10	♘c3	a6
11	b3	

11 ♗f4 ♘h5 12 ♗e3 ♘e5 13 ♘d5 ♘g4 14 ♗c1 c5 15 ♘f3 ♗f5∓ Jacobsen–J. Fries Nielsen, Esbjerg 1988.

11	...	♖b8 *(135)*
12	♗b2	

12 e4 ♘c5 13 f3 ♗d7 14 ♗e3 b5 15 b4 ♘e6 16 ♘xe6? (16 c5) 16 ... ♗xe6 17 c5 ♘d7 18 f4?! (18 ♖ac1) 18 ... a5 19 a3 a4 20 ♖d2 (20 ₩d2 fails to 20 ... dc 21 bc ♘xc5!) 20 ... ♗b3 21 ₩c1 ₩f6 22 e5 and now in Baburin–Van Wely, Berlin 1991, **22 ... de?!** 23 ♖xd7 ef

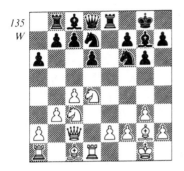

135
W

♘e4 25 ♖d4 ♘xg3 26 ♖xd6 ♕b6+
27 ♕d4 ♕a5 (Threatens 28 ...
♕xe1+!) 28 ♔f2 ♘h5 29 ♘h4
♗g4 30 c5 ♖e6!. White, presumably in serious time trouble, self-
destructed in this messy position:
31 a4? b6! 32 ♖d8+ ♖xd8 33
♕xd8+ ♔h7 34 cb? ♗f6! (A
pulverizing blow!) 35 b4 ♕xb4 36
♖e4 and 0–1.

24 ♗d4 ♕xd4+ led to a very
messy position. Instead **22 ... ♕e7**
would have left Black on top.

12	...	♘e5

12 ... c5 13 ♘f3 ♕e7 14 a4 ♘f8
15 ♕d2 ♖d8 16 ♘g5 gave White
a positional superiority in Kir.
Georgiev–Marin, Warsaw Z 1987.

13	♖d2

13 c5 d5 14 e4 c6 15 ed ½–½
Fominykh–Tseshkovsky, Balassagyarmat 1990.

13	...	h5!?
14	♖f1	

14 ♖ad1 is met by 14 ... ♗h6!
whilst 14 h3 h4 15 g4 ♘fxg4 16
hg h3! allows Black's queen to
participate in the attack.

14	...	h4
15	♘d5	♘fd7
16	e4	hg
17	hg	♘g4

White has, very classically,
played in the centre, but nevertheless Black has counterplay against
White's loosened kingside. Play
continued: 18 ♖e1 c6 19 ♘e3
♘de5 20 ♘xg4 ♗xg4 21 f4 ♘d7
22 ♘f3 ♘f6 23 e5 ♗f5 24 ♕d1

Mikhalchishin–Hellers
Copenhagen 1991

1 d4 ♘f6 2 c4 g6 3 ♘f3 ♗g7 4 g3
0–0 5 ♗g2 d6 6 0–0 ♘bd7 7 ♕c2
e5 8 ♖d1

8	...	♖e8
9	de	

Note that 9 ♘c3 not only
deprives White of the ♘bd2–c4
manoeuvre, but invites **9 ... c6** 10
e4 ♕c7!? (10 ... ♕e7) 11 b3 (11
h3!?) 11 ... b5 when the potential
pin on the c-file caused White
some problems in J. Piket–Cu.
Hansen, Hamburg 1991: 12 cb?!
(12 ♗a3) 12 ... cb 13 ♗a3 ♗b7
14 ♖ac1 (14 ♗xd6) 14 ... ♕b6!.
Black may also play **9 ... ♕e7**,
transposing to Romanishin–
Akopian, or 9 ... c6 10 e4 **ed** 11
♘xd4 ♕e7, transposing to Salov–
Kasparov.

9	...	de
10	e4	c6
11	h3 *(136)*	
11	...	♕c7

(a) **11 ... ♘h5** may well be
an important alternative — Black
simply plays on the kingside as

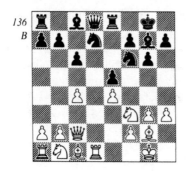

136
B

quickly as possible. Vaganian–Bronstein, Moscow Ch 1981 continued 12 ♗e3 ♕e7 13 a3 (13 c5 ♗f8 14 ♖c1; 13 ♘bd2) 13 ... ♘f8 14 c5 f5! 15 ♗g5 ♕f7 16 ♗c1!? ♘e6 17 ♘bd2 ♖d8 18 ♘c4 (18 b4!?) 18 ... ♖xd1+ 19 ♕xd1 ♘xc5 20 ♘cxe5 ♕e8 21 ef ♗xf5 22 ♗e3 ♖d8 23 ♗xc5 ♖xd1+ 24 ♖xd1 ♘f6 25 ♗xa7 ♗e4 26 ♗c5 ♗d5 27 ♖e1 ♘e4 ½–½.

(b) **11 ... ♕e7** is a solid move, quite possibly better than 11 ... ♕c7. Harmless is then 12 ♘c3 h6 (Black delays ... ♘c5 until White has spent time preparing b4) 13 ♖b1 ♘c5 14 ♖e1 (14 b4? ♘cxe4 15 ♘xe4 ♘xe4 16 ♕xe4 ♗f5) 14 ... ♘h5 15 ♗e3 ♘e6 16 ♖bd1 ♘g5 17 ♘xg5 hg 18 ♕c1 g4 19 hg ½–½ L. Hansen–Schandorff, Kerteminde 1991. White's main choices maintain the possibility of a ♘d2–c4–d6 manoeuvre:

(b1) **12 b3** ♘c5 13 ♘c3 ♘fd7 (13 ... ♘e6!? 14 ♘xe5 ♘c5 15 ♗f4 ♘h5 16 ♘xc6 bc 17 ♗d6 ♕g5 18 h4 ♕f6 19 ♘e2 ♘xe4 20 ♗xe4 ♗g4 gave Black compensation

in Mikhalchishin–Magerramov, Klaipeda 1988) 14 ♗a3 (14 ♗e3 is inconsistent, and after 14 ... a5 15 ♖d2 ♕f8 16 ♖ad1 ♗h6 17 ♗xh6 ♕xh6 18 ♖d6 ♘f8 19 ♕d2 ♕xd2 20 ♖1xd2 ♔g7 led to a promising ending for Black in Lysenko–Yurtaev, Pula 1990) 14 ... ♕f6 15 b4 ♘e6 16 c5 h5 17 ♗b2 g5 18 ♘e2 a5 19 a3 ab 20 ab ♖xa1 21 ♗xa1 h4?! 22 ♘h2! gave White the advantage in Mikhalchishin–Hazai, Kecskemet 1983.

(b2) **12 ♗e3** ♘c5 13 ♘c3 and now Black may try 13 ... a5!? △ 14 ... ♘fd7 or:

(b21) **13 ... ♘h5** 14 ♖ab1?! (14 b4 ♘e6 15 b5 ♘c5!? △ ... ♗f8 and ... ♕c7) 14 ... ♘e6 15 ♔h2 ♖f8 16 ♕d2 f5 17 ♕e1 f4 18 ♗c1 ♘d4 19 ♖d3 ♘xf3+ 20 ♖xf3 g5∓ Sloth–W. Watson, Herning 1991. White has spent too much time manoeuvring.

(b22) **13 ... h6** 14 b4 ♘e6 15 b5 ♘c5 16 ♘e1 ♘fd7. Now White's most promising is **17 a4** intending a further advance of the a-pawn. Instead of Romanishin–Yurtaev, Frunze 1985, after **17 ♖ac1** ♗f8 18 ♖b1?! (18 ♕d2) 18 ... ♘b6 19 ♗f1 ♗e6 20 ♗xc5 ♕xc5 21 ♘d3 ♕xc4 22 ♘xe5 ♕c5 23 ♘d3 ♕a3, Black's position was rather promising.

12   c5!?

Salov's idea. Previously played was **12 ♗e3 b6**:

(a) **13 a3** ♘f8 (13 ... a5 14 ♘c3 Mikhalchishin) 14 b4 ♘e6 15 ♘c3

♗b7 16 ♕a4 (16 c5!?) 16 ... a6 17 ♕b3 ♖ad8 18 c5 b5 19 a4 ♖xd1+ 20 ♖xd1 ♘d7 21 h4 ♘df8 22 ♖d6 ♗f6 23 ab ab 24 ♘d5!∞ Lysenko-Berelovich, Kislovodsk 1984.

(b) 13 ♘c3 ♗a6 14 ♗f1 ♗b7 15 ♖ac1 ♘f8 16 b4 ♘e6 17 c5 bc 18 bc ♖ad8 19 ♘b1 ♗c8 20 ♘bd2 ♗f8= Pigusov-Lautier, Sochi 1989. There is too much pressure on c5 for White to achieve much.

| 12 | ... | b6 |

12 ... a5 can be met by 13 ♗e3 b6 14 cb ♘xb6 15 ♘bd2 △ ♖ac1±.

| 13 | b4 |

Mikhalchishin suggests that 13 cb ab 14 ♗e3 ♗f8 15 ♘c3 ♘c5 (15 ... ♗c5 16 ♗g5±) 16 b4 ♘e6 17 a3 ♗b7 18 ♘g5!? may preserve a small advantage.

| 13 | ... | a5 |

Or 13 ... bc 14 bc and now Black may choose from:

(a) 14 ... ♘xe4? 15 ♕xe4 ♘xc5 16 ♕c4 e4 17 ♘d4 ♘d3 18 ♘c3 ♗a6 19 ♕xa6 ♗xd4 20 ♘xe4! is very good for White.

(b) 14 ... ♘f8 intending to attack c5 with ... ♘e6, ... ♗f8 and ... ♘d7, is suggested by Salov.

(c) 14 ... ♘h5?! 15 ♗e3 ♘f8 16 ♘bd2 ♗a6 17 ♘c4 ♗xc4 18 ♕xc4 ♖ed8 19 h4!± Salov-Lautier, Wijk aan Zee 1991.

(d) 14 ... ♗f8 15 ♗e3 ♕a5:

(d1) 16 ♖c1 ♗a6 17 ♘bd2 ♖ab8 18 a3 ♘h5 19 ♘c4 ♗xc4 20 ♕xc4 ♘g7 21 ♘g5 ♘e6 22 ♘xe6 ♖xe6 23 h4 ♖ee8 24 ♗h3 ♖b7 25 h5 ♘f6 26 hg hg 27 ♕c2

½-½ Greenfeld-Smirin, Tel Aviv 1991.

(d2) After 16 ♘bd2!?, *ECO*'s 16 ... ♗a6 may be met by 17 ♘b3 ♕a4 18 ♖ac1, whilst Romanishin-Tomaszewski, Polanica Zdroj 1980 saw 16 ... ♘xc5 17 ♖dc1 ♘cd7 18 ♕xc6 ♗a6 19 ♘c4 ♗xc4 20 ♕xc4, when Black's best try was 20 ... ♗a3!? 21 ♖c2 ♘b6.

| 14 | cb |

After 14 ba bc 15 ♗d2 ♘f8! 16 ♗c3 ♘6d7, Black intends ... ♘e6-d4, with plenty of central control.

| 14 | ... | ♘xb6 |

14 ... ♕xb6 is unpromising; Mikhalchishin gives 15 ba ♕xa5 (15 ... ♕c5 16 ♘c3±) 16 ♕xc6 ♘b6 17 ♗d2±.

| 15 | ba | ♖xa5 |
| 16 | ♗d2 |

Worthwhile alternatives are 16 ♘bd2 followed by 17 ♘b3 and 16 a4 intending ♗d2 and a5.

| 16 | ... | ♖a8 |
| 17 | ♗b4!? |

17 a4 is a clearer way to keep an edge.

| 17 | ... | ♗f8 |

17 ... ♘xe4 18 ♕xe4 ♗f5 19 ♕e1 e4 20 ♘d4 c5 21 ♗c3 cd 22 ♗xd4±.

| 18 | ♗xf8 | ♖xf8 |
| 19 | ♖c1 |

Mikhalchishin's preference afterwards was 19 ♘fd2! intending ♘c3 and a4 — the white knights are most effective on these squares.

| 19 | ... | ♗b7 |
| 20 | ♘bd2 | ♘fd7 |

21	a4	♖a5
22	♗f1	♖fa8
23	♗c4!	♘c5

23 ... ♖xa4 fails to 24 ♖xa4 ♖xa4 25 ♘g5 ♘xc4 26 ♕xa4 ♘xd2 27 ♕a2!±±.

24 ♘b3?

White's last chance to maintain an advantage was **24 ♘g5!** ♘xc4 25 ♘xc4 ♖xa4 26 ♖xa4 ♖xa4 (26 ... ♘xa4? 27 ♖a1 ♘b6 28 ♖xa8+ ♗xa8 29 ♘xb6 ♕xb6 30 ♕a2 ♕b7 31 ♘xf7! is disaster for Black) 27 ♖d1 followed by 28 ♘d6 with a serious initiative.

After the text, Black has adequate play. The game finished: 24 ... ♖xa4 25 ♖xa4 ♘cxa4 26 ♗b5 ♕e7 27 ♗xc6 ♗xc6 28 ♕xc6 ♖c8 29 ♕b5 ♘c3 ½-½.

Romanishin–Akopian
Moscow GMA 1989

1 d4 ♘f6 2 c4 g6 3 ♘f3 ♗g7 4 g3 0-0 5 ♗g2 d6 6 0-0 ♘bd7 7 ♕c2 e5 8 ♖d1

8	...	♕e7
9	♘c3	

9 de de 10 e4 is rather harmless when Black hasn't spent a tempo on ... ♖e8: 10 ... ♘c5 11 ♘c3 c6 12 b3 ♖e8 13 ♗a3 a5= Plachetka–Barczay, Trnava 1982.

9	...	♖e8

This is an interesting alternative to 9 ... c6 (see next game). Now White can try **10 b3**, which is best met by **10 ... c6**, considered in the note to White's tenth move in Salov–Kasparov below; instead

ECO gives **10 ... ♘f8** 11 e4 ♗g4 12 d5±.

10	♗g5	c6
11	♘e4!?	ed

Romanishin's idea is that **11 ... h6?** 12 ♗xf6 ♘xf6 13 ♘xd6 ♕xd6 14 de ♕e7 15 ef ♕xf6 16 ♖d2 leaves White on top.

12	♘xd4	

12 ♖xd4 is met not by **12 ... h6?** 13 ♗xf6 ♗xf6 14 ♘xf6+ ♘xf6 15 ♕d2!±, but **12 ... c5!** 13 ♗xf6 ♗xf6! 14 ♘xf6+ ♘xf6 15 ♖d2 ♗f5 with unclear play, according to Akopian.

12	...	h6

Now there is no tactical drawback with this move.

13	♘xf6+	♘xf6
14	♗f4	♘g4! (137)

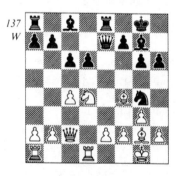

15	h3?	

White should instead play **15 e4**, when Akopian considers the position equal. The text allows Black to seize the initiative by tactical means.

15	...	♘xf2!
16	♔xf2	g5
17	♕d2	

The only move, since 17 &c1
&xd4+ 18 &xd4 &f6+ wins an
exchange and 17 &xc6 bc 18
&xd6 (18 &xc6 gf∓∓) 18 ...
&e3+ 19 &f1 &e6! leaves White
defenceless.

17	...	gf
18	&xf4	c5
19	&b5	&xe2+
20	&g1	&e3+!
21	&xe3	&xe3
22	&f2	

22 &xd6 &xg3! 23 &f2 (23
&d8+ &h7 doesn't help White,
e.g. 24 &ad1 &d4+ 25 &xd4
&xg2+ 26 &xg2 &xh3+ 27
&xh3 &xd8) 23 ... &e5 24 &d8+
&g7∓ (Akopian).

| 22 | ... | &e7 |
| 23 | &e1 | |

23 &xd6?! &e6 is also grim
for White; Akopian considered 23
&d2 the most stubborn.

| 23 | ... | &e6! |
| 24 | &xd6 | &d7! |

Now Black is clearly winning,
e.g. 25 &xb7 &b8, 25 &ad1 &ad8
or 25 &b5 &xc4.

The game in fact finished 25
&e4 &xb2 26 &ad1 &xd1 27
&xd1 &d4+ 28 &f3 &xc4 29
&d2 &e8 30 &d6 &d5+ 31 &g4
&e5! 32 &xb7 &g5+ 33 &h4
&f6 34 g4 &xb7 0-1.

Salov–Kasparov
Linares 1991

1 d4 &f6 2 c4 g6 3 &f3 &g7 4 g3
0-0 5 &g2 d6 6 0-0 &bd7 7 &c2
e5 8 &d1

| 8 | ... | &e7 |
| 9 | &c3 | c6 | (138) |

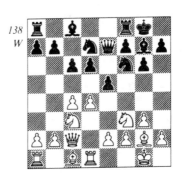

138
W

10 e4

There are two alternatives:
(a) 10 d5 c5 (10 ... cd 11 cd &c5
12 &d2 &d7 13 b4?! &a6 14 &b3
e4 15 &f1 &g4 16 &b2 f5 17 f3
&e3!? gave Black good play in
Nagatz–Vogt, Bad Lauterberg
1991) 11 a3 (11 h3 &h5 12 e4 f5
13 &g5 &df6 14 &h4 fe 15 &cxe4
&c7 16 &xf6+ &xf6 17 &f3 &e7
18 &d2 &g7 was nothing special
for White in Johansson–Tangen,
Gausdal [Arnold Cup] 1991) 11
... &b6 12 &d2 &f5 13 e4 &g4
14 &e1! (14 f3 &d7 intending ...
&h5 and ... f5–f4 gives Black good
counterplay; note that 15 b4 &ac8
16 &b1 &h6 17 bc &e3+ 18
&h1 &xc5∓ is one benefit of
provoking f3) 14 ... &h5 15 b4
&ac8 16 &b1 &d7 17 a4! cb 18
&xb4 &c5 19 &a2 &c7 20 &b3
&b8 21 a5 &c8 22 &db1!? &f6!
23 &a3 &g5 24 &ab5 &xb5 25
&xb5 &c5 26 &xg5 &xg5 27 a6!
&d8! 28 &a1 ba 29 &xa6 &b6
and now in McNab–M. Gurevich,

Ostend 1991, **30 ⟂xb6?!** ♕xb6 permitted Black adequate counterchances; instead Gurevich recommends **30 ⟂ba4±**.

(b) **10 b3** and now Black has two options:

(b1) **10 ... ed** 11 ♘xd4 ⟂e8. Now Kasparov considers **12 ♗f4!** ♘e5 (12 ... ♘h5? 13 ♘xc6!) 13 ♕d2 slightly to favour White. Instead **12 ♗b2** ♘c5 13 e3 (13 e4 is considered in the note to White's thirteenth move in the main game) 13 ... a5 14 a3 h5! gave Black good play in Timman–Kasparov, Tilburg 1991. After 15 b4 (15 h3 h4 16 g4 ♘xg4! 17 hg ♗xg4) 15 ... ♘ce4! 16 b5 ♗d7! 17 ⟂ac1 h4 18 a4? (18 ♘xe4 ♘xe4 followed by 19 ♘f3, 19 bc!? or 19 a4 is OK for White) 18 ... hg 19 hg, the sacrifice 19 ... ♘xf2! worked extremely well: 20 ♕f2 ♘g4∓ 21 ♕f3? ♘e3 22 ⟂e1 ♗xd4 23 ♘d5 ♘g4+?! (23 ... ♘d1+!) 24 ♗xd4 ♕xe1+ 25 ⟂xe1 ⟂xe1 26 ♗f1 cd∓∓ 27 ♕xd5 ⟂ae8 28 ♗f2 ♗e6 29 ♕xb7 ⟂c1 30 ♕c6 ⟂c8 31 ♕e4 ⟂8xc4 32 ♕a8+ ♔h7 33 b6 ⟂b4 34 ♕xa5 ⟂bb1 35 ♔g2 ⟂c2 0–1.

(b2) **10 ... ⟂e8** with a further division:

(b21) **11 e3** ♘f8 12 de (12 ♗a3 e4 13 ♘d2 ♗f5 14 b4 h4 15 b5 h4∓ K. Arkell–W. Watson, Ostend 1987; 12 e4 ♘e6! 13 de de 14 ♘xe5 ♘xe4 15 ♘xe4 ♗xe5 16 ♗b2 ♘c5= Birnboim–Blees, Tel Aviv 1987) 12 ... de 13 a4 (13 h3 e4) 13 ... e4 14 ♗a3 c5 15 ♘d4 (15 ♘d2 ♗g4∓) 15 ... ♗g4 (15 ...

b6 16 h3 ♗b7= Garcia Palermo–Vogt, Cienfuegos 1983) 16 ⟂d2 ♕e5 17 ♘db5 ⟂ad8 with reasonable prospects for Black in K. Arkell–Kochiev, Leningrad 1989.

(b22) **11 ♗a3** e4!? (11 ... ed) 12 ♘g5 e3 13 f4 (After 13 f3 ♘f8 Yusupov gives the lines 14 ♘ce4 ♗f5 15 ♕c3 ♘xe4 16 ♘xe4 c5∓ and 14 ♘ge4 ♗f5 15 ♕c1 ♗xe4 16 ♘xe4 ♘xe4 17 fe c5 18 e5 ♘e6 19 ed ♕xd6 20 ♗xb7 ♘xd4∞) 13 ... ♘f8 14 b4 ♗f5 15 ♕b3 h6 16 ♘f3 ♘g4 (16 ... g5!?) 17 b5 g5 18 bc bc 19 ♘e5!? gf 20 ♘xc6 ♕g5 21 ♗xd6 led to great complications in the final quickplay game of the Ivanchuk–Yusupov candidates match (Brussels 1991). There followed 21 ... ♘g6 22 ♘d5 ♕h5 23 h4 ♘xh4 24 gh ♕xh4, when, according to Yusupov's analysis, 25 ♗xf4!? would have given Black nothing better than a perpetual check with 25 ... ♕f2+ 26 ♔h1 ♕h4+.

10 ... ed

Knaak mentions the possibility **10 ... ♘b6** 11 b3 ♗g4 12 ♗e3 ♘fd7, whilst the position after **10 ... ⟂e8** was reached in Makarov–Magerramov, USSR Ch (Moscow) 1991. Bizarre complications quickly arose: 11 d5 (11 b3) 11 ... a5 12 ♘e1 cd 13 cd ♘c5 14 ⟂b1 ♗d7 15 ♘d3 b6 16 b4 ab 17 ♘xb4 ⟂ec8 18 ♕e2 ♘f8 19 ♗g5 ⟂a3 20 ⟂dc1 ♗h6!? 21 ♗xf6 ♗xc1 22 ♘b5 ⟂a5 23 ♘d4 ♘xe4 and the game eventually ended in a draw.

11 ♘xd4   ♖e8

Less effective was 11 ... ♘e5 12 ♕e2! a6 13 h3 c5 14 ♘c2 ♗e6 15 b3 ♘fd7 16 ♗b2 b5 17 f4± in L. Hansen–Mortensen, Kerteminde 1991.

12 b3

The old recommendation was tried in Isaev–Kovalëv, Podolsk 1990: 12 ♗f4 ♘e5 (12 ... ♘c5?? 13 ♘xc6) 13 b3 a6 14 h3 ♗d7 15 a4 a5 16 ♖d2 ♖ad8 17 ♖ad1 ♗c8 18 ♘de2 ♗f8 19 c5 d5 20 ed ♘xd5 21 ♘xd5 cd and Black could be happy.

12   ...   ♘c5
13   f3

A natural alternative is 13 ♗b2 a5 (Not 13 ... ♘fxe4? 14 ♘xe4 ♘xe4 15 ♖e1 ♗xd4 16 ♖xe4 ♗e5 17 f4 ♗f5 18 fe ♗xe4 19 ♕xe4 de 20 ♖e1± Ftačnik) 14 ♖d2 (14 a3 h5 15 b4 ab 16 ab ♖xa1 17 ♗xa1 ♘a6 18 ♕b1 ♘c7 19 ♘b3 h4= Foisor–Ciocaltea, Romanian Ch 1981) 14 ... h5 15 ♘a4! ♘xa4 16 ba. White's pawns appear ugly, but Black's are more easily attacked, while the exchange of knights has reduced Black's counterchances. In Salov–Hjartarson, Amsterdam 1991, Black had to play accurately for the half point: 16 ... ♘d7 (16 ... h4?! 17 ♘b3 hg 18 hg±) 17 ♘b3 ♗xb2 18 ♕xb2 ♘b6 (18 ... ♘e5 19 ♕c3! c5 20 ♖ad1 ♘c6 is considered unclear by Hjartarson, since on 21 ♖xd6 there would follow 21 ... ♘d4) 19 ♕d4 c5 20 ♕xd6 ♕xd6 21 ♖xd6 ♘xc4 22 ♖d5 b6 23 ♖c1

♘b2!? 24 ♖d2! ♘xa4 25 e5 ♖b8 26 ♗c6 ♖f8 (26 ... ♗e6!?; 26 ... ♗h3!?) 27 ♗b5 (27 ♗xa4 b5 28 ♗xb5 ♖xb5 29 ♖xc5 ♖xc5 30 ♘xc5 ♗h3 gives Black compensation; compare the game) 27 ... c4! 28 ♖xc4 ♘c5 29 ♘xc5 bc 30 ♖xc5 ♗h3 and White's problems with his king allowed Black to achieve a draw: 31 f3 ♖fc8 32 ♖xc8+ ♖xc8 33 a4 ♖c5 34 ♔f2 (34 ♖e2!?) 34 ... ♖xe5 35 ♖d8+ ♔g7 36 ♖a8 ♗e6 37 h4 (37 ♖xa5 ♗c4=) 37 ... ♗b3 38 ♖a7 ♖c5 39 ♖xa5 and a draw was agreed due to 39 ... ♗xa4.

13   ...   ♘fd7

The older move is 13 ... a5, but this is not yet necessary since White isn't ready to play b4.

14   ♖b1

Alternatively:

(a) 14 ♕f2 a5 15 ♖b1 ♘e5 16 ♗f1 ♕f8 gave Black a respectable position in J. Horvath–M. Pavlović, Stary Smokovec 1990.

(b) 14 ♗b2 appears less logical than on the previous move. 14 ... a5 15 ♖d2 ♘e5 16 ♖ad1 was Korchnoi–Qi Jingxuan, Lucern 1985; Black could try 16 ... h5.

14   ...   ♘e5

14 ... a5 15 a3 ♘b6 16 ♗f1 d5! 17 cd cd 18 b4 ♘e6 led to interesting play in Birnboim–Liberzon, Beersheva 1982, but Kasparov's plan looks more natural.

15   ♘ce2   a5
16   a3   h5! *(139)*

A useful thrust: White must

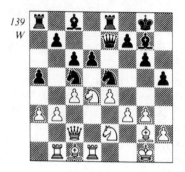

either allow the pawn to advance further, or play h4, after which the e5-knight is more secure.

17	h4	♗d7
18	♗e3	a4
19	b4	♘e6
20	c5	d5

Anand gives **20 ... dc** 21 ♘xe6 ♗xe6 22 ♗xc5 ♕c7∞. The text leads to equality, thanks to Black's grip on c4.

21	ed	cd
22	♗f2	♘c4
23	♕c3	♖ac8
24	♖bc1	b6
25	cb	♘xb6
26	♕d3	♘c4
27	♖e1	♕d6
28	f4	

White frees f3 for his queen. Kasparov's reply neutralises this idea due to possibilities of a knight invasion on d3. Therefore the players repeat moves.

28	...	♘b2
29	♕d2	♘c4
30	♕d3	♘b2
31	♕d2	♘c4

½–½

13 Classical Fianchetto: Gallagher Variation

**1 d4 ♘f6 2 c4 g6 3 ♘f3 ♗g7 4 g3
0-0 5 ♗g2 d6 6 0-0 ♘bd7**

7	♘c3	e5
8	e4	ed
9	♘xd4	♖e8
10	h3	a6!? *(140)*

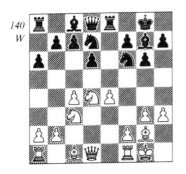

In the traditional lines, Black increases the pressure on the e4 pawn with ... ♘c5 at some point, and maybe ... ♕e7, while the queenside pawns are arranged to restrict White's expansion: ... c6 and often ... a5–a4.

Black's aims in the variation considered in this chapter, played many times with success by Knaak and especially Gallagher, are quite different; the idea is to expand on the queenside with ... ♖b8, ... c5 and ... b5. The queen's knight often goes to e5, as the c4 pawn is inconvenient for White to defend. White can prevent Black's plan by playing a4, but it is not clear whether this is a good idea; after the reply ... a5, White's normal plans with b4 are impossible, while Black's knight has a secure post on c5. A couple of specific positions to illustrate these points:

An obvious objection to Black's plan with ... c5 and ... b5 is the weakness left at d6. The following position *(141)*, from Csom–Bellón, Ter Apel 1991, shows that this is often not so relevant:

Play continued 14 ♕xd6 ♖b6! 15 ♕d1 b4! 16 ♘a4 ♖be6! 17 ♗b2 ♕e7 18 ♕d2 ♗b7. White's pieces are in rather a mess, while Black's are superbly coordinated. Csom decided 19 f3 ♘h5 was too uncomfortable and instead returned the pawn, but eventually lost an unpleasant ending.

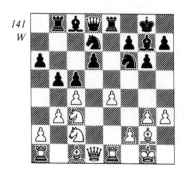

141
W

Black's bishop can often be effective from a6, e.g. *(142)*:

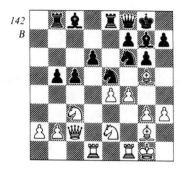

142
B

Black, in Draško–Gallagher, Aosta 1990, now played 18 ... ♘c4 19 ♕c1 ♗a6!, seeing various lines where the attack against e2 and f1 is valuable. In the game, 20 e5 de 21 fe ♘xe5 22 ♗xf6 b4 23 ♗xe5 ♖xe5 24 ♗d5 ♖xd5! illustrated this well.

There is little consensus in practice as to White's most effective plan. Generally White begins with 11 ♖e1 or 11 ♗e3, but in the first illustrative game we consider other approaches.

P. Nikolić–Gelfand
Belgrade 1991

1 d4 ♘f6 2 c4 g6 3 ♘f3 ♗g7 4 g3 0-0 5 ♗g2 d6 6 0-0 ♘bd7
7 ♘c3 e5
8 e4

This is by far the most popular move. After **8 h3 ♖e8, 9 e4** ed 10 ♘xd4 transposes to our main line. A rather harmless alternative is **9 de** de 10 ♗e3 ♕e7 11 ♖c1 (11 ♘d2 ♖d8 12 ♕b3 c6 13 ♖ad1 ♘f8 14 ♕a4 ♘e6 15 b4 ♘d4 16 ♘b3 ♗e6 17 ♗xd4 ed 18 ♘xd4 ♗xc4 19 b5 cb 20 ♘dxb5 ♖xd1 21 ♖xd1 ♗e6 22 ♘d4 ♗d7 23 ♕b3 ♖c8! held together Black's position in Kurajica–Damljanović, Yugoslavia Ch (Kladovo) 1991, leaving him with the better long-term prospects) 11 ... c6 12 ♕b3 ♘c5 13 ♕a3 ♗f8 14 ♖fd1 a5 15 b3 h6 16 ♔h2 ♗f5 17 ♕b2 ♕c7 18 ♘h4 ♗e6 ½–½ Fauland–Gallagher, Zug 1989. Black may also try **8 ... ed** 9 ♘xd4 ♖e8 10 b3 (10 e4 is our main line again) 10 ... ♘c5 11 ♗b2 ♗d7 12 ♕c2 (12 ♖c1 ♕c8 13 ♔h2 ♖e5 14 ♘f3 ♖h5 15 h4 a5 16 ♗a1 ♗c6 17 ♔g1 ♕d7 18 ♕c2 ♖e8∓ Lein–Tukmakov, New York 1990) 12 ... ♕c8 13 h4 (13 ♔h2 ♖e5) 13 ... ♗h3 14 ♖ad1 ♗xg2 15 ♔xg2 c6= P. Nikolić–Bischoff, Munich 1990.

Another transposition is **8 b3 ♖e8 9 e4** (9 e3 allows Black to construct a pawn centre with 9 ... c6 followed by ... e4 and ... d5) 9 ... ed 10 ♘xd4 a6 11 h3 ♖b8 12

♖e1 — see note (c) to White's twelfth move in Mirallès–Gallagher.

8	...	ed
9	♘xd4	♖e8
10	h3	

An advantage of Black's chosen system is that White has little real choice; thus Fominykh's 10 ♖e1 (10 ... ♘g4 11 h3!; 10 ... ♘c5 11 b4!?) can be met by 10 ... a6, when White can hardly do better than transpose with 11 h3.

| 10 | ... | a6!? |
| 11 | ♘b3 | |

This is a rather unnatural move, which does, however, prevent Black's plan, since ... b5 will be met by ♘a5. White has tried a number of other moves:

(a) 11 ♖b1 ♖b8 12 a4 ♘c5 13 ♖e1 a5 14 b3 c6?! (14 ... ♘fd7 refuses to give White a target) 15 ♗f4 ♘h5 16 ♗e3 ♕c7 17 g4 ♘f6 18 ♗f4± Scholz–Gallagher, France 1989.

(b) 11 ♘de2, withdraws the knight from the centre, which has its logic since it will normally be obliged to retreat anyway. Black may either continue normally, or seek to benefit from the fact that the long diagonal is now unclogged:

(b1) 11 ... ♖b8 12 ♕c2 ♘e5 13 b3 b5 14 cb (Van Wely gives the line 14 f4? ♘c6 15 e5 ♘b4∓ ∓) 14 ... ab 15 ♗g5 c6! 16 ♖ad1 b4 17 ♘a4 ♕c7 18 ♖fe1 (18 ♖d2 gives unclear play after 18 ... h6 19 ♗e3 ♗xh3 20 ♗xh3 ♘f3+ followed by ... ♘xd2, ... ♘xe4 and

... d5) and now, rather than forcing the bishop to a more effective diagonal with 18 ... h6?! 19 ♗f4 c5 20 ♕d2 ♗b7 21 ♕xd6 ♕xd6 22 ♖xd6 ♘xe4 23 ♖b6!± P. Nikolić–Van Wely, Wijk aan Zee 1992, Van Wely recommends 18 ... c5! 19 ♕d2 ♗b7∞.

(b2) 11 ... ♘b6!? 12 b3 ♘xe4 13 ♘xe4 ♖xe4 14 ♗xe4 ♗xa1. In P. Nikolić–Gelfand, Wijk aan Zee 1992, White demonstrated compensation, but no more: 15 ♗g2 ♗f6 16 ♘f4 ♖b8 17 ♗e3 ♗d7 18 ♗xb6 cb 19 ♕xd6 ♗c6 20 ♕xd8+ ♖xd8 21 ♘d5 ½-½.

(c) 11 ♗g5 h6 12 ♗e3 ♖b8. Gutman has now tried two squares for the queen; in both cases, Black should seek tactical counterplay, rather than meekly defend h6:

(c1) 13 ♕c1 and now Knaak's 13 ... c5! 14 ♘de2 b5 15 cb (15 ♗xh6 bc∞) 15 ... ab 16 ♗xh6 b4 17 ♘a4 ♘xe4∓ should be given preference over 13 ... ♔h7 14 ♖d1± c5?! 15 ♘de2 b5 16 cb ab 17 a4! b4 18 ♘b5 ♘xe4 19 ♗xe4 ♖xe4 20 ♘xd6 ♕e7 21 ♘f4! (Black would be delighted to give up an exchange to dominate the light squares around the white king) 21 ... ♗b7 22 ♘xb7 ♖xb7 23 a5!± Gutman–Gallagher, Biel 1989.

(c2) 13 ♕d2 c5 14 ♘de2. The queen is much more actively placed on d2 than on c1, but there is a tactical drawback: 14 ... ♘e5 15 b3 ♗xh3! (143).

Now 16 f4? ♗xg2 17 fe ♘xe4∓ ∓

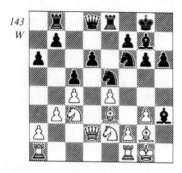

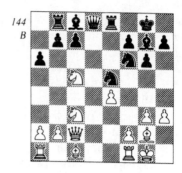

is no good, so Gutman–Knaak, Münster 1991 continued **16 ♗xh6 ♛d7 17 f3** (Necessary, since 17 ♗g5? fails to the far from obvious 17 … ♗xg2 18 ♔xg2 ♘f3!! 19 ♔xf3 ♛g4+ 20 ♔g2 ♘xe4 21 ♘xe4 ♛xe4+ when Black emerges with extra material) 17 … **b5 18 cb ab 19 ♗xg7 ♔xg7 20 ♘f4 ♗xg2 21 ♔xg2 ♖h8 22 ♖h1 b4 23 ♘cd5 ♘xd5 24 ♘xd5**, when instead of **24 … ♛e6? 25 ♖ad1!±**, Knaak analysed **24 … ♘c6! 25 ♛b2+ ♘d4 26 ♘f4** (△ 27 ♘e2) 26 … **f6!** with equality.

(c3) **13 a4 ♘e5 14 b3 ♗d7 15 ♖a2** can be met by 15 … c5 16 ♘de2 b5!? (Knaak) or 15 … ♛c8 16 ♔h2 h5, transposing to the final game of this chapter.

11	…	**♖b8**
12	**♛c2!**	

12 a4 ♘e5 13 ♛e2 c6 gives Black plenty of play.

12	…	**♘e5**
13	**c5**	

The c4-pawn is very often a target for Black's counterplay, so it is logical to liquidate it. Gelfand considers **13 ♘d5 ♘xd5 14 cd c6**

to be equal.

13	…	**dc**
14	**♘xc5** *(144)*	

This position is surprisingly awkward for Black. Gelfand recommends now **14 … ♛d6! 15 ♘b3 ♛d3 16 ♛xd3 ♘xd3 17 ♖d1 ♘xc1 18 ♖axc1** with just an edge for White. As played, Black has serious difficulties.

14	…	**♛e7?**
15	**♗e3!**	**b6**

15 … ♘c4 16 ♗d4 maintains White's plus, e.g. **16 … b6 17 ♘b3 c5? 18 ♗xf6 and 19 ♘d5±∓; 16 … ♖d8 17 ♗xf6 ♗xf6 18 ♘d5 ♖xd5 19 ed ♛xc5 20 ♖ac1 b5 21 b3±∓**.

16	**♘b3**	**c5**
17	**f4**	**♘c4**
18	**♗f2**	**♗b7**
19	**♖fe1**	

This move threatens 20 ♘d5. Note that **19 e5** doesn't advance White's cause: 19 … ♗xg2 20 ♔xg2 ♛b7+ 21 ♘h2 ♘d5 restricts White to an edge (Gelfand).

19	…	**♛d7**
20	**a4?**	

Now Black can execute a highly thematic combination. Better were

20 ♖ad1! ♕c6 (20 ... ♕c8) 21 ♔h2 △ ♗h1 and e5± (Gelfand) and **20 e5** ♗xg2 21 ♔xg2 ♘d5 22 ♘e4 (Knaak).

20 ... ♘xb2!(145)

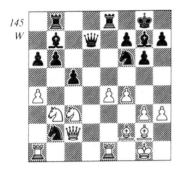

145
W

21 ♕xb2?!

Gelfand gave **21 e5** ♗xg2 22 ♔xg2 ♘d3 23 ♖ed1 ♕b7+ 24 ♔h2 ♘xf2 25 ♕xf2 ♘e4 as equal, presumably because Black's queenside is rather vulnerable.

21 ... ♘xe4
22 ♖ad1

22 ♗xe4 ♗xe4 23 ♔h2 ♗a8 gives Black strong threats on *both* long diagonals.

22 ... ♗xc3!
23 ♖xd7?

23 ♕xc3 was perhaps White's last chance. Black can then choose between **23 ... ♕xd1** and **23 ... ♕xa4.** After the text Black obtained a very promising ending: 23 ... ♗xb2 24 ♖xb7 ♖xb7 25 ♖xe4 ♖xe4 26 ♗xe4 ♖d7 27 a5 (Else 27 ... c4 wins the knight) 27 ... ba 28 ♘xc5?! ♖d1+ 29 ♔g2 ♗d4! 30 ♗b7? ♖d2 31 ♘e4 ♖c2 32 ♗xa6 ♗xf2 33 ♗d3 ♖b2 34

♘xf2 a4 35 ♗c4 a3 36 ♔f3 ♖c2 37 ♗d5 ♖d2 38 ♗c4 ♖c2 39 ♗d5 a2 40 ♗xa2 ♖xa2 0–1.

Miralles–Gallagher
Bern 1991

1 d4 ♘f6 2 c4 g6 3 ♘f3 ♗g7 4 g3 0–0 5 ♗g2 d6 6 0–0 ♘bd7 7 ♘c3 e5 8 e4 ed 9 ♘xd4 ♖e8 10 h3 a6

11 ♖e1 ♖b8
12 ♗e3

White has several alternatives:

(a) **12 ♖b1** is probably best met by **12 ... ♘e5** 13 b3 c5, though in Akopian–Piket, Groningen 1991/2, an entirely different approach turned out satisfactorily: **12 ... ♘c5** 13 b3 ♗d7 14 ♗b2 ♕c8 15 ♔h2 b5 16 cb ab 17 b4 ♘a4 18 ♘xa4 ba 19 a3 ♕a6∞. Black's play is similar to the line 10 ... ♘c5 11 ♖e1 ♗d7, introduced by Yurtaev; here Black is arguing that ♖b1 is not a terribly useful move in this position.

(b) **12 f4** appears rather weakening, but prevents the often annoying ... ♘e5. Gomez Esteban–Bellón, Spanish Ch (Lleida) 1991 continued 12 ... c5 (12 ... h5!? △ ... ♘c5, ... ♗d7) 13 ♘c2 ♘b6 (13 ... b5) 14 ♕d3 ♗d7 15 b3 ♘c8 16 a4 b5 17 ab ab 18 cb ♗e6 19 ♖a3 ♘b6 when Black had some compensation, but it never seemed enough for equality.

(c) **12 b3** c5 13 ♘c2 b5! is Black's most consistent. There can follow **14 ♕xd6 ♖b6!** 15 ♕d1 b4 16 ♘a4 ♖be6 17 ♗b2 ♕e7 18 ♕d2 ♗b7 when White must either play **19 f3 ♘h5** when Black has good play on the kingside, or return the pawn with a slight disadvantage: **19 e5 ♘xe5 20 ♗xe5 ♗xg2 21 ♔xg2 ♕b7+ 22 f3 ♖xe5∓** Csom-Bellón, Ter Apel 1991. Exchanging a pair of pawns first changes little: **14 cb ab 15 ♕xd6 ♖b6! 16 ♕d1 b4 17 ♘a4 ♖be6 18 ♗b2 ♕e7 19 ♘e3 ♗b7 20 f3 ♘h5 21 ♗xg7 ♔xg7 22 g4 ♘f4 23 ♕d2 ♘e5** and the black pieces were set to invade, in Whiteley–Gallagher, Royan 1989.

(d) **12 ♗f4 ♘e5**. Now White has three ways to defend c4:

(d1) **13 b3** h6 (Black may also opt for the immediate 13 ... c5, but this is a useful little move) **14 ♗e3 c5 15 ♘de2 b5 16 f4 ♘ed7 17 ♕xd6 b4 18 e5** (18 ♘a4? ♘xe4 19 ♗xe4 ♖xe4 20 ♗xc5 ♗xa1∓∓) **18 ... bc 19 ♘xc3!** was not too bad for White in D'Amore–Gallagher, Biel 1990, though Black is at least OK.

(d2) **13 ♗f1 ♗d7 14 ♖c1 h6 15 ♖c2 ♕c8 16 ♔h2 g5 17 ♗e3 g4 18 f4 gf 19 ♘xf3 ♘g6** secured adequate kingside play in Ervin–Benjamin, Santa Monica 1985.

(d3) **13 ♕e2 c5 14 ♘f3 ♘xf3+ 15 ♕xf3 ♘h5 16 ♗d2 ♗e6! 17 ♗f1! ♘f6 18 ♗f4 ♘h5 19 ♗e3 ♘f6 20 ♕d1** (20 ♗f4 ♘h5 repeats) **20 ... ♕b6 21 ♕c2 ♘d7 22 f4** f5 gave Black quite a promising position in Levitt–Gallagher, Hastings Masters 1990.

12 ... c5

After **12 ... ♘e5, 13 b3** c5 **14 ♘de2?!** (14 ♘c2) **14 ... b5 15 cb ab 16 ♖c1 b4∓** was Krählenbühl-Landenbergue, Lucern 1989, whilst **13 ♕e2** c5 **14 ♘c2** transposes to the note to White's fourteenth move.

13 ♘c2 ♘e5! (146)

Previously **13 ... b5** had been played, which does not seem adequate after **14 ♕xd6!**:

(a) **14 ... b4 15 ♘a4 ♘xe4** (15 ... ♗f8 16 ♕d3 ♕a5 17 b3 ♗b7 18 ♗g5 ♗g7 19 ♖ad1 ♖bd8 20 ♕f1 ♕c7 21 ♘e3! ♗xe4 22 ♗xe4 ♖xe4 23 ♘d5±± Schulze–Z. Ilić, Bern 1989) **16 ♗xe4! ♖xe4 17 ♖ad1! ♕f8 18 ♗f4±** *ECO*.

(b) **14 ... bc 15 ♘a3** (15 ♖ab1!?) **15 ... ♖xb2 16 ♘xc4** and now *ECO* gives the lines **16 ... ♖b4 17 ♕d3** △ ♘d6± and **16 ... ♖c2 17 ♕d3 ♖xc3 18 ♕xc3 ♘d5** (18 ... ♘xe4?! 19 ♕c1 ♗xa1 20 ♕xa1±) **19 ♕b3 ♘xe3 20 ♕xe3 ♗xa1 21 ♖xa1±**.

14 b3

14 ♕e2 is best met by Knaak's **14 ... b5!?**, rather than **14 ... ♗e6 15 b3 b5 16 cb ♕a5 17 ♘d5! ♗xd5 18 ed ab 19 b4!±** (*ECO*).

14 ... b5
15 cb

15 f4 ♘ed7 16 ♕xd6 bc (16 ... b4) **17 bc ♘h5**.

15 ... ab
16 f4 ♘ed7!

Of course not **16 ... ♘c6? 17 e5.** After the text, Black's knight manoeuvre ... ♘d7–e5–d7 has allowed White two free moves (b3

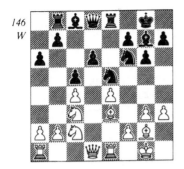

146
W

and f4) but these are both rather weakening.

17   ♕xd6   b4
18   e5

After **18 ♘a4**, Knaak mentions **18 ... ♖e6 19 ♕d2 ♘xe4 20 ♗xe4 ♖xe4 21 ♘xc5 ♗c3 22 ♕d3 ♖e7∓**, while Gallagher's preference is **18 ... ♘xe4 19 ♗xe4 ♗xa1**, when White can hardly expect compensation.

18   ...   ♖b6! *(147)*

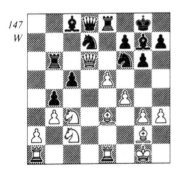

147
W

19   ♕d1

19 ♕d3 ♗a6 only helps Black.

19   ...   bc
20   ef   ♗xf6

Now Black is clearly better. White should now try 21 ♗f2,

but instead makes matters worse by playing ambitiously.

21   ♕d5?   ♗b7
22   ♕c4   ♗xg2
23   ♔xg2   ♖d6!

The clever point of this move is that now 24 ♖ad1 fails to 24 ... ♘b6 25 ♖xd6 ♕a8+!.

24   ♖e2   ♕c8!?
25   ♕b5!

The only defence to Black's threat of 25 ... ♕b7+ followed by 26 ... ♖e4, since **25 ♔f2 ♘b6!** 26 ♕xc5 ♕xc5 27 ♗xc5 ♖xe2+ 28 ♔xe2 ♖d2+ followed by 29 ... ♘d7 wins for Black.

25   ...   ♗d4
26   ♖ae1   ♕a8+
27   ♔f2   ♗xe3+!?
28   ♘xe3   ♖d2?

With this move Black starts to make things difficult for himself. After **28 ... ♘f6!** 29 ♘c4 ♖xe2+ 30 ♖xe2 ♖d1! White's days would be numbered.

29   ♘f1!   ♖exe2+
30   ♖xe2   c2?

30 ... ♕d5 31 ♕c4 ♕xc4 32 bc c2 33 ♖xd2 c1(♕) 34 ♖xd7 ♕xc4 (Knaak) and **30 ... ♖xe2+** 31 ♕xe2 ♘f6 (Gallagher) were still promising for Black.

After the text, Black no longer has any advantage. In the game a couple of time-trouble blunders actually left Black with a lost ending: **31 ♘xd2 c1(♕) 32 ♕xd7 ♔g7?** (Black should allow a perpetual: 32 ... ♕ah1 33 ♕e8+ ♔g7 34 ♕e5+) 33 ♖e7! ♕f8? 34 ♖e8 ♕xe8 35 ♕xe8 ♕xd2+ 36 ♕e2

♕d4+ 37 ♔g2 ♔h6 38 ♕c2
♕d5+ 39 ♔h2 ♔g7 40 ♕c3+ f6
41 h4 h5 42 a4 and White went
on to win this ending without
undue difficulty.

Kiril Georgiev–Knaak
Dortmund 1991

1 d4 ♘f6 2 c4 g6 3 ♘c3 ♗g7 4 g3
0–0 5 ♗g2 d6 6 0–0 ♘bd7 7 ♘c3
e5 8 e4 ed 9 ♘xd4 ♖e8 10 h3 a6
11   ♗e3   ♖b8
12   a4

Again White has a choice:

(a) 12 ♕c2 c5 13 ♘de2 b5 14
♖ad1 (14 cb ab 15 ♖ad1 b4 16
♘d5 ♘xd5 17 ♖xd5 ♘f6 18 ♖d2
♕e7 19 f3 ♗e6 20 b3 ♖bc8 21 ♘f4
d5 22 ed? ♗f5∓∓ Castiglioni–
Gallagher, Mendrisio 1989) 14 ...
♕e7 15 cb!? (15 ♗f4 ♘e5 16 cb
ab 17 ♗g5 ♕f8 18 f4 ♘c4 19 ♕c1
♗a6∓ Draško–Gallagher, Aosta
1990) 15 ... ab 16 ♘f4 ♗b7 17
♘xb5 ♗xe4 18 ♗xe4 ♘xe4 19
♘d5 ♕e6 20 ♘bc7 ♕xh3 21 ♘xe8
♖xe8 22 ♖fe1 ♕f5 23 ♗f4 ♗d4
24 ♖xd4 cd 25 ♘c7 ♖e7 26 ♕c6
g5 27 ♘d5 ♖e8 28 f3 gf 29 g4 ♕g5
30 ♕xd7 ♖e6 31 ♖xe4 ♕xd5 32
♖xe6 fe 33 ♕e8+ ½–½ Schroll–
Van Wely, Kecskemet 1991.

(b) 12 ♖c1 gives Black no problems: 12 ... c5 13 ♘de2 b5 14 cb
(14 ♕xd6) 14 ... ab 15 ♕xd6 (15
♕c2?! b4 16 ♘b1 ♗a6 17 ♖fd1
♘xe4! 18 ♗xe4 ♗xe2 19 ♖xd6
♕e7∓ 20 ♖d2 ♗b5 21 ♗g2 ♖bc8
22 a3 ♘b6 23 ♗xc5 b3 won
material in Radulov–Gallagher,

Biel 1989) 15 ... b4 16 ♘a4 ♗f8
17 ♕d3 ♕a5 18 b3 ♗a6 19 ♕c2
♖bc8 was comfortable for Black
in Szekely–Gallagher, Hastings
Challengers 1990/1.

(c) 12 b3 is a move Black is often
willing to use a tempo to provoke,
so can hardly pose problems: 12
... c5 13 ♘de2 b5 14 ♕xd6 (14 cb
ab 15 a4 b4 16 ♘b5 ♘xe4 17
♗xe4 ♖xe4 18 ♘xd6 ♕e7!? gave
Black an excellent position in Gutman–Benjamin, Dortmund 1985)
14 ... b4 15 ♘a4 (15 e5 ♘h5 16 f4
bc 17 g4 ♗f8 18 ♕d3 ♘g7∓
Grün) 15 ... ♘xe4 16 ♗xe4 ♖xe4
17 ♖ad1 ♕e8 18 ♘f4 ♗f8 ½–½
Zarković–Z. Ilić, Cetinje 1990.

(d) 12 g4 intends to reduce the
pressure on e4 by driving away
the f6 knight. Black must reply
sharply to exploit the loosening
effect of this move: 12 ... ♘e5 13
b3 c5 14 ♘de2 b5 15 f4 ♘exg4
(*ECO*'s suggestion 15 ... ♘ed7 can
be met by 16 g5! ♘h5 17 ♕xd6 b4
18 ♘d5 ♗xa1 19 ♖xa1 ♖e6 20
♕c7±) 16 hg ♘xg4 17 ♗f2 bc!
(Neither 17 ... f5? 18 ef b4 19
♗d5+ ♔h8 20 ♘e4 ♗xf5 21
♘g5± Stangl–Vazquez, World
Junior (Tunja) 1989, nor 17 ...
b4 18 ♘d5 ♗xa1 19 ♕xa1 ♗b7
20 ♗f3 ♗xd5 21 cd ♘xf2 22
♖xf2 when the black king comes
under attack, are good enough)
18 bc ♗e6 19 ♕d3 ♖b4 20 ♖ad1
(148).

Now, rather than 20 ... ♖xc4??
21 e5!±± (since 21 ... ♕a5 fails
to 22 ♗d5! ♗xd5 23 ♘xd5 ♖a4

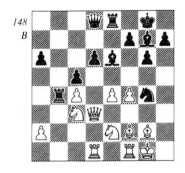

148
B

24 ed± ±) Dautov-Knaak, Bad Lauterberg 1991, Dautov recommends **20 ... ♗xc4 21 ♕xd6 ♕xd6 22 ♖xd6** with the possibilities **22 ... ♗xc3 23 ♘xc3 ♗xf1 24 ♗xf1 ♘xf2 25 ♔xf2 ♖b2+ 26 ♔f3** (26 ♔e3!?) **26 ... ♖c2 27 ♘d5 ♖b8! 28 ♖xa6 ♖bb2 29 ♘e3 ♖f2+ 30 ♔g3 ♖xa2 31 ♖c6=** and **22 ... ♖b2 23 ♗f3 h5! 24 e5! g5! 25 ♖fd1 gf 26 ♖d8 ♖xd8 29 ♖xd8+ ♔h7 30 ♗xc5 ♗xe5**, considering the position to be unclear.

12 ... ♘e5!?

Alternative methods, resulting in more traditional King's Indian positions, are **12 ... a5 13 ♕c2 c6 14 ♖ad1 ♕c7 15 ♖fe1 ♘c5 16 f4±** (Dautov) and **12 ... ♘c5 13 ♕c2 a5 14 ♖ad1 ♕e7 15 ♖fe1 c6 16 f4 ♘fd7 17 ♗f2 ♘f8 18 ♖e2 ♗d7 19 ♘b3**, as in Cvitan-Gallagher, Lenk 1989. White ought to be a little better here, though Black emerged victorious from the complications following **19 ... ♘xb3 20 ♕xb3 ♗e6 21 ♘d5 ♕d7 22**

♘b6 ♕c7 23 ♖ed2 ♖bd8 24 ♕c2 f5 25 c5 dc 26 ef ♗xf5 27 ♕xc5 ♘e6 28 ♕xa5 ♖xd2 29 ♖xd2 ♘xf4!.

13 b3 ♗d7
14 ♖a2

14 f4!? must be critical. A further possibility is **14 ♖e1 c5 15 ♘de2 ♗c6 16 ♕c2 b5 17 cb ab 18 ab ♗xb5 19 ♘xb5 ♖xb5 20 f4 ½-½** Adorjan-Groszpeter, Hungarian Ch 1991.

14 ... ♕c8
15 ♔h2 h5!
16 ♖d2 h4 (149)
17 gh

17 g4? is met by **17 ... c5 18 ♘de2 ♗xg4 19 hg ♘fxg4+ 20 ♔g1 h3 21 ♗xh3 ♘xe3 22 ♗xc8 ♘f3+ 23 ♔h1 ♘xd1∓** (Knaak).

17 ... c5
18 ♘de2 ♗xh3!

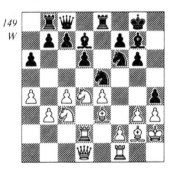

149
W

Forcing a draw.

19 ♗xh3 ♘f3+
20 ♔g3 ♘h5+
21 ♔g2 ♘xh4+
       ½-½

14   Lines with ♘ge2

These ideas are quite closely related to the Sämisch. White retains the option of supporting e4 with f2–f3, but meanwhile develops some pieces.

In the first game we see the move 5 ♘ge2. The problem with this is that the knight will have to move again to allow the completion of kingside development. The knight's subsequent posting on g3 appears awkward, but from here the knight covers the important squares e4 and f5, while White's thrust h4–h5 is often a useful possibility — after the possible reply ... h7–h5, Black must watch out for sacrifices on h5. Black's most promising methods take advantage of the slowness of White's development by opening the queenside, in some cases combined with a well-timed ... h5, i.e. when h2–h4 in reply may just leave White's h-pawn weak.

With 5 ♗d3, the subject of our second game, White develops the bishop before playing ♘ge2. In answer to this, standard play by Black allows White a flexible position with good control of the central light squares — all the benefits of the Sämisch, but without losing time and weakening the dark squares with f2–f3. It is therefore no surprise that Black's best approach is to strike at the weakened square d4, threatening to sink a knight into the heart of White's position.

Korchnoi–Nunn
Wijk aan Zee 1992

1 d4 ♘f6 2 c4 g6 3 ♘c3 ♗g7 4 e4 d6

5   ♘ge2 *(150)*

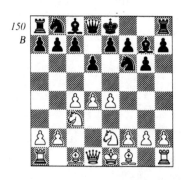

5   ...   0–0

Black has a few ways to try to benefit from delaying or omitting castling. The only argument against these is possible transposition to lines of the Sämisch. Thus:

(a) **5 ... e5 6 d5** (Exchanging queens is harmless since White cannot develop a quick initiative with the knight on e2) 6 ... ♘a6 7 ♘g3 h5 8 ♗e2 h4 9 ♘f1 ♘c5 is quite a good idea. There can follow **10 ♕c2** a5 11 ♗g5 ♗f8 12 b3 b6 13 ♖g1 ♗e7 14 ♗e3 ♘h5 15 g3 ♗g5 16 ♕d2 ♗xe3 17 ♕xe3 ♗d7 18 0-0-0 ♕e7 19 f4 0-0-0= Serper–Akopian, USSR Ch (Moscow) 1991, or **10 ♗g5** ♗h6 11 ♗xh6 ♖xh6 12 ♘d2 ♘h5 (12 ... a5!?) 13 b4 ♘d7 14 ♗xh5 ♖xh5 15 0-0 ♘f6 16 ♕e2 ♖g5 17 ♘f3 ♘h5!? 18 ♘xg5 ♕xg5 19 ♕e3 ♘f4 20 g3 hg 21 ♕xg3! ♕f6 22 ♔h1 ♗d7 23 ♕e3 ♔e7 24 f3 ♖h8 25 ♖f2 (Novikov–Gelfand, USSR 1987) and now 25 ... ♘h3! would have maintained Black's counterchances. White, however, has other options on move six. **6 ♗g5** can be met by 6 ... h6 7 ♗h4 g5 8 ♗g3 ♘h5 9 de ♘xg3 followed by 10 ... ♗xe5, but **6 f3!** leaves Black in one of the less dynamic lines of the Sämisch (6 ... ♘fd7 7 ♗e3 ♗h6 8 ♗f2 0-0 9 h4 c5 10 d5 f5 11 h5 ♗g5 might be worth investigating).

(c) **5 ... a6**. Now after 6 f3, it is a matter of taste which line of the Sämisch Black chooses, but note that ... ♘c6 has less bite when the bishop is not committed to e3. One idea is after 6 ... 0-0, to meet 7 ♗g5 with 7 ... c6, and 7 ♗e3 with 7 ... ♘c6. If White steers clear of the Sämisch, we have after **6 ♘g3**:

(c1) **6 ... h5** 7 ♗e2 c6 8 0-0 ♘bd7 9 ♖e1! e5 (9 ... ♕b6 10 ♘a4 ♕c7 11 h3!±) 10 ♗g5 ♕c7 11 ♖c1?! (11 d5 c5 12 ♖b1± — Piket) 11 ... 0-0 12 d5 c5 13 ♘f1 ♘h7 14 ♗d2 h4 15 ♗d3 ♘df6 16 ♘e3 ♗d7 17 a4 ♘h5 18 g3 ♗h6 19 ♖c2 ♔h8 20 ♘g2 left White marginally for preference in Korchnoi–J. Piket, Wijk aan Zee 1992.

(c2) **6 ... c6** 7 a4 (7 ♗e2 b5 8 0-0 bc 9 ♗xc4 d5 10 ♗b3 de 11 ♘gxe4 ♘d5 12 ♕f3 0-0 13 ♗g5 ♖a7 14 ♖ad1 h6 15 ♗c1 e6 16 ♖fe1 a5 gave Black a playable game in Novikov–Kruppa, USSR Ch (Moscow) 1991 7 ... a5 8 ♗e2 e5 (8 ... 0-0 9 0-0 e5 10 ♗e3 ♘a6 11 ♕d2 ♘g4 12 ♗xg4 ♗xg4 13 f3 ed 14 ♗xd4 ♗e6 15 ♖ad1 ♘c5 16 ♗xg7 ♔xg7 17 ♔h1 f6 led to a draw after careful defence by Black in Gulko–Benjamin, USA Ch (Los Angeles) 1991) 9 d5 ♘a6 10 h4 (10 ♗e3 0-0 11 h3 ♘c5 12 ♕c2 ♕e7 13 0-0 ♘fd7 14 ♖ad1 ♘a6 15 ♕d2 ♖e8 Remlinger–Vladimirov, Gausdal International 1991) 10 ... h5 11 ♖a3 ♘d7! 12 ♗g5 ♗f6 13 dc bc 14 ♕xd6 ♘b4 15 ♕d2 ♗xg5 16 hg ♘c5 gave Black fantastic compensation in K. Rasmussen–Berg Hansen, Danish Ch (Århus) 1992; there followed 17 ♘a2 ♕xd2+ 18 ♔xd2 ♔e7 19 ♔c3 ♖b8 20 ♘c1

♖d8 21 ♘b3 ♘xb3 22 ♖xb3 ♖d4
23 f3 ♗e6 24 ♖d1 ♗xc4!∓.

6 ♘g3   e5

Piket suggests **6 ... a6** 7 ♗e2
c5 8 d5 (8 dc) 8 ... b5, while **6 ...
♘fd7!?** 7 h4 (7 ♗e3) 7 ... ♘c6 8
d5 ♘d4 9 ♗e3 c5 10 dc ♘xc6 11
h5 ♕a5 12 hg hg led to a short
sharp fight in Alber–Degenhardt,
Frankfurt 1990: 13 ♕d2 ♘c5 14
♖c1 ♘e6 15 b3 ♗d7 16 ♗d3
♘e5 17 ♗e2 ♖fe8 18 ♘f5?! gf 19
ef ♘f8 20 ♗h6 ♗f6 21 ♕f4? ♘eg6
22 fg ♗xc3+ 0–1.

One point to note is that 6 ...
a6 7 ♗e2 **c6** 8 0–0 b5 fails to 9
e5! ♘e8 10 f4 ♘d7 11 ♗e3 ♗b7
12 c5± Miles–Nunn, Amsterdam
1985.

7 d5   a5

The extravagant **7 ... ♘g4** was
tried in Serper–Dannevig, Gausdal International 1991. After 8
♗e2 ♕h4 9 ♘b5 ♘a6 10 ♗d2
♗h6!? (10 ... c6 11 ♕c1!) 11
♗xh6 ♘xh6 12 0–0 f5 13 ef gf 14
f4! ef 15 ♘h5 f3! 16 ♗xf3 ♕xc4
17 a4, Black should have tried **17
... ♕h4**, since in the game 17 ...
♗d7? 18 ♕d2! f4 19 ♖fc1! left him
in a real mess.

The main alternative is **7 ... c6
8 ♗e2 a6** *(151)*. Then White may
choose to push a rook's pawn:

(a) **9 a4?!** a5! 10 h4 h5 11 ♗g5
♕b6 12 ♖a3!? (12 ♕c2 ♘a6) 12
... ♘bd7 (Black is careful not to
allow the typical blow 12 ... ♘a6?!
13 ♗xf6 ♗xf6 14 ♗xh5! gh 15
♘xh5) 13 ♕c2 ♘c5 14 ♗e3. Now
14 ... ♘g4! 15 ♗xg4 ♗xg4 would

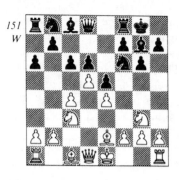

151
W

threaten both 16 ... ♕xb2 and 16
... ♕b4, but in Ionov–Bologan,
USSR Ch (Moscow) 1991, **14 ...
♗d7** 15 ♘f1 ♖ac8 16 ♘d2 ♕b4
17 ♘a2 ♕b6 18 ♘c3 ♕d8 19 ♕b1
♔h7 20 b4 ab 21 ♕xb4 ♗h6 was
pleasant for Black in any case.

(b) **9 0–0** cd 10 cd ♘bd7 (10 ...
b5 11 b4 △ a4) 11 ♗e3 (11 a4)
11 ... b5 12 b4 ♘b6 13 a4 ♘xa4!
14 ♘xa4 ba 15 ♖xa4 h5!∞ *ECO*.

(c) **9 h4** cd (9 ... b5 10 h5 cd 11
cd ♘bd7 12 ♗e3 ♘b6 13 b3±
Ermenkov–Topalov, Šumen 1991)
10 cd h5 11 ♗g5 ♕e8 12 ♕d2
♘bd7 13 ♗h6 ♕d8 14 a4 ♖e8 15
a5 ♘f8 16 ♗xg7 ♔xg7 17 ♘a4
♖b8 18 ♖a3 ♗g4 19 f3 ♗d7 20
♘b6 ♕e7 21 ♖c3 ♖ed8 22 ♕g5
♔g8 23 0–0 ♘8h7 24 ♕e3 ♗e8
25 ♘h1 ½–½ Hort–Wahls, Munich
1991.

8 ♗e2   ♘a6
9 h4

A more conservative approach
led nowhere in G. Georgadze–
Akopian, Tbilisi 1989: 9 0–0 ♘c5
10 b3 ♗d7 11 ♖b1 h5 12 ♗g5
♕e8 13 ♕d2 ♘h7 14 ♗h6 h4 15

♗xg7 ♚xg7 16 ♘h1 ♕e7 17
♖be1 ♕g5∓.

	9	...	c6
	10	h5	cd
	11	cd	♘c5 *(152)*

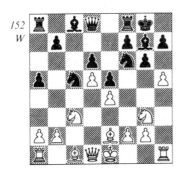

152
W

12   ♗e3

White has two other tries for an
advantage:

(a) **12 a4!?** ♗d7 (12 ... ♕b6!?)
13 ♖a3 ♖c8 14 ♗e3 ♕b6 15 hg
fg 16 f3 gave White an edge in
Novikov–G. Hernandez, Pamplona 1991/2.

(b) **12 ♗g5** a4 13 ♕d2 ♕a5 14
f3 ♗d7 15 ♔f2 b5 16 b4 ab 17
ab ♕b6 18 ♗e3 b4 19 ♘a4 ♗xa4
20 ba ♗h6 was played in Novikov–J. Polgar, Pamplona 1990/1.
There followed 21 ♖hb1 ♗f4 22
♗b5 b3 23 ♕e2 ♗xe3+ 24 ♕xe3
♘xd5!? 25 ed f5 26 ♔e2 f4 27 ♕f2
fg 28 ♕xg3 e4 30 hg ♕c7 31
gh+ ♔h8 and Black had some
problems to solve.

12   ...   ♕b6!

12 ... ♗d7 13 a4!± ♘e8 14
♖a3!? ♘c7 15 ♕d2 ♘7a6? (15 ...
♕e7) 16 ♘b5 was terrible for Black

in Hort–Schöne, German Ch
1991. Note that **12 ... a4?** 13 ♗xc5
dc 14 ♘xa4 gives Black no real
compensation.

Nunn's move eyes the potential
weakness b3 and in some cases
the b2-pawn.

13   b3

13 0–0 and **13 ♕d2?!** would
both be met by 13 ... ♗d7 to
prepare ... a4.

	13	...	♗d7
	14	0–0	♕b4!?

More adventurous, but not
necessarily better, than **14 ... ♖fc8**.

15   ♕d2!

Korchnoi avoids **15 ♗d2**
♕d4∓, and prepares to kick back
the queen with a3, seeing that the
b-pawn is poisoned.

	15	...	♖fc8
	16	a3!	♕b6
	17	♖ab1	♕d8
	18	h6!?	

This committal move eventually
gets White into trouble; safer is **18
hg**.

	18	...	♗f8
	19	♖fc1	

More consistent is **19 ♗g5!?**
♗e7 20 f4 ♘e8! 21 ♗xe7 ♕xe7
22 f5 ♕h4 23 ♕e3 ♘f6 (Nunn), but
Black has plenty of play here.

	19	...	♘g4
	20	♗xg4	♗xg4
	21	b4	ab
	22	ab	♘a4
	23	♘xa4	♖xa4
	24	♖xc8	♗xc8
	25	b5	♗e7
	26	♕c2?!	

Nunn considers **26 ♕b2** followed by ♖a1 good enough to maintain equality; with the rooks exchanged the weakness of Black's back rank balances the weakness of h6.

26	...	♖a8
27	b6	♕f8!
28	♖f1?!	♗d8
29	♕c3?!	♗d7
30	♕d2	f5!

Now White's problems are serious. However, Korchnoi managed to survive, despite some further time-trouble mistakes: **31 f4** ♕xh6 **32** ♕f2 ♖a3 **33** ef gf **34** ♘e2 ♗b5? (34 ... ♕h4!) **35** ♖c1! ♗h4 **36** g3 ♗xe2 **37** gh ♕h5 **38** ♖c8+ ♔f7 **39** ♖c7+ ♔g6 **40** fe ♕g4+ **41** ♔h2 de∓ **42** ♖c8?! (42 ♖c1!) 42 ... ♕e4?! (42 ... ♔f7!) **43** ♕xe2 ♖xe3 **44** ♕g2+ ♕xg2+ **45** ♔xg2 f4!∓ **46** ♖c7 ♖d3?? (Now White can make a draw. Instead 46 ... ♔f5! coordinates Black's pieces, whereupon the connected passed pawns triumph) **47** ♖xb7 ♖xd5 **48** ♖b8 ♖b5 **49** b7 ♔h5 **50** ♖e8 ♖xb7 **51** ♖xe5+ ♔g4 **52** ♖g5+ ♔xh4 **53** ♖g8 ♖b3 **54** ♖f8 ♖g3+ **55** ♔f2 ♖g4 ½-½.

Seirawan–Kožul
Wijk aan Zee 1991

1 d4 ♘f6 2 c4 g6 3 ♘c3 ♗g7 4 e4 d6

5	♗d3	0-0

5 ... ♘c6 can also be played, but generally transposes.

5 ... e5 6 d5 a5 (6 ... 0-0 7 ♗g5!?) **7 ♘ge2 ♘a6** was tried in Seirawan–I. Ivanov, USA Ch (Los Angeles) 1991. Best was then immediate queenside play with 8 a3, ♖b1 and b4 (Seirawan).

6	♘ge2 *(153)*

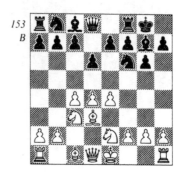

153
B

6	...	♘c6

This is by far the most logical response for Black, attacking the weakened d4-square. If Black tries to reach a more traditional King's Indian position, then White's pieces turn out to be rather well placed, controlling e4, while the f-pawn can easily advance if appropriate. A further use of the d3-bishop is to support a queenside advance by covering some crucial light squares. The alternatives are:

(a) **6 ... e5 7 d5 ♘h5** (7 ... c6 8 0-0 cd 9 cd ♘bd7 10 a3 ♘c5 11 ♗c2 a5 12 ♗g5 h6 13 ♗e3 ♘g4 14 ♗d2 f5 15 f3 ♘f6 16 b4± Arkhipov–Gallagher, Kecskemet 1990) 8 0-0 ♘d7 (8 ... f5 9 ef gf 10 f4) 9 ♗e3 f5 10 ef gf 11 ♘g3 ♘xg3 12 fg ♘c5 13 ♗c2 ♗d7 14 b4 ♘a6 15 ♖b1 ♕e7 16 ♕d2±

Aleksandrov–Shchekachev, Jurmala 1991.

(b) **6 ... ♘bd7 7 ♗c2** (7 0-0 a6!?) 7 ... a6 8 0-0 (8 a4 e5 9 d5 a5 10 h3! ♘c5 11 ♗e3 ♘fd7 12 0-0 ♘a6! 13 ♘a2 ♘dc5 was decent for Black in Seirawan–Ivanchuk, Reykjavik 1991) 8 ... c6 (8 ... c5 9 d5 b5 10 cb ab 11 ♘xb5 with a4 and ♘ec3 to follow, hardly offers Black compensation) 9 a4 a5 10 h3 (10 f4) 10 ... e5 11 ♗e3 ♖e8 12 ♕d2 ed 13 ♗xd4 ♘c5 14 ♘g3 ♕b6 (14 ... ♗e6 15 ♖fd1! ♗xc4 16 e5±) 15 ♖ad1 ♕b4 16 f4! ♕xc4 17 f5 ♘bd7 18 ♗b1! left Black in grave difficulties in Piskov–Wahls, Bundesliga 1991/2, due to White's direct threats against f7.

7 0-0 e5

7 ... ♘d7 is a logical idea, increasing the pressure on d4, but may not completely solve Black's problems. After **8 ♗e3 e5 9 d5 ♘d4**, White has:

(a) **10 ♗xd4?!** ed 11 ♘b5 ♘e5! 12 ♘bxd4 c5! 13 dc bc intending ... ♗a6 and ... d5 gives Black great compensation (Kulikov–Gerber, USSR 1987).

(b) **10 ♗c2** ♘xc2 11 ♕xc2 a6 (11 ... f5 12 ef gf 13 f4 ♘f6 14 h3 ♗d7 15 ♕d2 ♕e8 was Olafsson–Khalifman, Wijk aan Zee 1991) 12 ♖ae1 ♔h8 13 ♕d2 f5 14 ef gf 15 f4 e4 16 ♗d4 ♘f6! 17 ♘d1 ♕e8. Now 18 ♘ec3?! c5! 19 dc bc 20 ♘e2 ♗e6 21 ♘e3 ♖d8 22 ♕a5 c5 23 ♗c3 ♕g6 gave Black counterplay in Marin–Kožul, Sitges 1991. Marin's suggestion is **18 ♘e3±**.

(c) **10 ♗b1** ♘xe2+ 11 ♕xe2 a5 12 ♗c2 ♘c5 13 a3 f5 14 ef (14 f3!) 14 ... gf 15 f4 e4 16 ♕d2 a4 17 ♗xc5 dc 18 ♘xa4 ♗d4+ was reasonable for Black in Arbakov–Belov, Katowice 1990.

(d) **10 ♘b5!?** ♘xe2+ 11 ♗xe2 f5 (11 ... a5 12 ♕d2 ♘c5 13 ♘c3 b6 14 f3 f5 15 ef ♗xf5 16 ♖ac1 ♖f7 17 ♘d1! ♕e7 18 ♘f2 ♖ff8 19 ♖fe1 ♖fe8 20 ♗d1 left White with an enduring structural edge in Kiselëv–A. Kuzmin, USSR Ch (Moscow) 1991) 12 f3 (with b2 undefended, 12 ef gf 13 f4 is not a good idea) 12 ... a6 13 ♘c3 a5 14 a3 b6 15 b4 ♘f6 16 c5 ab 17 ab ♖xa1 18 ♕xa1 bc 19 bc fe 20 fe ♘g4 21 ♖xf8+ ♕xf8 22 ♗xg4 ♗xg4 was Glek–A. Kuzmin, Moscow 1991. White's edge is not so troublesome since the white king is rather exposed to perpetual checks.

8 d5 ♘d4
9 f3

9 ♗g5 h6 10 ♗h4 c5 11 dc bc 12 b4 ♖e8 13 b5 cb 14 cb g5 15 ♗g3 ♗b7 was wonderful for Black in Dzindzichashvili–Benjamin, USA Ch (Los Angeles) 1991.

More normal is **9 ♘xd4 ed** *(154)* and now:

(a) **10 ♘e2** ♖e8 11 f3 c5 (Ermolinsky analysed the alternative 11 ... ♘d7!? 12 b3 ♘c5 13 ♗b2 f5 14 ♗xd4 fe 15 fe ♘xe4=) 12 ♗g5 ♕c7 13 ♕d2 (13 h3!?; 13 ♘g3 ♘d7 14 f4 h6 15 ♗h4 b5! gave Black good play in Yudasin–Temirbaev,

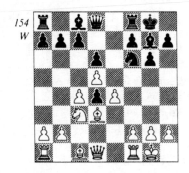

154
W

Kuybyshev 1986) 13 ... ♘d7!? (13 ... a6?! is unnecessary preparation for ... b5 and effectively loses a tempo) 14 f4 b5 15 b3 (15 cb a6 hands Black the initiative) 15 ... bc 16 bc ♖b8 17 ♘g3 ♖b4! 18 e5 de 19 f5 ♕b6 20 ♘e4 f6 21 d6! ♖b2 22 ♕c1 gave White enough activity to secure a perpetual check in Nenashev–Ernolinsky, Pavlodar 1987.

(b) 10 ♘b5 ♖e8 (After 10 ... ♕e7 11 ♖e1 ♘g4 12 h3, 12 ... a6 13 hg ab 14 cb ♕h4 15 g3 favours White, whilst 12 ... ♘xf2?! 13 ♔xf2 a6 14 ♘a3 ♗e5 15 ♖f1! arranged a successful king evacuation in Seirawan–Gelfand, Wijk aan Zee 1992; after 15 ... ♕h4+ 16 ♔e2 f5 17 ef ♗xf5 18 ♗xf5 ♖xf5 19 ♖xf5 gf 20 ♔f1 (the f-file is now safe) 20 ... ♕g3 21 ♕f3 ♕h2, 22 ♘c2!±± would have left Black with nothing) 11 ♖e1 and now:

(b1) 11 ... ♘g4 12 h3 gives Black problems: 12 ... a6 13 hg ab 14 cb ♕h4 15 g3! (discovered by endgame specialist Shereshevsky) 15

... ♕xg4 (15 ... ♕h3 16 ♗f1 ♕xg4 is a slight improvement) 16 ♕xg4 ♗xg4 17 ♔g2 with a very good ending for White due to the potentially passed a-pawn (Yusupov–Ehlvest, USSR Ch (Minsk) 1987); 12 ... c6 13 dc bc 14 hg cb 15 cb ♕h4 16 ♗e2! d5 17 g3! ♕h3 18 ♗f3 de 19 ♖xe4 ♖xe4 20 ♗xe4 ♗xg4 21 ♕f1! with a similarly advantageous ending (Olafsson–Mortensen, Espoo Z 1989).

(b2) 11 ... a6!? 12 ♘xd4 ♘xd5 13 cd ♗xd4= 14 ♕c2 ♗d7 15 ♗e3 ♗g7 16 ♖ad1 (16 ♕b3!?) 16 ... c5 17 dc ½–½ Seirawan–Benjamin, USA Ch (Los Angeles) 1991.

9 ... c5
Black may consider also **9 ... ♘d7**.

10 ♘xd4! cd?!
Much more natural is 10 ... ed 11 ♘e2, which after 11 ... ♖e8 transposes to note (a) to White's ninth move. After the text, White obtains a substantial queenside preponderance.

11 ♘a4! ♗d7
After 11 ... ♘d7?! 12 b4 f5 13 c5 ♘f6 14 ♘b2 △ ♘c4 Black's attacking chances are stillborn.

12 b4 a5
13 b5! b6?
White's next move, threatening 15 fe de 16 c5, shows this to be a bad decision; Black cannot cover b6 in a convenient manner. Seirawan instead proposes 13 ... ♕c7, with the point that 14 b6? fails to 14 ... ♗xa4; but he judges 14

♗g5 intending ♕d2 and ♖ac1 quite pleasant for White.

14	f4!	♘g4
15	f5	gf!
16	ef	♕h4
17	h3	♘e3
18	♗xe3	de	*(155)*

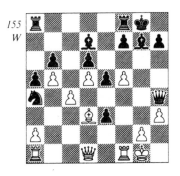

155
W

19   ♕g4!

Seirawan also considered **19 ♘xb6!?** ♕d4 **20** ♔h1 e4 (20 ... ♕xb6 21 f6! △ ♗xh7+) **21** ♘xd7, which is pretty strong, but the text is clearer — Black wins an exchange, but none of his pieces have any scope.

19	...	♕xg4
20	hg	e4
21	♗e2!	

Naturally, opening the e-file would be a disaster for White.

21	...	♗xa1
22	♖a1	♖ab8

An unfortunate necessity. Now White has time to bring the king to f4, which followed by rook penetration to h6 would be decisive.

23	♔h2	h5!
24	gh	♗xf5
25	♔g3?!	

As it happens, **25 ♖f1!** ♗h7 26 ♖f6! ♖fd8 27 g4! is even nastier.

25	...	♔g7
26	♔f4	♗h7
27	g4!	

Black is entirely without activity and can only wait for White to create a strong passed pawn with the c5-pawn break. In some time trouble, Kožul was tricked into allowing this rather quickly: 27 ... f6 28 ♘c3 ♔h6 29 ♘d1 ♖be8 30 ♘xe3 ♖e5 31 ♖f1 (31 ♖d1 is more direct) 31 ... ♖g8 32 ♗d1 f5? (Black sees the undefended rook on f1, but after White's reply, finds that he has only ruined what was left of his own position) 33 ♗e2! ♖g5 34 c5! bc 35 b6 ♖e8 36 gf ♖b8 37 ♖b1 ♖gg8 38 b7 ♔g7 39 ♖b6 ♔f7 40 ♗a6 ♔e7 41 ♖c6 ♔d7 42 ♖c8 1–0.

15 5 ♗g5 and 5 ♗f4

In this short chapter we consider a few ideas for Black against two lines in which White avoids playing e4, and instead develops his queen's bishop. These systems are not terribly threatening, but Black must be careful to avoid an entirely passive position.

Knaak–H. Grünberg
E. German Ch (Zittau) 1989

1 d4 ♘f6 2 c4 g6
3   ♘c3

It is worth mentioning the slightly bizarre **3 ♗g5 ♘e4 4 ♗f4**. Then Speelman–Ehlvest, Reykjavik 1991 continued **4 ... c5 5 ♕c2 ♕a5+ 6 ♘d2 f5 7 ♘f3**, when 7 ... ♗g7 would have been equal. The players analysed the Budapest-like **4 ... e5!? 5 de ♗b4+ 6 ♘d2 (6 ♗d2 ♘xd2 7 ♘xd2 ♘c6 8 ♘f3 ♕e7=) 6 ... d6! (6 ... f6) 7 ♘f3 (Not 7 ed? ♕f6!?) 7 ... ♘c6=.**

3   ...   ♗g7
4   ♘f3   0–0

The alternative King's Indian move-order is **4 ... d6**. Then:

(a) **5 ♗g5 c6 6 e3 ♕a5 7 ♕d2 (7 ♗e2 ♘e4) 7 ... ♗g4 *(165)* is** an interesting way to attack the g5-bishop.

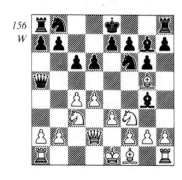

156
W

Then **8 ♗e2 (8 ♗xf6 ♗xf6 9 ♗e2 ♘d7 10 ♘e4=; 8 b4!? ♕xb4 9 ♖b1 ♕a5 10 ♖xb7 ♘bd7!∞** S. Pedersen) **8 ... ♗xf3 9 ♗xf6 ♗xf6 10 ♗xf3 ♘d7 11 0–0 0–0 12 a3 ♕c7 13 b4 a6 14 ♖fd1 ♗g7 15 ♖ac1 ♖fd8** was reasonable for Black in Danielsen–Schandorff, Danish Ch (Århus) 1992. There followed **16 c5?! dc 17 bc ♘xc5 18 ♘d5 cd 19 ♖xc5 ♕d6 20 ♖xd5 ♕xa3 21 ♖xa5 ♕b3 22 ♖aa1 ♕e6 23 ♗xb7 ♖a7 24 ♗f3 ♖b8** when Black's chances were preferable.

(b) **5 ♗f4 ♘h5!? 6 ♗g5 h6 7 ♗e3 (7 ♗h4 g5 8 ♗g3 c5!** is promising for Black after **9 e3**

♘xg3 or 9 d5 ♕a5 10 ♕d2 ♘xg3⩲
Farago–Szabo, Hungarian Ch
1969) 7 ... 0–0 8 ♕d2 ♔h7 9 h3
f5!? 10 g4!? fg ll hg ♗xg4 12 ♘h4?!
(12 ♗g2 e5 13 0–0–0 ♘c6 14 d5
♘e7 15 ♖dg1∞ Kupreichik) 12 ...
e5! 13 de ♘c6! 14 ed ♕xd6⩲
Vaganian–Kupreichik, USSR Ch
1979.

5 ♗g5

5 ♗f4 d6 (5 ... c5 6 d5 d6 7 e4
is a Benoni line) 6 h3 (6 e3 c5 7
♗e2 ♘h5!?) 6 ... ♘bd7 7 e3 ♕e8!?
(7 ... e6 followed by ... ♕e7 is a
safer way to prepare ... e5, whilst
7 ... c6 8 ♗e2 a6 9 0–0 b5 10 ♖c1
♗b7 11 ♘d2 was Andersson–
Kamsky, Tilburg 1990; Kamsky
then gave 11 ... b4 12 ♘ce4 c5 13
♘xf6+ ♗xf6 14 ♘b3 ♕b6=) 8
♗e2 e5 9 ♗h2 ♘h5 10 de?! (10
0–0 f5) 10 ... de 11 ♘b5 ♕d8 12
g4 ♘hf6 13 ♘xe5 ♘e4 14 ♘d3 (14
♘xd7!? ♗xd7 △ ... ♕h4) 14 ...
♕h4 15 ♗f3 ♘dc5 16 ♗xe4 ♘xe4
17 ♕f3 ♗d7! 18 ♘xc7 f5! 19 ♘xa8
♗c6 gave Black excellent play in
Fedder–T. Sørensen, Copenhagen
Ch 1992.

5 ... c5
6 e3

6 d5 d6 7 ♕d2 b5 8 cb a6 9
e4 ♕a5 10 b6 ♘bd7= Yusupov–
Balashov, USSR 1983.

6 ... cd
7 ed

7 ♘xd4 gives White nothing
after 7 ... ♕a5 △ ... ♘e4. Instead
Dražić–J. Polgar, Novi Sad OL
1990 continued 7 ... ♘c6 8 ♗e2
d6 (8 ... ♕a5) 9 0–0 ♗d7 10 ♕d2

♖c8 11 ♖fd1 a6 12 ♖ac1 h6 13
♗h4 g5 14 ♗g3 ♕a5 15 h4 g4
16 ♘xc6 bc 17 ♘d5! ♕d8 18
♘xf6+ ♗xf6 18 c5!±.

7 ... d5!? (157)

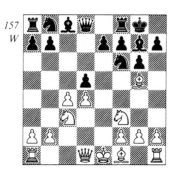

This pawn sacrifice is the point
of Black's play. If White declines,
Black is left with a very satisfactory Panov Attack position.
Acceptance, on the other hand,
entails exchanging a bishop for
knight while losing time and opening the position.

8 ♗xf6

8 cd ought not to be harmful,
but was successful in Smyslov–
Martinović, Groningen 1989/90:
8 ... ♘xd5 9 ♕b3 (9 ♗c4?! ♗e6!)
9 ... ♘xc3 10 bc ♘c6 11 ♗e2 b6
12 0–0 ♕d6 13 ♖ad1 e6 14 ♘d2!?
♘a5 15 ♕b4 ♕c7 16 ♘e4 h6 17
♕e7 ♕xe7 18 ♗xe7 ♖e8 19 ♘f6+
♗xf6 20 ♗xf6 ♗b7 21 ♖d3 ♗d5
22 ♖h3 ♔h7 23 ♖e1 e5 24 de
♘c4 25 ♗xc4 ♗xc4 and 1–0 due
to 26 ♖e4.

8 ... ♗xf6
9 ♘xd5

9 cd gives Black three possibilities:

(a) **9 ... e6!?** is Carsten Hansen's suggestion, which is probably best met by 10 ♗c4!?.

(b) **9 ... ♗g4** 10 ♗e2 ♘d7 (10 ... ♕b6 11 0–0!? ♕xb2?! 12 ♘e4!± S. Pedersen) 11 0–0 ♗xf3 12 ♗xf3 ♕b6 13 ♕a4 ♕xb2 14 ♕xd7 ♕xc3 15 ♕xb7 ½–½ Pekarek–Züger, Prague 1989.

(c) **9 ... ♘d7!?** 10 ♗c4 (10 ♗e2 ♘b6 11 ♕b3) 10 ... ♘b6 11 ♗b3 ♗g4 12 0–0 ♘c8 13 ♘e4 ♗g7 14 ♖e1 ♘d6 15 ♘xd6 ♕xd6 16 ♖e4 ♗f5 17 ♖e3 ♖ac8 18 ♕e1 ♖c7 19 ♖c3 ♗h6 led eventually to a Black win in Allan–Nunn, Szirak IZ 1987.

9 ... ♗g7
10 ♘e3

The alternatives do not promise much either:

(a) 10 ♘c3 ♗g4 11 ♗e2 (11 d5 ♕a5 12 ♕c2 ♗xf3 13 gf ♘d7 14 ♗e2 ♖ac8 15 0–0 ♘b6 16 ♕b3 ♗xc3 17 bc ♖c7 18 ♖fd1 ♖fc8∓ Moore–Burgess, Frome 1991) 11 ... ♘c6 12 d5 ♗xf3 13 ♗xf3 (13 gf ♘d4) 13 ... ♘e5 14 ♗e2 ♖c8 15 ♕b3 ♕c7= *ECO*.

(b) 10 ♗e2 ♘c6 11 0–0 ♕d6 12 ♘c3 ♘xd4 13 ♘xd4 ♕xd4 14 ♕b3= Kristinsson–H. Olafsson, Reykjavik 1984.

10 ... ♘c6
11 d5?

11 ♘c2 is met by 11 ... ♗g4=, but the text leads to trouble.

11 ... ♕a5+
12 ♘d2

Neither 12 ♕d2 ♗xb2 nor 12

♔e2 ♘e5 helps White at all.

12 ... ♗xb2! *(158)*

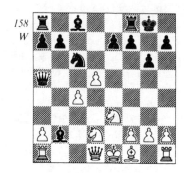

158
W

13 ♖b1

Grünberg gave the variation 13 dc ♗xa1 14 ♕xa1 ♖d8 15 ♕b2 bc 16 ♗e2 ♖b8! 17 ♕c2 ♖b7 which leaves White tied up, e.g. 18 h4 ♖bd7 19 ♘f1 h5 20 ♖h3 ♖xd2.

13	...	♗c3
14	dc	♖d8
15	♘d5	♗xd2+
16	♕xd2	♕xd2+
17	♔xd2	bc

The smoke clears; Black will have a sound extra pawn.

18	♗d3	cd
19	c5	♖d7!
20	c6	♖c7
21	♖hc1	♔f8
22	♖b4	e6
23	g4	♔e7
24	g5	♔d6
25	♖h4	♖b8
26	♖xh7	e5!

26 ... ♖b2+ gives White some counterchances.

The more careful text left White with little hope (0–1, 48).

Index of Variations

Section 3: Classical Main Line

Section 4: Fianchetto and Other Lines